Marketing in Practice
2003–2004

Marketing in Practice 2003–2004

Mike Hyde

AMSTERDAM BOSTON HEIDELBERG LONDON NEW YORK OXFORD
PARIS SAN DIEGO SAN FRANCISCO SINGAPORE SYDNEY TOKYO

Butterworth-Heinemann
An imprint of Elsevier
Linacre House, Jordan Hill, Oxford OX2 8DP
200 Wheeler Road, Burlington MA 01803

First published 2003

Copyright © 2003, Elsevier Ltd. All rights reserved

No part of this publication may be reproduced in any material form (including
photocopying or storing in any medium by electronic means and whether
or not transiently or incidentally to some other use of this publication) without
the written permission of the copyright holder except in accordance with the
provisions of the Copyright, Designs and Patents Act 1988 or under the terms of
a licence issued by the Copyright Licensing Agency Ltd, 90 Tottenham Court Road,
London, England W1T 4LP. Applications for the copyright holder's written
permission to reproduce any part of this publication should be addressed
to the publisher

Permissions may be sought directly from Elsevier's Science and Technology Rights
Department in Oxford, UK: phone: (+44) (0) 1865 843830; fax: (+44) (0) 1865 853333;
e-mail: permissions@elsevier.co.uk. You may also complete your request on-line via the
Elsevier homepage (http://www.elsevier.com), by selecting 'Customer Support'
and then 'Obtaining Permissions'

British Library Cataloguing in Publication Data
A catalogue record for this book is available from the British Library

ISBN 0 7506 5956 4

For information on all Butterworth-Heinemann publications
visit our website at www.bh.com

Typeset by Integra Software Services Pvt. Ltd, Pondicherry, India
www.integra-india.com
Printed and bound in Italy

Contents

Preface	Welcome to the CIM coursebooks	vii
Unit 1	**Marketing in practice – an overview**	**1**
	Introduction	1
	Exam or continuous assessment?	2
	The role of the front-line marketer	3
	Audit of necessary skills for marketers	3
	The five elements of activity that make up the syllabus	4
	Analysis of exam questions	5
Unit 2	**Gathering information from inside and outside the organization**	**7**
	Introduction	8
	Gathering information from inside the organization	8
	Gathering information about competitors	13
	Gathering information about potential suppliers	15
Unit 3	**Assembling and presenting information**	**22**
	Introduction	23
	Choosing a database	23
	Presenting information for comparison and to influence decisions	26
	Managing the database	32
	Using the database in segmentation	33
Unit 4	**Gathering and analysing financial and numerical information**	**35**
	Introduction	36
	Using spreadsheets	37
	Basic statistical techniques	45
	Comparing financial information	49
	Balancing financial decisions with other factors	50
Unit 5	**Making contacts for marketing**	**53**
	Introduction	54
	Who's who in marketing?	54
	Understanding the organization	56
	Marketing-orientated organizations	57
	E-relationships – using electronic media to communicate with customers and suppliers	58
	Dealing with external agencies	59
	Dealing with customers	62
	Personal selling	64
	Dealing with contacts up and down your supply chain – suppliers and distribution channels	67
Unit 6	**Practical networking skills**	**73**
	Why networking is important	74
	Building your list of contacts	75
	Personal skills for building relationships	76

Contents

	Promoting yourself at work	80
	Handling the press	82
	Meeting your goals through networking	83

Unit 7 Planning events — 86
- Approaches to planning — 87
- Venue selection — 94
- Conference and event costings and budgets — 96
- Event evaluation and selection — 98
- Meeting customer needs — 99
- Detail planning, anticipating and on-the-day management — 100
- Analysis of the results of a marketing event — 104

Unit 8 Marketing activities and events – exploring their diversity and application — 106
- Conferences and events – a truly international business — 107
- The scope of marketing events and activities — 108
- Exhibitions and shows — 111
- Meetings and conferences — 115
- Hosting international visitors — 118
- New outlet launches — 119

Unit 9 Co-ordinating the promotional effort — 123
- The promotional mix introduced — 124
- Advertising — 125
- Managing the print production process — 133
- Public relations — 133
- Sales promotion — 139
- Sales and the promotional sub-mix — 143

Unit 10 Co-ordinating the marketing mix — 146
- The development of the marketing mix — 147
- The extended marketing mix — 148
- Co-ordinating the mix — 149

Unit 11 Introduction to budgeting — 165
- The scope of the marketing budget — 166
- The marketing budget analysed — 167
- Methods of setting the marketing budget — 168
- Budget negotiation — 169
- Cost behaviour for marketing — 170
- Marginal costing — 173
- Apportioning the costs — 174

Unit 12 Calculations in the examination — 177
- Introduction — 178

Appendices
1. Guidance on examination preparation — 182
2. Undertaking CIM assignments and the integrative project — 194
3. Answers and debriefings — 204
4. Curriculum information and reading list — 221

Index — 227

preface
welcome to the CIM coursebooks

From the author

Mike Hyde has had a long involvement with CIM, teaching many groups at all levels. Mike ran a large CIM Marketing Programme at Solihull College and was also involved in course delivery at Marketing Academy Budapest before joining Bournville College as Head of the Business School. Mike was appointed Senior Examiner for Marketing in Practice in 1999.

Mike had a career in marketing before joining the world of education and feels that this syllabus, and this book, reflect the needs of today's marketers and their current or future employers.

An introduction from the academic development advisor

In the last two years we have seen some significant changes to the CIM Professional Series initiated by the Chartered Institute of Marketing. The changes have been introduced on a year-on-year basis, with Stage 1 (Certificate) changes implemented last year in 2002, and the Stage 2 (Advanced Certificate in Marketing) being implemented this year. It is anticipated that next year in 2004 the Stage 3 (Postgraduate Diploma) changes will be implemented.

As a result the authoring team, Butterworth-Heinemann and I have aimed to rigorously revise and update the coursebook series to make sure that every title is the best possible study aid and accurately reflects the latest CIM syllabus.

The revisions to the series this year included continued development in the Stage 1 and Postgraduate Diploma Series, and complete rewrites at Stage 2 to align with the radical overhaul of the CIM syllabus. There are a number of new authors, and indeed Senior Examiners, in the series who have been commissioned for their CIM course teaching and examining experience, as well as their research into specific curriculum-related areas and their wide general knowledge of the latest thinking in marketing.

We are certain that you will find these coursebooks highly beneficial in terms of the content and assessment opportunities and a study tool that will prepare you for both CIM examinations and continuous/integrative assessment opportunities. They will guide you in a logical and

Preface

structured way through the detail of the syllabus, providing you with the required underpinning knowledge, understanding and application of theory.

The editorial team and authors wish you every success as you embark upon your studies.

Karen Beamish
Academic Development Advisor

How to use these coursebooks

Everyone who has contributed to this series has been careful to structure the books with the exams in mind. Each unit, therefore, covers an essential part of the syllabus. You need to work through the complete coursebook systematically to ensure that you have covered everything you need to know.

This coursebook is divided into units each containing a selection of the following standard elements:

- **Learning objectives** Tell you what you will be expected to know, having read the unit
- **Syllabus references** Outline what part of the syllabus is covered in the module
- **Study guides** Tell you how long the unit is and how long its activities take to do
- **Questions** Are designed to give you practice – they will be similar to those you get in the exam
- **Answers** (at the end of the book) Suggest a format for answering exam questions. *Remember* there is no such thing as a model answer – you should use these examples only as guidelines
- **Activities** Give you a chance to put what you have learned into practice
- **Debriefings** (at the end of the book) shed light on the methodologies involved in the activities
- **Hints and tips** Are tips from the senior examiner, examiner or author which are designed to help you avoid common mistakes made by previous candidates and give you guidance on improving your knowledge base
- **Insights** Encourage you to contextualize your academic knowledge by reference to real-life experience
- **Key definitions** Highlight and explain the key points relevant to that module
- **Definitions** May be used for words you must know to pass the exam
- **Summaries** Cover what you should have picked up from reading the unit
- **Further study** Provides details of recommended reading in addition to the coursebook

While you will find that each section of the syllabus has been covered within this text, you might find that the order of some of the topics has been changed. This is because it sometimes makes more sense to put certain topics together when you are studying, even though they might appear in different sections of the syllabus itself. If you are following the reading and other activities, your coverage of the syllabus will be just fine, but don't forget to follow up with trade press reading!

About MarketingOnline

With this year's coursebooks Butterworth-Heinemann is offering readers free access to MarketingOnline (www.marketingonline.co.uk), our premier online support engine for the CIM marketing courses. On this site you can benefit from:

- Tutorials on key topics every two weeks during the term, comprehensive revision support material and access to revision days from Tactics – the highly acclaimed independent trainer for CIM courses
- Fully customizable electronic versions of the coursebooks – annotate, cut and paste sections of text to create your own tailored learning notes
- Instant access to weblinks related to the coursebooks
- Capacity to search the coursebook online for instant access to definitions and key concepts.

Logging on

Before you can access MarketingOnline you will first need to get a password. Please go to www.marketingonline.co.uk where you will find registration instructions for coursebook purchasers. Once you have got your password, you will need to log on using the onscreen instructions. This will give you access to the various functions outlined below.

Using MarketingOnline

MarketingOnline is broadly divided into four sections which can each be accessed from the front page after you have logged on to the system:

1. *The coursebooks* Buttons corresponding to the three levels of CIM marketing qualification are situated on the home page. Select your level and you will be presented with the four coursebook titles for each module of that level. Click on the desired coursebook to access the full online text (divided up by chapter). On each page of the text you have the option to add an electronic bookmark or annotation by following the onscreen instructions. You can also freely cut and paste text into a blank Word document to create your own learning notes.
2. *Revision material* Click on the 'Revision material' link and select the appropriate CIM level and coursebook to access revision material.
3. *Useful links* Click on 'Useful links' to access a list of links to other sites of interest for further reading and research.
4. *Glossary* Click on the 'Glossary' button to access our online dictionary of marketing terms.

If you have specific queries about using MarketingOnline then you should consult our fully searchable FAQ section – again, this is accessible through the appropriate link on the front page of the site. Please also note that a **full user guide** can be downloaded by clicking on the link on the opening page of the website.

unit 1
marketing in practice – an overview

Learning objectives

In this unit you will:

- Be introduced to the rationale for the introduction of this new module
- Undertake a personal skills audit.

By the end of this unit you will be able to:

- Understand the framework for the module
- Recognize your own strengths and weaknesses in the skills for this module.

Introduction

You are sitting at your office desk in Croydon, Kuala Lumpur or Colombo, and things are very hectic. You have many things to do and only three hours to do them. You need to work out some costings for a proposed advertising campaign, write a brief for your PR consultants and put together a presentation for your manager. Also you have some information to sort out to help the rest of the marketing team come to an important decision. And then there is the sales conference with all its attendant problems.

How does this sound to you? Does this sound like a really good job with plenty of variety and pace where every day is different?

The location does not matter too much, the guiding principles of marketing and associated tasks and activities are similar throughout today's technological world. (Although we all still have to be mindful of important cultural differences when dealing with customers, colleagues and suppliers from other nations or cultural backgrounds, see 'Making contacts for marketing' and 'Practical networking skills' in this coursebook, plus the other certificate texts.)

Unit 1 Marketing in practice – an overview

The above is the world of the front-line marketer; you may be in such a role or are perhaps looking at such a first career move in the near future and that is precisely why you are studying the Chartered Institute of Marketing's Certificate in Marketing.

Front-line marketing positions can often be among the most varied and interesting posts in the marketing industry, as although they are lower in a traditional company hierarchy, the scope of involvement and activity can be far greater than the more specialized and focused roles a marketer might undertake later in their career.

The pace of change in marketing is increasing rapidly, as you will have learnt in your studies for the Marketing Environment exam. A grasp of the basic concepts of marketing gained from the Marketing Fundamentals coursebook plus an ability to communicate (from the Customer Communications module) are vital to survive and thrive in the global marketing industry.

Now the time has come in your studies to apply all that you have learnt, plus more besides, into challenging situations. This is what Marketing in Practice is all about, taking your knowledge and using it to solve marketing problems set within an organization. Just as the geographical location might differ, then so might the industry context in which you find yourself. Indeed, previous Marketing in Practice exam papers have been set around:

- A tyres /batteries/car servicing chain (June 99)
- A property development company (Dec 99)
- Food and leisure (June 00)
- A retail chain (Dec 00)
- A conference centre (June 01)
- An IT company in Hungary (Dec 01)
- A football club (Jun 02)
- A car importer in Ghana (Dec 02).

In the future, your exam could be based around a company in the business-to-business sector, or it could be in an advertising agency, or one of the new e-commerce operations.

It could also be based anywhere in the world to reflect the mobile nature of employment.

In summary: Marketing in Practice is an applied subject, and should not be attempted until the other three modules at certificate level have been studied. (To attempt it without would very likely result in failure.) It is based around a case study which could be in any sector anywhere in the world and all questions should be answered in this context. It should prove enjoyable and lead on to further success at CIM Advanced Certificate level.

It is well worth remembering that there is a growing emphasis on ICT throughout the syllabus to reflect the reality of the marketplace.

Exam or continuous assessment?

With such a practical bias, Marketing in Practice lends itself particularly well to continuous assessment (go to Appendix 2 for approaches to studying and being assessed in this way). For those taking an examination, there are important changes in format and, as such, these affect your approach. Go to www.cimeduhub.com or www.bh.com/marketing for online access to specimen examination papers – there are references to the questions on these papers in each unit so that you will know which part of your studies equips you to answer each one.

Unit 1 Marketing in practice – an overview

The role of the front-line marketer

The module is written to reflect the role of Marketing Assistant or Marketing Executive. Many also fulfil this role with the title of Personal Assistant to the Managing/Marketing Director. The main feature of their work is the variety and scope involved. Their work often spans the whole spectrum of marketing activity – usually at a very tactical level. For example, you may not deal with national advertising, but may deal with the local press.

Activity 1.1

If you work in marketing, or a marketing-related environment, what does your job entail?

If you are studying at a CIM approved centre, how does this compare with your co-students?

Now think wider still. What might a marketing assistant do at a software design company in Singapore? How would the role of a PA to the marketing director of a bus manufacturer in Hungary compare with the equivalent job in Leeds?

Compare your experience and thoughts on job content with the syllabus contained at the end of this coursebook. If you have examined a selection of jobs, the chances are that the entire syllabus is within the collective experience of a group of people, but each will be different to each other. There is probably no such thing as the average marketing role, but there are many common threads across industry sectors and geographical locations.

Audit of necessary skills for marketers

As students of the Certificate in Marketing you will come from widely diverse backgrounds; some of you will work in marketing and some will be looking to move into marketing. Some of you will work in large organizations and carry out very focused roles, and some in small organizations and carry out a wide range of activities. Some of you may not currently be working, and may be looking to acquire a new range of skills to help you find work in the future.

The key skills needed are considered to be skills that apply to many roles in business today, and these are detailed in a checklist in 'Approaching the Module for Continuous Assessment' at www.cimeduhub.com or www.bh.com/marketing. These have then been specifically linked to skills you will need and tasks you will undertake in a marketing role, and these are detailed in a second checklist in 'Approaching the Module for Continuous Assessment' at www.cimeduhub.com or www.bh.com/marketing.

Depending on your current level of experience and your current role you will have different levels of expertise in each of these areas, and it is suggested that you look at these checklists and undertake a personal skills audit before you go any further with this module. This is a useful exercise whether you will be doing assignments as your assessment for this module, or taking the Case Study examination. Go to www.cimeduhub.com or www.bh.com/marketing for guidance on approaching the module for continuous assessment and, if you are being assessed through the continuous assessment route, return to it at the end of your studies.

When you know where your weaker areas are, you will be able to spend longer on your studies of these areas as you progress through the coursebook. Do not be tempted to neglect your strong points, however. We never stop learning – and marketing changes at a fast pace. Continuous Professional Development is a way we can match that pace, and is a habit worth forming now, in readiness for your progression to Chartered Marketer status in the future.

This module has been designed to provide a practical focus for the theory covered in the other three modules of the Certificate in Marketing. This will apply whether you work in consumer marketing, a small business, business-to-business marketing, services marketing, or the not-for-profit sector.

The five elements of activity that make up the syllabus

The syllabus is made up of five elements which are outlined and explained below.

Gathering, analysing and presenting information

There is a need for business decisions to be based on information, and this section deals with sources of information which can be accessed, and the need to evaluate the information. There is a strong practical element, and market research techniques are examined, in particular, from a DIY angle.

Segmentation is also touched upon – not in any great depth but as a practical tool to use in marketing situations. As in the rest of the module, you are encouraged to explore the practice of your own organization.

Building and developing relationships

This section is concerned with the 'people' aspect of marketing. Commencing inside the marketing department, it then looks across the organization, before examining relationships outside – whether with suppliers or further down the supply chain. It covers both the human aspects, and the procedural and contractual, to give a realistic view of the real world. Aspects covered here also include 'managing your manager' – a key task many of us have to perform.

Organizing and undertaking marketing activities

Research has shown that many Marketing Assistants have responsibility for organizing a variety of events, from sales meetings to full-blown conferences, and from exhibitions to corporate hospitality. This part of the syllabus compares and contrasts different approaches. Again, it takes a strong practical approach, and it is essential that you have a grasp of costing and can evaluate the success of activities undertaken.

Co-ordinating the marketing mix

'Co-ordinating' is a key word – this is not strategic management of the mix. For example, at this level you are unlikely to be asked to decide pricing strategy, but may be asked to report on the effects of a pricing decision. You may not deal with strategic advertising, but may control local advertising. Similar demarcations apply across the mix, and it is this level of activity that is covered.

In line with research findings, there is a heavy emphasis on promotional activity, but all 7 Ps and their application are explored, building on the input in Marketing Fundamentals. Budgeting and dealing with information are also important features in this section.

Administering the marketing budget (and evaluating results)

This need not strike you with fear! Practical and tactical are again watchwords for this section. Company accounts, discounted cash flows, etc. are not needed at this level.

There is, however, a need for an appreciation of costs, how they are apportioned, and how cost-effective marketing activities are. As such, basic manipulation of figures is essential. Overall, the section seeks to answer the following questions: 'How much does it cost? How do we split the costs? What will the result be? Is it worth doing?'

This module offers the opportunity to put into practice the entire Certificate syllabus, integrate key skills, and draw on your experience. It should be lively and fun for all involved – just as your career in marketing should be!

> **Exam tip**
>
> This examination is based around a case study and to help you pass, all exam papers produced to date are available on the CIM students' website. It is recommended that early on in your studies you read and become familiar with the two most recent papers. These are Newtown United (Jun 02) which is set at a football club and Africars (Dec 02) which is based around a car importer situated in Ghana. Throughout the text at appropriate junctures you are invited to answer appropriate questions related to each of these cases. It is also recommended that you do not read the previous papers just yet, but attempt each of them in their entirety at the end of your learning to gain valuable experience.

Analysis of exam questions

It is a dangerous and risky strategy to try to 'question spot', that is to try to anticipate specific questions, with a subsequent revision strategy based around only a fraction of the syllabus. This exam above all other is best approached with a broad grasp of the syllabus coupled with an ability to apply whatever knowledge you have.

However, Senior Examiners have to ensure that in each exam sitting their syllabus is sufficiently covered. In the case of Marketing in Practice, there are a total are five distinct areas of the syllabus, as we have previously identified. As there are a total of seven questions, it should come as no surprise that all five areas have at least one question attached to them. The following is a table of questions by broad syllabus area.

QUESTION	1	2	3	4	5	6	7
DEC 99	OIB	M	R	M	R	I	M
JUN 00	BBM	I	M	M	I	R	I
DEC 00	MBR	M	I	M	R	O	M
JUN 01	BIR	M	I	M	O	I	M
DEC 01	BRM	I	O	M	B	M	I

Key: B = budgets, M = mix, I = information, R = relationships, O = organizing events

Unit 1 Marketing in practice – an overview

Job scope and career progression

The figure shows progression through a marketing career and the scope of typical jobs. First marketing jobs are often very varied, not with a great deal of responsibility or specialization. When promotion or a career move follows it is likely to be into a narrower role although with greater responsibility and control, such as a product manager's job. Many marketers wish to progress beyond marketing into more strategic roles within the organization. At this stage, the width of scope returns often with greater people and financial responsibility, with 'pure' marketing. The academic progression route on the right will assist in preparing you for your future career.

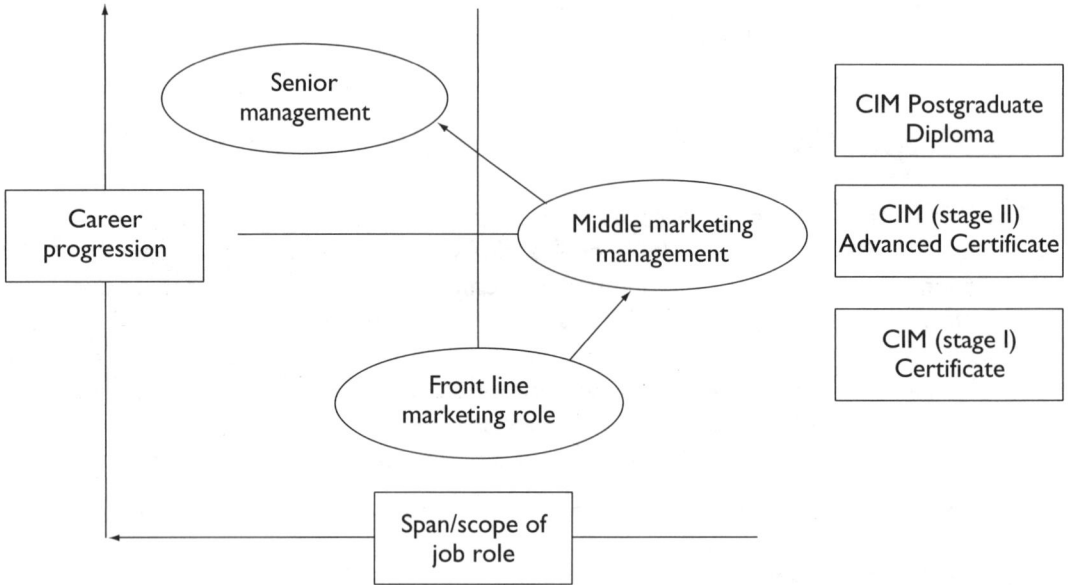

Figure 1.1

unit 2
gathering information from inside and outside the organization

Learning objectives

In this unit you will:

- Examine the various sources of relevant information within the organization (4.1.1)
- Consider how information about competitors can be obtained (4.1.5)
- Assess the value of information obtained from the internet (4.1.1).

By the end of this unit you will be able to:

- Identify sources of information within your own organization (4.1.1)
- Gather information on competitor pricing and promotional activity (4.1.5)
- Use the internet as an information source, particularly to gather information from overseas (4.1.1, 4.1.7)
- Detail external sources of information relevant to your own situation and environment (4.1.1)
- This unit covers the key skills Using ICT and the internet and Presenting information
- It also covers the statements of practice for marketers Exchange information to solve problems and make decisions and Collect, synthesize, analyse and report measuremant data.

Unit 2 Gathering information from inside and outside the organization

Study Guide

This unit covers a range of information that you may be asked to gather in your marketing role. With the next unit on 'Assembling and presenting information', it covers the 20 per cent of the syllabus devoted to 'Gathering and Assembling Information for Marketing' (Section 4.1). It focuses mainly on desk research, but includes basic questionnaire design for customer satisfaction surveys, and basic sampling methods. Completion of the unit will take approximately 10–12 hours, including the completion of all activities.

Introduction

Marketing is about making decisions – decisions about which products and services should be offered to best meet the needs of our customers, and which should be withdrawn; decisions about how they should be priced; where we should advertise; what trade show we should attend; what combination of strategies will give us the edge over our competitors. These decisions will be much more reliable if sufficient, relevant information is gathered to inform them. Any organization that is prepared to make significant changes to its marketing mix without researching the likely market reaction is taking a very high risk of failure.

Definition

Marketing mix – The core decisions taken by management about the 4/7 Ps, i.e. Product, Pricing, Promotion, Place (distribution), People, Process and Physical evidence.

Gathering information from inside the organization

This unit focuses upon desk research, i.e. the collection of secondary data, rather than the collection of primary data, which is covered in Marketing Fundamentals (Syllabus Reference 1.2.1) and Customer Communications (Syllabus References 2.2.2 & 2.2.3). In 'Assembling and presenting information' you will consider ways to display data collected, and in 'Gathering and analysing financial and numerical information' be introduced to some analytical techniques that help make sense of your findings.

There are many sources of information that you may be asked to access within your organization. These may include sales reports, customer complaints and enquiries, management information gathered proactively on a regular basis, minutes of meetings, monthly reports, newsletters which show new contracts won and activity within different departments, etc. You may be asked to assemble information from a series of these sources, and in a different format to that which they are in already. For example, monthly reports from the sales force may include comments on competitor activity. You may be asked to compile this information and highlight key points for your manager or other departments. Alternatively, you may be asked to produce a comparison of competitor pricing for a particular product in your portfolio. These monthly sales reports may be your first research point.

Unit 2 Gathering information from inside and outside the organization

Activity 2.1

Look at the information that is on your desk. What pieces of paper are there – memos, reports, newsletters, etc.? Who have they come from? What information do you need regularly to do your job? Where do you get it from and how long does it take you? What information do you pass on to other people, either within your own department or in other departments? Draw up a table which shows *what* information you need, *when* or how often you need it, *who* provides it, *where* you need to obtain it from if it is not sent automatically, and then *why* you need it. Are there patterns emerging? Are there actions you can take now to make this process easier in the future?

Using the intranet

What is an intranet? It is a private, organizational network that uses internet technologies. Access to an organization's intranet remains within its control and is usually limited to its employees, which provides it with an obvious advantage of confidentiality. More recently, organizations have started to develop extranet facilities which make part of their intranet accessible to customers and suppliers. Intranets can be developed to meet the specific needs of an organization. They can be used to communicate general information that was previously held only in hard copy, such as the annual report and financial statement, the product catalogue and price list, quality manuals, training manuals, etc. They can also be used interactively to update all staff about new contracts which have been won, new staff taken on, internal job ads, newsletters, etc.

Often organizations will use their intranet to publish the minutes of recent meetings, rather than circulate them to all employees, publish confidential management information that they can update easily and quickly, and reduce the amount of paper-based communication.

An intranet also offers advantages to you if you work in sales or regularly work from home. In the past you would have had to either carry heavy catalogues and reports with you, or phone or call at the office to obtain information. Using an intranet you can access the same information anywhere, by connecting your PC or laptop to the intranet via a modem.

Activity 2.2

Find out if your organization has an intranet and use an hour to identify what information you can usefully obtain from it both now and in the future. If your organization does not have an intranet, ask your colleagues at college to see if you can visit one of their organizations to look at their service. Companies are increasingly using their intranets as a source of competitive advantage as the scope for improved customer service through speedy and effective communication is vast. Don't be too disappointed if you are refused access!

Analysing reports

This section deals with an activity in which you may be involved when gathering and presenting information. You may be asked to compile a summary report from the reports submitted by others.

Do individuals in your organization submit reports in a standardized format? Are they standardized within departments, but does structure and style vary from department to department? If reports are standardized, then your job is much easier when asked to compile certain information from them. Computerized formats make extraction of information speedier and easier still.

When you know what information it is that you need to compile and summarize, consider setting up a spreadsheet to make life easier in subsequent months or reporting periods. (See 'Gathering and analysing financial and numerical information' for working with spreadsheets.) If you do not have access to a computer on a regular basis, or a suitable computer package to set up a spreadsheet, consider setting up a suitable standardized tabular report into which you can transfer the information. Figure 2.1 shows a table that is used to present information gathered on a monthly basis from regionally based salespeople.

	Jan	Feb	Mar	Apr	May	Jun	Jul	Aug	Sep	Oct	Nov	Dec	Total
NW & Scotland	23	22	39	21									
NE	11	14	23	13									
Midlands	16	14	23	15									
SE	52	49	72	50									
SW	13	11	19	20									
Total for month	115	110	176	119									

Figure 2.1 Monthly sales per region – 2003 (£000s)

Sales reports are only one form of report that you may have to handle in the sales and marketing department. You may be asked to compile a report from various secondary data sources. There is a danger when researching of going into 'information overload' – having so much information that it is impossible to identify key points. The busier we all become, the more senior decision makers rely on summaries and briefing papers that have been prepared by others. Summarizing is a skill involving identifying and focusing on key information. The stages are:

- Clarifying your objectives – what exactly are you being asked for? Who are you writing for and what do they already know? Do you need to precis everything in a number of documents, or are you focusing on one specific area?

- Considering reliability and validity – what do you know about the source of your information? Is it from a reliable source? What was it collected for? There may be evidence of bias and one-sided argument in the cases of some sources, and it is important that you are able to establish whether this is the case. How valid is the information – and how accurate is the result of your analysis therefore likely to be?

o Reading and examining material – how well do you understand the arguments put forward in the documents you are examining? If you are examining a lengthy document, it may help you to use a highlighter pen to identify key points in each section. Does the document you are examining already have a summary? This may not cover all that you need to know, but will help to identify the key points it raises.

o Drafting – who are you writing for? You need to consider your audience when you start to draft your document as it will shape your decisions about the language you use. The main principle here is KISS – keep it short and simple. You need to cut out all detail, including statistics, figures and examples.

o Checking – reread your draft and ensure that you have transferred the key points accurately. It is easy to change meaning when you are summarizing, unless you are very careful. You will also need to check that you have included all the information that you identified when you first clarified your objectives. Have you included any personal bias that you may feel? It is important that this does not happen when you are summarizing someone else's work. If you have strong views, they should be put forward in an accompanying document, as they are not part of a summary.

o Preparing final document – before you write it up, check to see if you can delete any further 'waffle' from your document. Check that you have kept to a logical format and that your summary flows.

Activity 2.3

Select two articles on a similar topic from *Marketing* or *Marketing Week*. Write a summary of the two articles, aiming your document at a new marketing assistant who has been employed to help you.

Getting the best from meetings – as meeting leader

Many organizations quite rightly rely heavily on meetings as a means of communication. They are an important way of communicating with others both inside and outside the organization. However, their effectiveness is often limited by a lack of training in managing meetings well. You may not currently run meetings – nevertheless, your contribution towards an agenda topic can make a significant difference. The key to a meeting's effectiveness is often in the amount of preparation that an individual undertakes. This applies whether you are running the meeting, or attending as a participant.

Every meeting will have a mix of personalities – some will be more talkative than others, and some more confident. We also vary our behaviour depending on what is happening at the time. For example, an individual may feel that he or she should not be at a particular meeting, and therefore act resentfully and not take any active part.

Unit 2 Gathering information from inside and outside the organization

 Activity 2.4

If you are running the meeting, how will you deal with the following types of behaviour?

- *Aggressive behaviour* Shows itself as an individual being too opinionated, too quick to jump to conclusions, and generally too noisy.
- *Silent behaviour* Quiet and reserved. However, is this because the individual is nervous, or because he or she is hostile to the topic under discussion?
- *Abusive behaviour* Can be abrasive, and quick with reasons why something will not work or should not be done. This behaviour will demoralize the meeting if you do not control it quickly.
- *Rambling behaviour* Often turns up late, is easily distracted, and tells stories that go off at a tangent.
- *Sniping behaviour* Quick with one-line statements and witty retorts. These can be damaging if they are aimed at individuals rather than issues.

If you are leading a meeting, your main responsibility is to keep the attention of the participants focused upon its objectives. You need to think about the following:

- *The structure* – keeping to the agenda set before the meeting, watching the time
- *The interaction* – ensuring that all participants have an opportunity to put their points across, fostering an atmosphere of co-operation and openness
- *The content* – ensuring that the discussion does not drift away from the subject, drawing on all the information, knowledge and experience that participants bring to the meeting.

Meetings may be formal or informal in their style. If you are leading a meeting, your activities will vary depending on the style that is most appropriate. Most work-based meetings will have a degree of formality to help make them efficient in their use of time and effective in their achievement of an objective.

Each should be well planned and organized. They should have a clear purpose, and this should be understood by, and agreed to by all participants. Ideally, those who are to take part should be given the opportunity to contribute items for the agenda before it is set. This avoids surprise items being raised under 'Any other business' at the end of the meeting. If an item is important enough to be raised, then assessment as to whether it is relevant to the purpose of the meeting should take place in advance to enable people to prepare.

At the end of the meeting, action points should be agreed, and responsibility for these actions clearly allocated to individuals.

Getting the best from meetings – as a participant

You also have responsibilities if you are attending a meeting called by someone else. You should check the following points before you go.

- Do I need to go? Is the subject of this meeting sufficiently relevant to me to make it more important than other priorities I have? You may have no choice – you may be asked to attend on behalf of your manager or because you have particular experience that is essential to the discussion.
- Where did the last meeting leave things and what did I agree to do? Have I completed all that I promised to do?

- What is on the agenda of this meeting? Am I fully prepared to make a valuable contribution? Have I collected together all the information I need? Am I ready to listen to others as well as put across my own point of view?

If you have answered 'Yes' to all of the above questions, you can be confident that you will be a welcome participant at any meeting, and that meetings you attend and run will be useful rather than a waste of time.

Rules for behaviour at meetings should include:

- Be well prepared and knowledgeable about the subject
- Keep your own contribution short and simple (*KISS*)
- Try to retain your sense of humour – without becoming flippant
- Listen to others' points of view without interrupting
- Contribute only when you have something constructive to add – don't use the meeting as a platform for airing personal grievances that are irrelevant
- Be prepared to compromise if necessary and appropriate
- Acknowledge others' strengths
- Don't become defensive.

Gathering information about competitors

There are many questions that can be answered, at least in part, through desk research. You need to know everything there is to know about your competitors. Who are they? Where are they based? What are their strengths and weaknesses? What range of products do they offer? How much do they charge? What discount strategies do they employ? What are their terms of trade? What is their reaction likely to be if you lower your prices by x per cent? You can also see from the above questions that this research is likely to be ongoing – finding the answers on a single occasion is not going to be sufficient.

Another common question asked by new marketers is 'How do I find out how big the market is, and how fast it is growing?' Size can often be established through secondary research sources and growth rate by tracking results over time. However, figures obtained are often given in terms of sales volume and are restricted to general broad descriptions of the market. For example, it may be relatively easy to discover total sales volumes of salad dressings broken down into mayonnaise, salad cream and salad dressings, but you may need more detail to help you make decisions. In this particular example, there was a Mintel Report on the bottled sauce market prepared in December 1998, and this may be your second source of information.

Case history

Information gathering in a 'secret' environment

The international defence equipment market contains only a few hundred customers. Because it is quite small, you might think it would be easy to gather market information. However, much of the information that the marketer needs in order to plan is politically and militarily sensitive and so is covered by the Official Secrets Act. So where do marketers get their information in such a 'hush-hush' market?

Information gathering in this market is not easy. All the information ultimately comes from customers, who are reluctant to talk in detail or in advance about their equipment programmes. Firms competing in the defence market usually use a combination of three sources for their information.

o **The defence press**
Jane's Defence Weekly, International Defence Review and *Flight International* are examples of sources which contain valuable 'low-level' information on new equipment entering service, current major equipment programmes, contracts and competitors. These periodicals are well informed and enjoy wide circulation. Many also have an associated 'yearbook' which catalogues customers' equipment in service and current procurement programmes. More specialist magazines containing more specific details are also available on restricted circulation.

o **Secondary research reports**
As in most markets, research agencies specialize in providing reports which provide forecasts of forthcoming equipment programmes in various regions. Many of these play on the concept of 'intelligence' in its military sense to increase their perceived value in this marketplace. The forecasts are usually three to ten years out of date but, with customers being reluctant to give details of their programmes and equipment purchases being at the political whim, their accuracy and completeness are sometimes questionable.

o **The sales force**
Most companies rely heavily on their sales force staff to get close to their customers to find out about equipment programmes of interest and the main players wanting a stake in the programmes. The quality of the relationships with their customers will determine the quality of the information they are able to obtain. So sales staff have a dual role to play: to gather intelligence, and to sell the company's equipment. In many companies staff performing this role have job titles such as Sales and Marketing Manager. A key task for marketing support staff in this kind of environment is persuading sales staff to remember to collect and report intelligence and to provide and maintain an information system into which this information can be entered.

Defence firms do also use primary research, but it is not as common as in other markets. Customers are reluctant to divulge information to people they do not know, which is why the role of the sales staff takes on far greater significance in this market.

Competitor pricing

Organizations need to set up systems which ensure that information about their competitors is gathered on a regular basis.

- o The sales team, if briefed well, are the most useful source of information about the prices your competitors are charging. They will be meeting customers face-to-face, and, particularly where the relationship is well established, will be very willing to share any information they have regarding competitor activity.
- o The internet can also be a useful source of information. Many companies are now putting both their product catalogues and their price lists onto their website. If you are new to using the internet, there is a section later in this unit that will help. Have a look at www.ghengineering.co.uk to see an example of this.

- If your products or services sell through retail outlets, then you may be able to visit retailers that stock your competitors' products to check out prices. There are also agencies that specialize in collecting competitor intelligence – however, this is an expensive service and the benefits need to be considered carefully.
- Finally, there is the obvious option that can easily be forgotten – the telephone is a useful method of checking competitor prices.

No matter how you collect the information, it is important that the exercise is continued on a regular basis.

Activity 2.5

Select one of your products or services. Identify your three main competitors for this product or service and find out their current prices.

- How do these compare?
- Are there reasons for the differences?
- Do you sell to the same target group of customers?

Competitor promotional and other mix activity

How do you find out what your competitors are doing in terms of promotional activity? The ease with which you can do this will vary across industry sectors. For example, if your target market is made up of consumers, then you will quickly know about any change in activity. If you provide goods or services in business-to-business markets or in industrial markets, then you will have to look more selectively. The trade press can be a useful source of information, as will published data sources. Keynote and Mintel produce reports about various industries which may give you some background data to help your search.

When looking for information on promotional activity, *Marketing* (www.marketing.haynet.com) and *Marketing Week* (www.mad.co.uk) as well as *Campaign* are all useful weekly sources of information. If your company does not subscribe to these magazines, you will find that they are widely available in libraries.

Companies' Annual Reports and Accounts sometimes contain details of activity undertaken during the year and planned for the future. For example, J. Sainsbury's Annual Review for 2002 outlined plans for new 'city-centre' format stores and also details of their home delivery service. As mentioned previously, do not underestimate the importance of collecting this information in a systematic way. Look at their latest Report & Accounts on the internet at www.j-sainsbury.co.uk to see an update on their situation. Click on 'Investor centre' and then on 'Annual Reports' and then on '2002' to see their current plans on improving customer service, taking advantage of e-commerce and designing stores to meet customer needs.

Gathering information about potential suppliers

Business today is about a linked chain of processes that ends with the supply of a product or service to the end-customer. It is therefore as important to develop good relationships with your suppliers as with your buyers. Suppliers are stakeholders in your organization's future. Arranging the supply of materials or components will probably not involve you – however, you

Unit 2 Gathering information from inside and outside the organization

may be asked to gather information on suppliers for a specific purchase. Perhaps you have to arrange the printing of a brochure or catalogue (this is covered in more depth in co-ordinating the promotional effort) or you may be asked to obtain suitable quotes for the supply of a new contact management database.

The first step is to check whether your organization operates a 'preferred supplier' database. Other departments may have made similar purchases and your organization may have specific selection criteria for suppliers that you use. Some organizations require suppliers to hold ISO9002, for example, to help ensure the quality of products purchased. If your organization does not operate such a system, then it is good practice for you to decide on a list of criteria for selection of an appropriate product or service. Which is most important to you – quality or price? If it is new technology you are purchasing, how important is it that it is user-friendly? Will it be used by specialists, or will staff need training? If training will be required, how important is it that this is provided as part of the package? What else is important about the specific purchase?

One source of information about suitable suppliers is your personal network of contacts (this is covered in 'Practical networking skills'). You may also be able to find specialist trade magazines that cover the type of product you require. The internet may be another source of information. You may also have close relationships with certain customers who have made similar purchases, and will be happy to pass on their experience and recommendations. When you have identified two or three companies that could supply suitable products, ask them to visit to present their products to you for consideration. It may be that a demonstration of a product is necessary for you to make a choice confidently. If it is to be a product that will be used for some considerable time, then it will be important that you are able to build a relationship with the firm of suppliers, and a face-to-face meeting will help to establish this.

Activity 2.6

Find out whether your organization has a 'preferred supplier' list. Ask how companies get on this list – what are the criteria used for selection?

Using the internet

The internet can be used to collect information in two ways: through a search for specific information, and through asking visitors to your own website to register, thus giving you demographic data and potential sales leads. The use of your own website to collect data is covered further in 'Assembling and presenting information', in the section on using the database for segmentation. This section will focus on using the internet to search for the information you need.

When you first start searching the internet the mass of information available can seem daunting. Search engines such as 'Yahoo', 'Altavista', 'Lycos' and 'Excite' will help you find the information you need. If you have not used the internet before, don't worry – if you can use a word processor you can use the internet. When you log on through your Internet Service Provider (ISP) there will be a means of accessing search engines. Alternatively, you can visit website www.search.com, where you will see a box in which you type 'key words' relating to the subject you are looking for. The search engine then checks its database of sites for matching entries and lists them – the closest matches to the words you specified will be at the top of the list. You can then read the summaries of the sites and choose the one you want to see. If you receive the message 'No matching entries found', then check your spelling, as this is often the

16

Unit 2 Gathering information from inside and outside the organization

source of the problem. If this still does not work, then try adding words to define your search more accurately. Each search engine has a 'Hints on searching' section to help you. The key to searching successfully is knowing what you are looking for and expressing it carefully.

General tips

- The more terms you can add to your search enquiry, the more chance you have of finding it successfully. Practice makes perfect.
- Use a capital letter when appropriate and the search will only select matches that start with capital letters.
- Using + before a word in your search means that the match must include that particular element. Using a − means that the search will look for sites that exclude that part.
- For more information about which search engine to use, visit www.searchenginewatch.com. This is a website address or URL (Uniform Resource Locator). If you want to go directly to a site and you know the address, then you just need to type it into the box marked 'URL' or 'Go to' and press 'Enter'.

If you are gathering information about your competitors, you can add their URLs to your 'Favourites' (a file of preferred websites). You can access this from a pull-down menu at the top of your screen. Click to open the menu and then click 'Add to favourites'. The next time you need to access the site you can access it from your 'Favourites' list and find it in seconds.

If you do not know whether the company you want has a website, then either use a general search or try www.yell.co.uk, a directory of business website addresses in the UK that is provided by *Yellow Pages.*

There are many sites that provide general information on companies. Try the following:

- www.dunandbrad.co.uk (the Dun & Bradstreet site). See Figure 2.2 on p.18
- www.dis.strath.ac.uk/business/index.html. This is a guide to business information sources across the web that is maintained by Strathclyde University.

Unit 2 Gathering information from inside and outside the organization

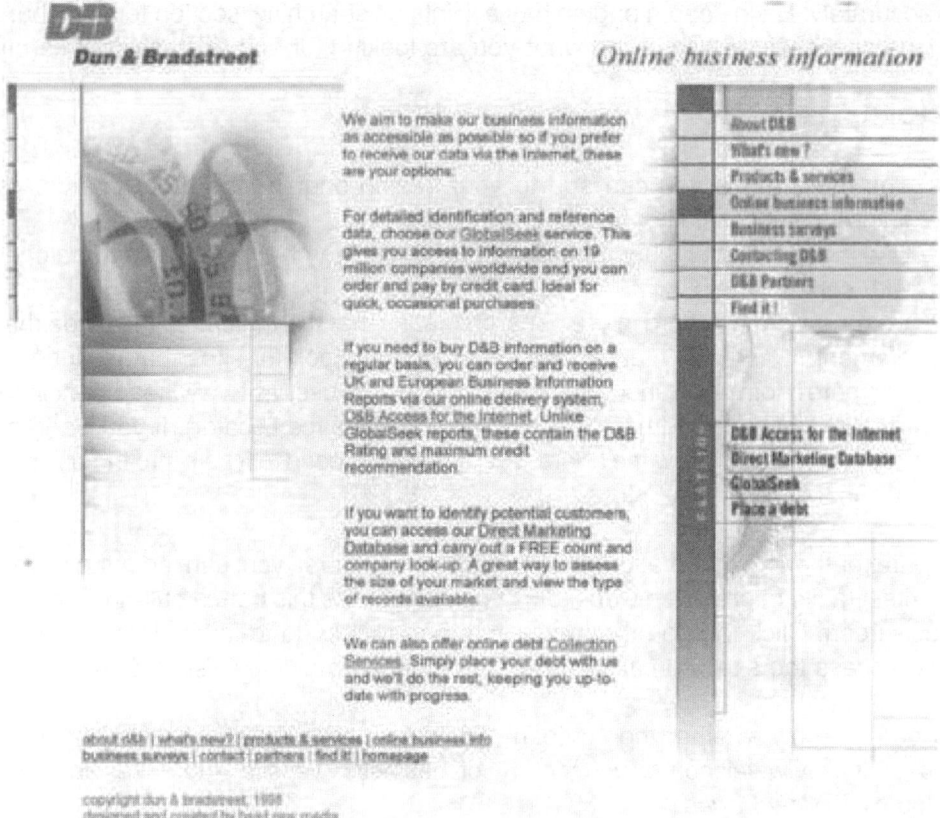

Figure 2.2 Online business information

Other sources of information

Desk research is widely used as a 'first step' because it tends to be more easily accessible and relatively low-cost. However, you need to bear in mind the fact that it was not collected for your specific purpose and therefore may not be sufficient to satisfy research objectives that you have identified.

Figure 2.3 shows where this step falls within the overall marketing research process.

So many different sources of secondary data exist that it would be impossible to state them all, and you need to select the sources which are most relevant to your specific need at any one time.

One source of information you may find useful is Government-gathered data. The Central Statistical Office publishes vast amounts of data in the form of the *Monthly Digest of Statistics* (UK imports, information on various markets such as agriculture, food, drinks and tobacco, textiles, retail trade, overseas travel and tourism, and general information which is relevant to most market sectors). Other publications include *Financial Statistics* (personal income and expenditure, consumer credit, borrowing and house purchase, etc.); *General Household Survey* (a continuous sample survey of households and families, housing, pensions, health, smoking, etc.); and *Key Population and Vital Statistics* (annual review of population trends). The Office for National Statistics (ONS) has a website at www.ons.gov.uk and publishes 'Selected Monthly Indicators' on this site. An example is shown in Figure 2.4 on p. 20.

Unit 2 Gathering information from inside and outside the organization

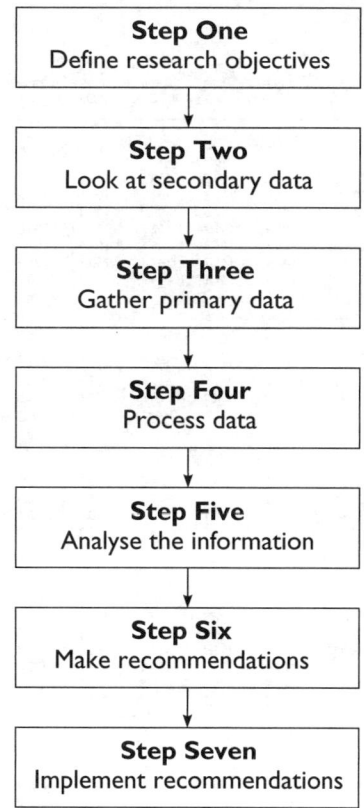

Figure 2.3 The marketing research process

There are also many non-government organizations that publish information. These include the:

- Confederation of British Industry (CBI) (industrial trend surveys, monthly reviews of retail and distributive trades) www.cbi.org.uk
- Halifax Building Society (regular report on house prices), www.halifax.co.uk (Click on 'Company Information' and then 'House Price Index')
- www.nua.ie This organization publishes internet surveys
- Kompass Register of British Industry & Commerce (trading and financial data on 42,000 UK companies) www.kompass.co.uk
- Mintel International Group Ltd (300 reports per year covering approximately 92 per cent of all UK consumer markets), www.mintel.com.

Trade associations and professional bodies also provide useful information which is focused on a narrower market. For example, The Food and Drink Federation produces statistics on individual sectors such as the Dessert and Cake Mixes Association and the Pickles and Sauces Association.

As stated above, there are many sources of information, and you need to identify which are the best to serve your purpose. Find out if your library is a member of the Business Information Network. This is an association of libraries and information units that supply business information to users. Visit your local library to see what is available, and, if you have a specific need for information, contact the CIM Information Service – a search is available free to members, and copies of the information you need can be supplied for a small charge. It holds an extensive range of product and service market data and statistics, as well as general business, industry and social data.

Unit 2 Gathering information from inside and outside the organization

		1997	1998	1998 Q2	1998 Q3	1998 Q4	1999 Q1	1999 Jan	1999 Feb	1999 Mar	% Change Latest 3 months avg over previous 3 months 1999 Mar
Output in constant prices											
(1995 = 100 unless otherwise stated)											
Gross value added at basic prices	CGCE	106.0	108.5	108.3	108.8	108.9	..	..	..	..	..
Industrial production	CKYW	101.9	102.5	103.1	103.1	102.2	..	101.3	101.3	..	..
Oil and gas extraction	CKZO	104.8	107.5	108.8	109.3	109.5	..	106.9	108.1	..	..
Manufacturing	CKYY	101.4	101.7	102.2	102.1	100.8	..	100.5	100.4	..	..
Construction	GDQB	104.7	106.4	105.5	105.4	105.5	..	..	..	..	..
Car production (thousands)	FFAO	141.5	145.7	147.1	150.2	135.4	..	..	..	..	..
GB housing completions (thousands)	CTPA	178.2	41.1	44.4	42.0	40.1	..	13.5	13.7	..	..
Domestic demand											
Retail sales volume (1995 = 100)	EAPS	108.6	111.7	111.7	112.3	112.1	113.3	113.3	113.0	113.5	..
GB new registrations of cars ('000s)[1]	BCGT	2 157	2 261.5	512.7	712.7	416.2	640.9	184.1	82.7	374.1	
Manufacturing: change in inventories (£m 1995 prices)	DHBM	-93	404	376	255	-171	..	..	..	..	
Prices & wages (12 monthly % change)											
Retail prices index[1]	CZBH	3.1	3.4	4.0	3.3	2.9	2.2	3.4	2.1	2.1	
Retail prices index[1] (less MIPS)[2]	CDKQ	2.8	2.6	2.9	2.5	2.5	2.6	2.6	2.4	2.7	
Producer output prices (less FBTP)[3]	EUAA	0.3	-0.1	0.1	-0.1	-0.6	0.6	-0.6	-0.5	-0.6	
Producer input prices	EUAB	-8.3	-9.0	-8.0	-9.3	-9.0	-5.5	-6.8	-6.1	-3.7	
Foreign trade[4]											
(1995 = 100 volumes unless otherwise stated)											
UK balance on trade in goods (£ million)	BOKI	-11 910	-20 598	-4 785	-5 267	-6 293	..	-2 734	-2 614	..	
Non EU balance on trade in goods (£ million)	ENRX	-7 874	-15 298	-3 184	-4 026	-4 856	-4 589	-2 026	-1 577	-986	
Non EU exports of goods (excl oil & erratics)	ENUA	118.2	113.7	114.6	113.8	109.7	110.5	102.6	111.5	117.5	0.8
Non EU imports of goods (excl oil & erratics)	ENTS	122.4	133.5	130.1	134.1	138.0	139.9	138.5	141.2	140.1	1.4
Non EU import & price index (excl oil)[5]	ENXR	-5.4	-5.0	-4.8	-5.5	-5.0	-4.0	-5.1	-4.2	-2.8	
Non EU export & price index (excl oil)[5]	ENXS	-2.5	-3.2	-2.9	-3.9	-3.8	-2.6	-3.0	-2.5	-2.2	
Labour market and productivity											
(1995 = 100 unless otherwise stated)											
UK claimant unemployment (thousands)	BCJD	1 586.1	1 346.9	362.6	1 333.2	1 323.3	1 306.7	1 306.7	1312.4	1314.4	-0.6
UK vacancies (thousands)	DPCD	283.6	296.3	293.5	299.2	312.0	..	305.0	301.3	301.7	-3.0
UK employees in manufacturing (thousands)	YEJA	4 166	4 142	4 142	4 142	4 122	4 064	..	4 064	4 044	..
Whole economy productivity	LNNN	103.1	104.2	104.3	104.5	104.4	..	..	..	..	..
Manufacturing productivity	LNNX	99.8	100.2	100.2	100.7	100.5	..	100.9	101.3	..	..
Unit wage costs – whole economy	LNNK	104.6	108.4	107.8	108.6	110.1	..	..	..	..	
Unit wage costs – manufacturing	LNNQ	109.0	113.5	112.9	113.5	114.4	..	115.1	114.7	..	
Financial markets[1]											
Sterling ERI (1990 = 100)	AJHX	100.6	103.9	105.3	104.4	100.6	101.1	99.6	100.8	102.8	
Average exchange rate / US $	AJFA	1.6382	1.6574	1.6537	1.6531	1.6762	1.6329	1.6509	1.6276	1.6220	
Average exchange rate / DM	AJFH	2.840	2.914	2.965	2.911	2.787	2.850	2.784	2.843	2.915	
FTSE (100 share)	AJNO	4 691.28	5 632.48	5 919.42	5 571.63	5 451.68	6 051.73	5 975.54	6 010.79	6 168.5	
3 month inter-bank rate[6]	HSAJ	7.59	6.28	7.72	7.28	6.28	5.22	5.69	5.38	5.22	
3 month interest on US Treasury bills[7/8]	AJIA	5.36	4.53	4.99	4.38	4.53	..	..	..	..	
Monetary conditions/government finances											
M0 (year on year percentage growth)	EUAC	6.2	6.1	6.2	6.0	5.4	5.5	5.6	5.2	5.6	
M4 (year on year percentage growth)	EUAD	11.2	9.7	10.0	9.5	8.7	7.4	7.7	7.4	7.0	
PSNB (£ million)[1/9]	RURQ	1 056	-7 357	5 391	-2 868	-3 957	-5 923	-11 942	-1 375	7 394	
Net lending to consumers (£ million)(broader)	RLMH	12 059	14 240	3 530	3 793	3 069	..	1 303	935	..	

		1998 Mar	1998 Apr	1998 May	1998 Jan	1998 Jul	1998 Aug	1998 Sep	1998 Oct	1998 Nov	1998 Dec	1999 Jan	1999 Feb	1999 Mar	1999 Apr
Activity and expectations															
CBI output expectations balance[1]	ETCU	12	3	-2	-3	-8	-15	-13	-29	-27	-13	-13	-10	-8	-1
CBI optimism balance[1]	ETBV	..	-22	..	..	-44	..	..	-58	..	..	-40	..	..	-6
CBI price expectations balance	ETDQ	-10	-8	-12	-20	-111	-13	-11	-19	-31	-29	-28	-25	-24	-16
GB housing starts (thousands)	CTOZ	15.6	14.1	16.1	14.0	16.1	13.7	14.9	14.0	15.5	14.6	15.3	15.8	..	..
New engineering orders (1995 =100)	FGWB	110.8	105.4	111.7	117.3	105.5	105.0	110.6	106.9	100.9	114.0	117.3	111.7	..	..

1 Not seasonally adjusted
2 MIPS: mortgage interest payments
3 FBTP: food, beverages, tobacco and petroleum
4 All Non EU figures exclude Austria, Finland & Sweden
5 12 monthly percentage change
6 Last Friday of the period
7 Last working day
8 Discontinued series due to the introduction of the Euro
9 Annual figures are for financial years 1997/8 & 1998/9

Figure 2.4 Selected monthly indicators

Summary

This unit has introduced the many needs you may have to gather information within your marketing role as well as the many different sources of information that are available. The list of sources is long, but not exhaustive, and you will need both to add to it and select from it as you work on different projects.

You will normally search secondary data sources first, as they are usually less costly. However, you need to bear in mind the fact that data has not been gathered specifically for your purpose when doing so. Questions that need to be asked include: why was this information gathered, who collected it and for what purpose, and when was it gathered?

Primary data is more relevant, as it is gathered for your specific need at the time. However, it is obviously more expensive to do this.

Further study and examination preparation

When you have completed this unit you will be able to answer Question 3 from the December 2002 examination paper. Go to www.cimeduhub.com to access Specimen Answers and Senior Examiner's advice for these exam questions.

It is also worth recapping on some of the useful internet sites listed throughout the unit, in particular

www.dunandbrad.co.uk

www.dis.strath.ac.uk/business/index.html

www.kompass.co.uk

www.mintel.com

unit 3
assembling and presenting information

Learning objectives

In this unit you will:

- Consider suitable criteria for selection of a database for use within your marketing role (4.1.2)
- Consider the practical aspects of database selection (4.1.2)
- Look at what is involved in managing a database (4.1.2)
- Gain an understanding of the way in which a database can be used in segmentation (4.1.3)
- Examine how best to present information in various aspects of your marketing role (4.1.6).

By the end of this unit you will be able to:

- Identify factors that influence the choice of a database for use in your organization (4.1.2)
- Explain the necessity to manage a database (4.1.2)
- Explain the practical aspects of using a database to assist segmentation (4.1.3)
- Present information in various formats for comparison purposes (4.1.6) & (4.5.3)
- Present information in a suitable format to influence others (4.1.6) & (4.5.7)
- This unit covers the key skill Presenting information
- It also covers the statements of marketing practice Collect, synthesize, analyse and report measurement data and Exchange information to solve problems and make decisions.

Study Guide

This unit covers a range of information that you may be asked to gather in your marketing role. With the previous unit on 'Gathering information from inside and outside the organization', it covers the 20 per cent of the syllabus devoted to 'Gathering and Assembling Information for Marketing' (Section 4.1). It considers how to go about selecting an appropriate database, and, when the database is operational, how it can be effectively managed. It looks briefly at how the database can be used to assist segmentation decisions. Finally, it suggests how information can best be presented for a variety of purposes. For example, you may be asked to undertake some competitor analysis, and therefore need to present information for comparison. On another occasion you may be asked to recommend a venue for a new product launch to existing customers – in this case you will be presenting information you have gathered in order to persuade your audience to accept your recommendation. Completion of the unit will take approximately four to six hours, including the completion of all activities, some of which will contribute to your assignments if you are being assessed on a continuous basis.

Introduction

Direct marketing is now widely used as a means of promoting and developing better relationships with carefully targeted customers. Direct mail relies on an effective database, direct response advertising can be used to build up that database of interested customers, and telemarketing using the database can give an organization a cost-effective way of maintaining a close link with those customers. For these reasons it is very important to create and maintain a database that can keep pace with customer profiles and their buying behaviour.

Choosing a database

A database is a collection of files that are in some way logically interrelated. It contains information that is organized in list format. For example, a database may contain names, addresses, contact numbers, etc. It replaces the card file or address book that you might keep manually.

A database will usually allow you to store almost limitless amounts of information, and organize this information in a way that makes sense to you and your way of working. It allows you to input information to tables of rows and columns, and, having done so, search that information through 'queries'. Queries are questions you ask to locate specific information and select information that matches your query. For example, you might want to identify all customers in a particular area that have placed orders in the past month. You will set up a query that identifies postcode areas to be included and dates in the 'Order placed' column which start one month ago. When you have identified the information you need, you can create a 'report' and print it off if appropriate.

You may choose to purchase a generic database package that you can design to your own specification, or have designed on your behalf. However, an increasing number of pre-designed customer management packages are becoming available, and purchasing one of these packages may be a time- and cost-effective way of making a first move.

The first stage in selecting a database is to set out your criteria for selection. For example, how much is available to spend, what is the level of IT literacy in your organization, and how important is it that the database is user-friendly? You may need it to be up and running within a set period of time, and you certainly need to identify what you need it to do. Will you need the company that supplies it to customize it for you and to provide training for the staff who are going to use it?

Case history

Robert Horne Paperlink

Robert Horne Paper Company is a national paper merchant, selling over 9000 products to printers. A specialist 'backselling' division called Paperlink was set up to target the customers of the printers (i.e. the design agencies) who are able to influence the choice of paper – commonly for the premium, specialist products. Paperlink has over 9000 clients who are managed by a team of 13 individuals – six office-based, and seven on the road. These are segmented in various ways, the most important of which is by potential profit they could generate. This allows Paperlink to decide how to manage each account:

- Visits, corporate entertainment, telephone contact and direct mail
- Telephone account management and direct mail
- Direct mail only.

Until 1998 Paperlink's only IT support was in the form of a basic order-processing system (to log samples and promotional material sent), and one PC for writing letters, etc. The whole company recognized the need for an upgrades system to take them into the next century – one that would allow improved segmentation and storage of customer information, more efficient internal communication and better account management. The Paperlink division was selected to trial a system for the following reasons:

- *Low risk* Paperlink does not have trading accounts, so key financial information could not be lost
- *Geographical coverage* Although it is a small team, members are based over the whole of the UK, so a wide variety of needs could be trialled
- *IT-literate* Being a fairly young team, everyone has good IT skills and no 'fear' of computers
- *Need* The Paperlink team has the highest staff/customer ratio and therefore has to manage accounts through more direct mail and telephone account management, rather than through face-to-face relationship building.

Paperlink identified several 'off-the-shelf' contact management software programs available (such as Maximiser, Tracker, etc.). Eventually a new system called 'Pursuit' that is totally customizable was chosen. The criteria for choice were identified as follows:

- The system needed to work in parallel with existing Robert Horne IT programs
- The system needed to be flexible to allow for the specialist role Paperlink fulfils within the organization
- The Paperlink manager and IT department needed to feel a good rapport with the system suppliers
- The system needed the capacity to store detailed information about each account and contact

- The system needed to have the ability to sort the information and select actionable segments (e.g. all large graphic design agencies with more than ten designers who do work for local authorities and are based in Yorkshire)

- The system needed to be user-friendly, easy to learn and easy to train people to use

- The system needed to have the ability to prompt action (e.g. one week after sample products had been despatched the team member would be prompted to telephone for feedback; two days after a specific order had been placed the team member would be prompted to send a thank-you letter, etc.)

- The cost of the system needed to fit budget requirements

- The system needed to be designed and implemented in 12 months.

The success of the system relies on accurate and up-to-date detailed information being captured and input. The team already knew much of the basic information, but everything had to be checked and supplementary information collected for all 9000 accounts. This was a very time-consuming and laborious task. The need for accuracy was also stressed by highlighting incoming direct mail that had errors – and the negative effect of those errors. Each individual was allocated a number of accounts for which they were responsible. Priority was given to key accounts, followed by smaller ones, and an achievable number was given as the target for each week. During this process the old system continued to be used in tandem to minimize disruption.

Results

The efficiency, motivation and performance of the team were noticeably improved through the implementation of the new system. In addition, customers enjoyed a higher level of relevant contact with the company, and received direct mail and promotions which were specific to their needs.

In summary:

- Time is spent more effectively – less on administration, more on customer contact

- Information stored is actionable – on an individual customer level, and by segment

- Internal communication efficiency has been improved

- External communication professionalism has been achieved.

When you are about to make your final selection of database, consider one more aspect – the Data Protection Act 1998. The Data Protection Registrar has a duty to ensure that all users of personal data comply with the eight enforceable principles of good practice. They say that data must be:

- Fairly and lawfully processed
- Processed for limited purposes
- Adequate, relevant and not excessive
- Accurate
- Not kept longer than necessary
- Processed in accordance with the data subject's rights
- Secure
- Not transferred to countries without adequate protection.

Unit 3 Assembling and presenting information

A booklet is available to provide guidance to direct marketers, and this can be obtained from: Office of the Data Protection Registrar, Wycliffe House, Water Lane, Wilmslow, Cheshire SK9 5AF.

The Market Research Society also publishes *Guidelines for Handling Databases*, and this can be obtained from: The Market Research Society, 15 Northburgh Street, London EC1V 0AH.

Presenting information for comparison and to influence decisions

When you have collected data, whether from internal reports or external sources, it is important that you present it in the best way possible. If you are presenting competitor prices for decisions on whether to adjust your own in response, then the information, and any trends to be drawn from it, must be clear to assist with decision making.

The following represents a summary of information you will have covered within Customer Communications, together with examples of how it may be used.

Bar charts

These are commonly used to show the relationships between variables, and the differences between figures are shown by the height or length of the bars drawn. See Figure 3.1 for an example of how the data from the table in Figure 2.1 is displayed using a bar chart.

Bar charts can be in the form of single bars or columns, multiple bars or columns, or stacked (component) bars or columns. Each is suited to a particular purpose. The example in Figure 3.1 is a multiple bar chart, as it is used to highlight the changing figures for several regions over time. You will see in Figure 3.2 that this also represents a suitable format for displaying a comparison of changing competitor prices over a period of time.

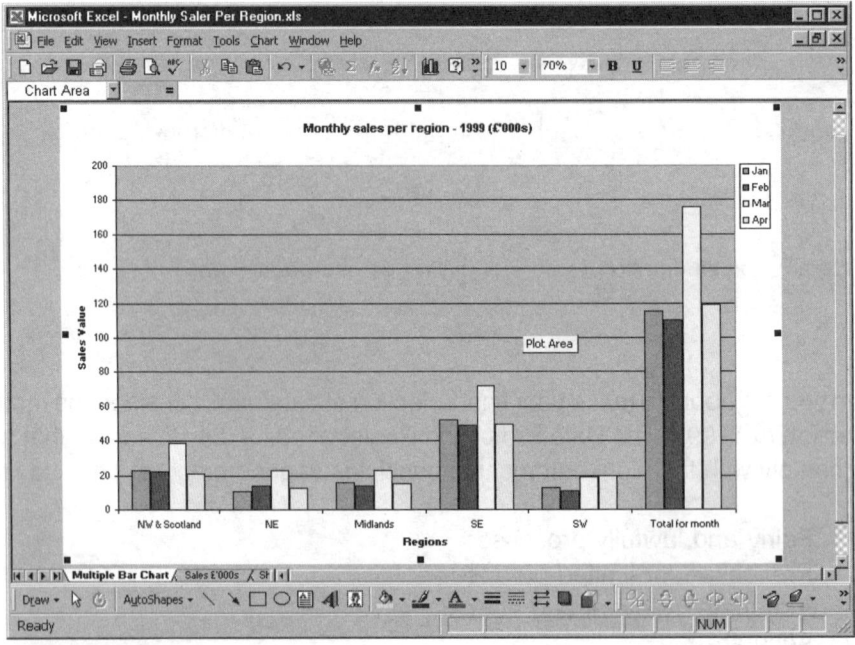

Figure 3.1 Multiple bar chart

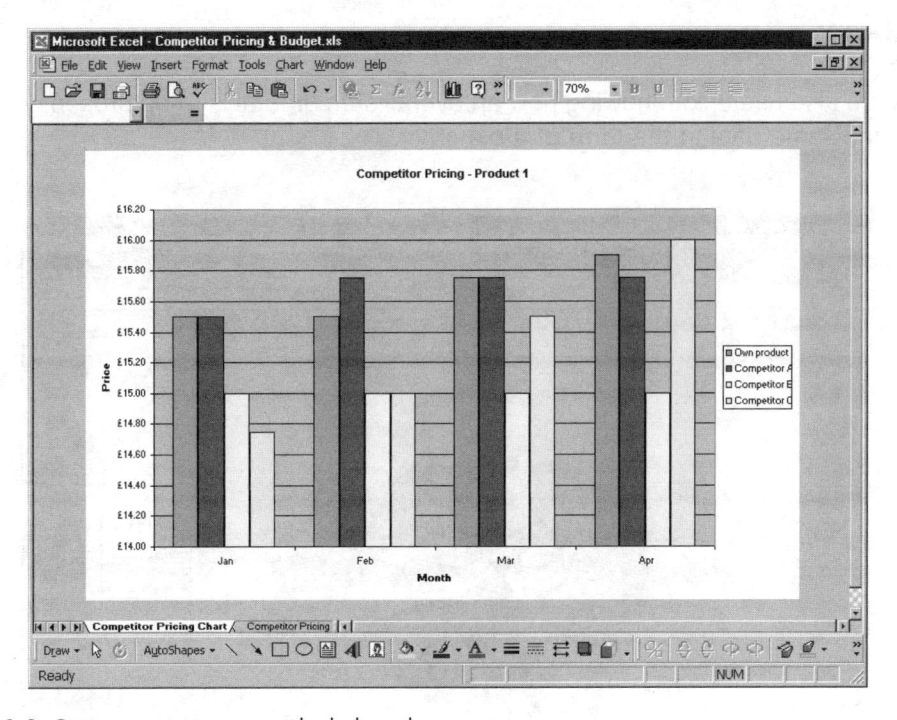

Figure 3.2 Competitor pricing – multiple bar chart

A component bar chart is more suitable for presenting the relative sizes of the components of an overall figure. An example of how a component bar chart can be used to show how a budget for an event is to be broken down is shown in Figure 3.3.

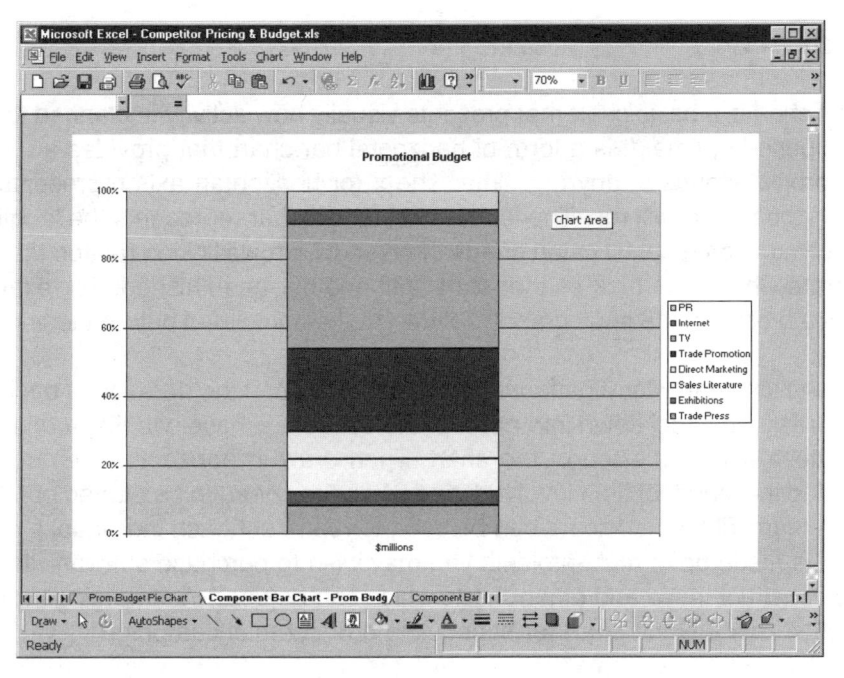

Figure 3.3 Component bar chart – breakdown of promotional budget

Pie charts

These are also useful for showing how an overall sum or total is to be broken down. Figure 3.4 shows the same data in the form of a pie chart.

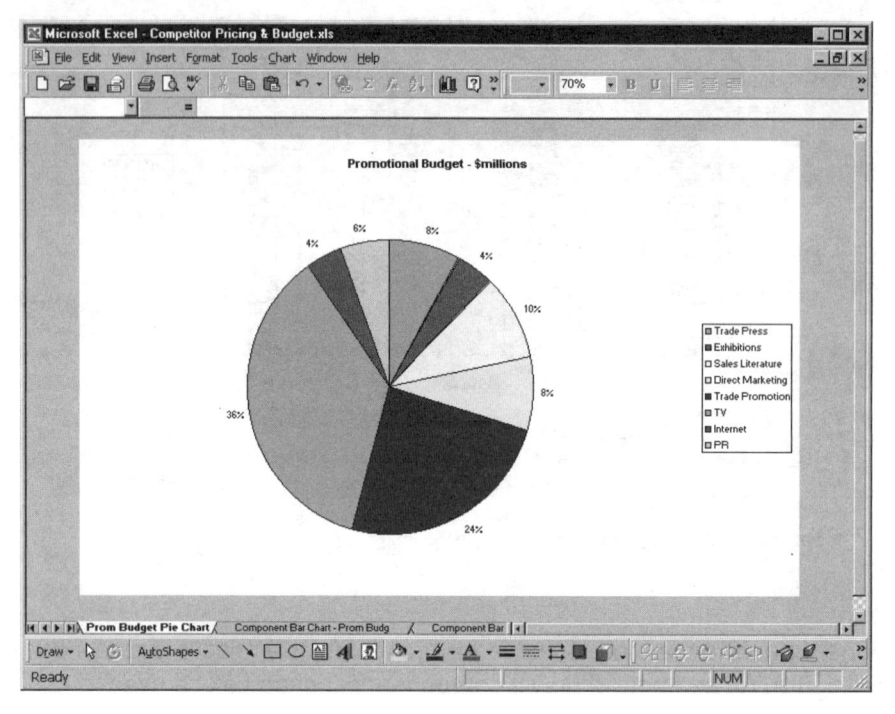

Figure 3.4 Promotional budget breakdown – pie chart

Gantt charts

The Gantt chart is a basic chart that presents visually how activity is planned to take place over a specific period of time. It is a form of horizontal bar chart that provides a useful overview of where a project stands at any one time. The x (or horizontal) axis represents the time scale over which the project will run. The length of each task bar represents the length of the specific tasks involved. More sophisticated charts often show arrows linking related tasks. This helps to demonstrate where one task cannot start until another has finished. For example, if you are producing a brochure, the photography will need to be completed before the printing takes place.

Constructing the chart is straightforward. List the tasks and the duration of each in the left-hand column. Break the 'time' down into appropriate sections – days, weeks, months, quarters, etc. and put these across the top of the chart. Then draw in horizontal lines against each task, representing the length of time involved, and when they need to be carried out. Where a project involves a team, different colours can be used to represent each individual's responsibilities. If your work is made up of multi-projects you may wish to purchase software that is designed to help you construct these and other charts which can be used in managing projects effectively. Figure 3.5 shows a Gantt chart for scheduling a direct mail campaign.

Persuasive language

When you are presenting information to make a recommendation, whether in report format or verbally, you need to consider the language that you use and how persuasive it sounds. Your audience will be more likely to accept your recommendation if it is presented confidently and based on sound logic. It is your job to signpost them through the information you are presenting to illustrate clearly the reason for your recommendations. The need for persuasive language becomes even more important when you are involved in Public Relations and are looking to change or reinforce attitudes towards your organization and its activities. In order to present a persuasive argument you need to consider the following points:

- Who is your audience?
- What do they already know?
- How well do they know you?
- Have you 'persuaded' them successfully before?
- What sort of questions or objections will they have?

Weeks	1	2	3	4	5	6	7
Print							
Envelopes (standard)	■	■	■				
Print proofs	■						
Completed print		■	■	■			
Laser proofs					■		
Laser print						■	
Delivery						■	
Insert and mailing							■

Figure 3.5 Gantt chart showing planned print activity for a direct mail campaign

These questions are equally important whether you are writing or speaking. In both cases you need to anticipate the audience's reaction and how you will counter any argument. In the case of written reports you will need to think more carefully, as you will not have the same opportunity to overcome issues you have not identified prior to writing.

What is the message that you are looking to communicate? How complex is the argument you need to put forward? How understandable will it be to the audience? What 'emotions' are you likely to arouse through your argument? It is recognized as being far harder to persuade people to accept new and/or controversial ideas. The best way to do this is to express your argument in clear language that is straightforward and easily understood. Can you add to this by demonstrating? It would be much easier to convince a group of people of the need to set up a lively website if you are able to show them some examples of what others have done. It may be even more effective if you can demonstrate that your competitors already have such a presence! Use the 'benefits' of what you are presenting – word your argument in such a way that it is obvious to the audience exactly how it will benefit them as an organization or as individuals. For example, say: 'This new system will provide each of you with the information you require, in detail, whenever you need it – saving you time and effort' rather than 'This system offers quotation management, opportunity profiling and qualification, and contact histories'. Use and repeat positive phrases such as 'We will ...', and summarize the key points of your argument.

When presenting face-to-face, try to make as much personal contact with your audience as you can. Use names, and terms such as 'our team' to involve the audience as closely as possible. Use strong eye contact – without intimidating.

Unit 3 Assembling and presenting information

Do not underestimate the need to see the argument from your audience's perspective. If you try to argue from your own perspective, which is a mistake many of us make, you are unlikely to achieve your objective.

Activity 3.1

You have been asked to obtain quotes from three companies for a new stand to use in the Reception area of your building. It needs to be:

- no taller than eight feet
- easy to put up and take down (you will also take it to exhibitions)
- lightweight and easy to transport
- free-standing
- within an overall budget of £1000.

You have received the following information (Figure 3.6) – present your findings in such a way that you make a clear recommendation as to which should be chosen.

Dear Sir

Thank you for your enquiry regarding our equipment. The information you require is shown below:

Easi-stands

Height   7'

Easy to put up and take down. Unlike other brands, our stand is durable and will not be damaged by frequent dismantling and transporting.

Weight   23–35lbs (packed)

Free-standing

Price   £1200 + VAT

If you require any further information, please do not hesitate to contact me.

I will telephone you in the next three days to ensure you have the information you need to make your decision.

Many thanks

Yours faithfully

A. Stand-seller
Easi-stands plc

Figure 3.6(a) Quote received following your enquiry about display stands

Dear Sir

Thank you for your enquiry regarding our equipment. The information you require is shown below:

Flexi-stands

Height   7' 6"

Dismantled in minutes. We will provide instructions to enable it to be put up within 45 minutes.

Weight   36lbs

Free-standing

Price   £875 + VAT

If you require any further information, please do not hesitate to contact me.

Many thanks

Yours faithfully

B. Stand-seller
Flexi-standsplc

Figure 3.6(b) Quote received following your enquiry about display stands

> Dear Sir
>
> Thank you for your enquiry regarding our equipment. The information you require is shown below:
>
> **Lite-stands**
>
> Height   8' 3"
>
> Easy to put up and take down.
>
> Weight   42lbs (packed)
>
> Free-standing
>
> Price   £1000+VAT
>
> If you require any further information, please do not hesitate to contact me.
>
> Many thanks
>
> Yours faithfully
>
>
> C. Stand-seller
> Lite-standsplc

Figure 3.6(c) Quote received following your enquiry about display stands

Managing the database

Once the database is up and running, it is very easy to neglect it in favour of other priorities. For this reason a 'database manager' should be nominated. This person should be the only one able to change the 'fields' of the database, and should actively manage input and updating of the database on a regular basis.

As database manager, the sales force becomes one of your most important suppliers of new data, and it is essential to set up a dialogue with them. You may wish to set up a proforma, or a report that they send to you on a weekly basis, updating information. You may have the facility through your intranet for the updating to be done by them directly, saving you time. In either case you will need to set up training sessions to ensure that everyone is aware of the benefits of keeping the information updated and the methods which are to be adopted.

Remember that your database should also be 'cleaned' on a regular basis. If you sell direct to consumers, you need to develop an effective way of ensuring that information is accurate and maintained that way. How will you deal with mailings that are returned as 'Gone Away'? How will you ensure that, when you are notified that a customer has died, you do not continue to send mail marked 'deceased'? – this can be extremely distressing for relatives and will not enhance the reputation of your organization.

Using the database in segmentation

The first source of data you will use will be your existing customers, and once they are input to the database you are in a position to cross-sell to them. You can target them more effectively as you will be able to 'sort' the database by any field or combination of fields. Fields you may use to set up your database will vary but will include some or all of the following:

- Customer name
- Customer title
- Address
- Postcode
- Company name (if applicable)
- Type of company (if applicable)
- Purchases made
- Date of first purchase
- Frequency of purchase
- Value of previous purchases
- Key Account Manager (if applicable)
- Geodemographic detail (if applicable)
- Source of original lead
- Past contacts
- Past responses.

If you used a software house to advise you on setting up your database originally, they will have considerable experience in guiding you through your 'needs' concerning what it is you want the database to do, and therefore what data you need it to contain.

From the above fields you can see that you would be able to use the database to help you segment your market and target your communications more effectively. You can target a complimentary product to those who have previously purchased a particular product from your existing portfolio. If your database reveals that a core group of customers re-buy approximately every two years, then you can send out a targeted mailing just before the end of that period to assist their 'information search' and encourage them to remain loyal to your organization. Your database provides the ideal tool for tracking customer needs and satisfaction.

Analysis of your database can help your search for new customers. You can carry out analysis to see in what postcode areas your most profitable sales are made, or what type of companies buy your products. You can then add to your list by buying more contacts from a list broker, or from the Electoral Roll (held in the local library), or from organizations such as Kompass who provide lists of companies.

If you have a website you can collect information about enquirers 'online'. Online surveys are an effective and affordable data collection tool. The information collected, however, needs to be qualified before it is assumed to be accurate and useful. For example, you can use an interactive form to collect data about visitors to your website. However, they may have visited by chance and not be potential customers. You can capture information about an enquirer to enable you to send information about your products and services to them, either via e-mail or more traditional methods. If you do use your website for this purpose, be ready to deal through

Unit 3 Assembling and presenting information

e-commerce – if you have to e-mail an enquirer later to ask for their name and address this will not be consistent with the technological advantage of convenience that they will have previously perceived!

You can also add to your database through attendance at events, as is mentioned in the example shown in 'Making contacts for marketing'. It is important to qualify contacts so that you are using your resources to best effect. Efficient target marketing will be more cost-effective.

Summary

In this unit we have considered the increasing use of the database in marketing activities. In particular, we have considered its use in segmenting your customers in various ways, and so improving the targeting of contacts.

We have also considered various means of presenting information for comparison and how to influence decisions to be made by an organization. Unit 2, 'Gathering information from inside and outside the organization', covered the collection of data for various marketing purposes – in this unit we have looked at ways of presenting this data so that others can make sense of it and follow trends identified from it.

Further study and examination preparation

When you have completed this unit you will be able to answer Question 6 from the June 2002 examination paper. Go to www.cimeduhub.com to access Specimen Answers and Senior Examiner's advice for these exam questions.

You may also wish to visit the following websites

www.roberthorne.co.uk for further information on a company featured in this unit

www.mrs.org.uk the market research society's website

unit 4
gathering and analysing financial and numerical information

Learning objectives

In this unit you will:

- Consider some basic uses for spreadsheets within your marketing role (4.5.7)

- Learn how a spreadsheet can be used to make calculations (4.5.4 & 4.5.5)

- Consider how basic statistical techniques can be used to analyse marketing and business information (4.5.3 & 4.5.5)

- Consider other factors which impact on decisions made in a marketing context, and how these relate to financial factors for consideration. (4.5.3 & 4.5.5).

By the end of this unit you will be able to:

- Use a spreadsheet to make basic calculations and to analyse the results of a customer satisfaction survey (4.1.4 & 4.5.5)

- Use basic statistical techniques to assist in making business decisions (4.5.3 & 4.5.5)

- Carry out a cost/benefit analysis (4.5.3)

- This unit covers the key skills Using ICT and the internet and Presenting information

- It covers the statements of marketing practice Collect, synthesize, analyse and report measurement data and Exchange information to solve problems and make decisions.

Unit 4 Gathering and analysing financial and numerical information

Study Guide

This unit provides an introduction to techniques that will help you make sense of quantitative information that contributes to marketing decision making. In Unit 3, 'Assembling and presenting information', we covered the presentation of data descriptively, through the use of tables and graphs. This unit follows on from this and considers a number of techniques used to analyse data, including summarizing data in terms of averages. It also looks briefly at probability, forecasting and trend analysis and how they can be used to inform an organization's decisions for the future.

With 'Gathering information from inside and outside the organization' and 'Assembling and presenting information', it covers the 20 per cent of the syllabus devoted to 'Gathering and Assembling Information for Marketing', and with 'Introduction to budgeting' (Unit 11), it covers the 20 per cent which is dedicated to 'Introduction to budgeting'. Completion of the unit will take approximately six to eight hours, including the completion of all activities, and depending on your existing level of competence with figures. The activities and questions are to check that you have the required level of understanding necessary to apply the techniques within your marketing role, and to tackle the questions on the Case Study. It is strongly recommended that you work through all of these activities before moving on in your studies.

Introduction

Most, if not all, organizations measure their success through some form of financial and numerical analysis. Even 'not-for-profit' organizations need money to ensure continued survival. In the past, marketers have been criticized for their lack of understanding of finance and figures – and yet, as a business area, use numerical analysis constantly. They may not express themselves using the same terminology as accountants, but the use of figures in the overall marketing planning process is widespread:

- What is the size of the market?
- How big is our share of this market?
- What does it cost to make this product?
- How shall we price this product?
- What impact will a ten per cent reduction in price have on profit?
- How much will it cost to book a stand at this exhibition?
- Will the cost involved be justifiable in terms of the objectives we have set?
- Which magazine shall we advertise in?
- How many insertions shall we plan?
- What targets will we set the sales force?
- How much will it cost to mail 30,000 potential customers in a specified geographical area?

Several specialized software packages exist to assist with data analysis and accurate statistical interpretation. One example would be SPSS which is used by many organizations. This package assists with customer segmentation and profiling, customer satisfaction surveys and effective direct mailing, as well as providing other tools. Your organization may already use such a package. If so, try to become familiar with it.

There are various tools and techniques that will help you in this area of your role – this unit introduces just some of these tools and techniques. The finance department of your organization is an internal customer. Marketing is all about meeting your customers' needs and being able to communicate with them. You will do this more confidently with an improved numerical ability.

Using spreadsheets

The use of database and spreadsheet software can be confused. The simple way to decide which to use is to consider what type of data you are working with and what you want to be able to do with it.

A *database* is a collection of files that are in some way logically interrelated. It contains information that is organized in list format. For example, a database may contain names, addresses, contact numbers, etc. It replaces the card file or address book that you might keep manually.

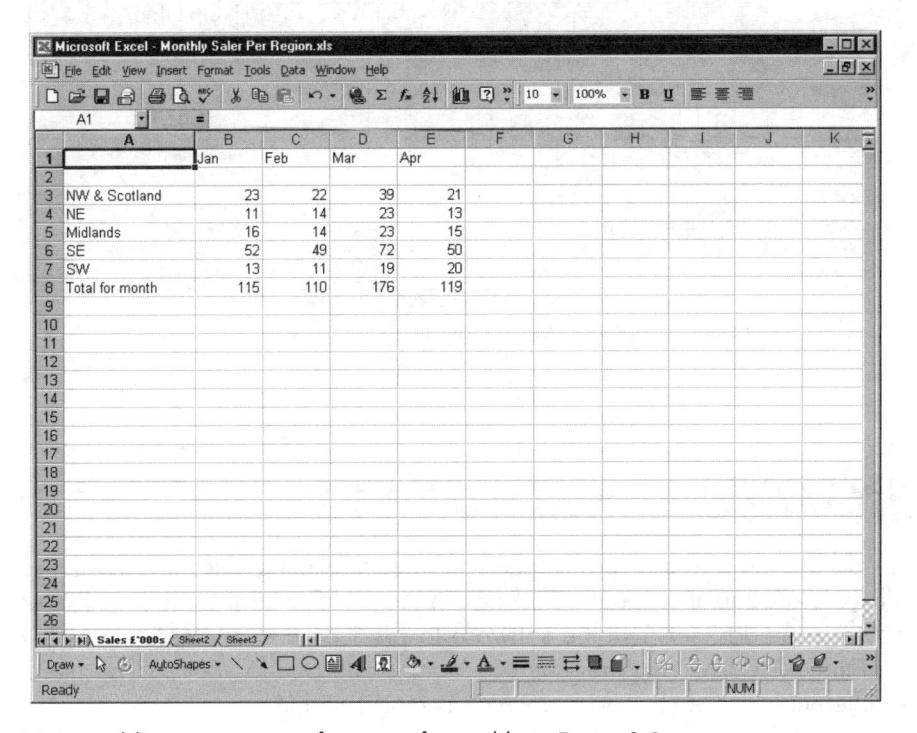

Figure 4.1 Spreadsheet containing information from table in Figure 2.1

The *spreadsheet* provides an electronic alternative to many tasks that have traditionally been carried out manually – for example, budget monitoring, sales reports, etc. It is used to store, analyse and present quantitative data. To enter information onto a spreadsheet, you simply move the cursor to the cell in which you want to put the data and input the number. You can type in words (as labels), numerical data (the data itself), and formulas (to make calculations for the analysis of your data).

Figure 4.1 shows a spreadsheet which contains the same information as Figure 2.1. The difference is that Figure 2.1 is shown in the form of a table and would be presented in this format or be manually converted into a chart. Figure 4.1 shows the spreadsheet and Figure 4.2 the chart that was automatically produced from the spreadsheet package.

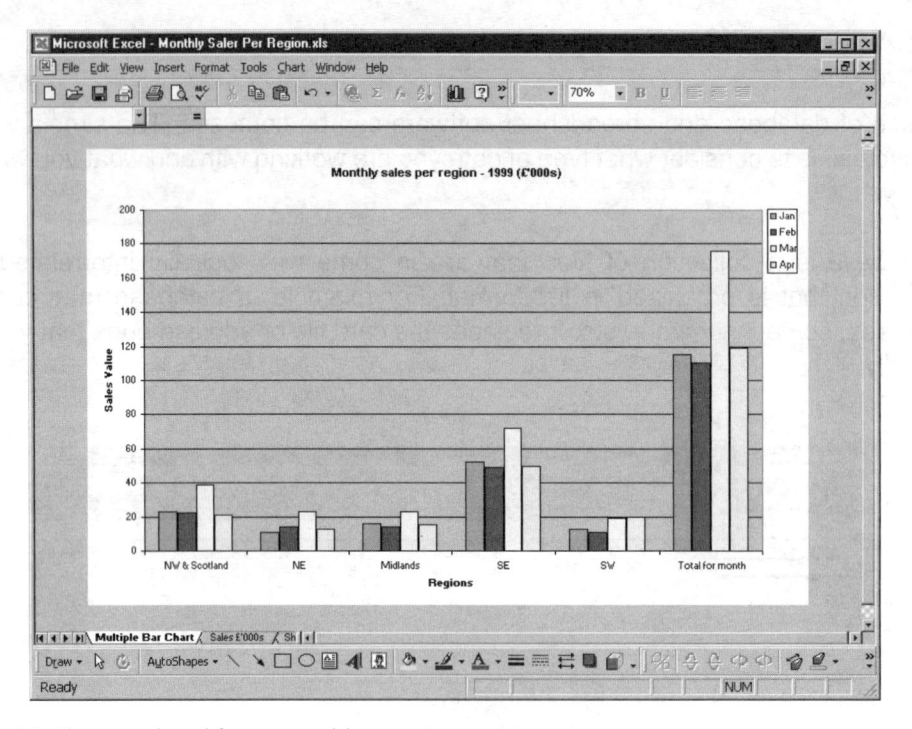

Unit 4 Gathering and analysing financial and numerical information

Figure 4.2 Chart produced from spreadsheet in Figure 4.1

Activity 4.1

If you do not already use spreadsheets in your marketing role, find out whether anyone within your organization does. Go back to Activity 2.5 and transfer the information you found to a spreadsheet. Use the software to produce a chart presenting the information. Repeat the exercise during the next two months and add to your spreadsheet. Experiment with different forms of chart to see which is most suitable.

Using the spreadsheet to calculate

The main advantage that a spreadsheet has over a database is its sophisticated ability to make calculations. You simply need to learn how to use the formula that the software contains. Most packages have tutorials that you can work through to learn how to use different elements of the software, and there are many books that provide easy reference guidance in the use of various packages. The large number of packages available means that it would be impossible to show the full potential of spreadsheets in this coursebook. This section simply looks to introduce the type of calculation that can be used to help you in your marketing role.

Calculations include simple arithmetical calculations (which allow you to add, subtract, multiply or divide the figures you have input). You can extend these calculations to a range of data within the spreadsheet and the package will make the calculations automatically.

Most spreadsheets are also programmed with 'functions' that carry out more complicated tasks, such as calculating averages, counting the number of entries in a range, or calculating the monthly payment on a loan. Commonly used functions include the following:

SUM	This displays the sum of a specific range of cells	= SUM(B4:B11)
AVERAGE	This calculates the average of a range of cells	= AVERAGE(A3:A25)
COUNT	This calculates the number of entries in a range	= COUNT(C11:C79)
MAX	Shows the largest value in a range	= MAX(B11:B55)
MIN	Shows the smallest value in a range	= MIN(D3:D29)

Figure 4.3 shows sales per sales representative over a four-month period.

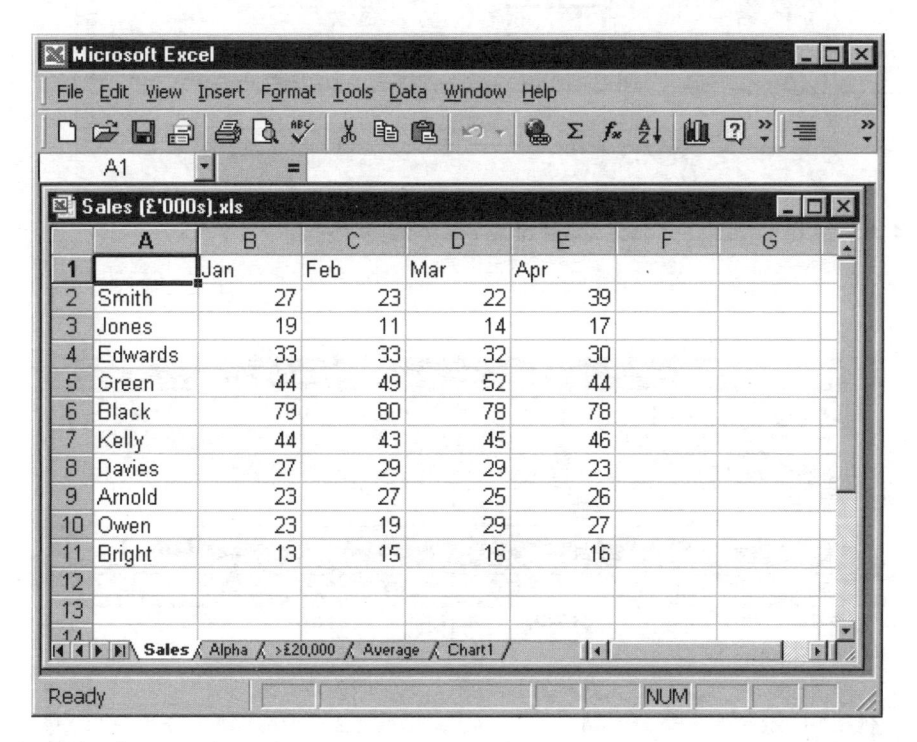

Figure 4.3 Sales figures achieved

Data can also be 'sorted' and 'filtered'. Lists of data can be 'sorted' into ascending or descending order, either numerically or alphabetically.

Figure 4.4 shows the same figures, and the salespeople are listed alphabetically. 'Filtering' can be used to display only information that meets criteria that you specify.

Figure 4.5 shows the same data 'filtered' to display only those salespeople who achieved sales of over £20,000 in any month during the four-month period.

Figure 4.6 shows the average achievement for each month – you will see the function that has been used in calculating the average automatically highlighted below the toolbars on the spreadsheet.

Figure 4.7 shows the same data displayed as a multiple bar chart produced automatically via the spreadsheet package.

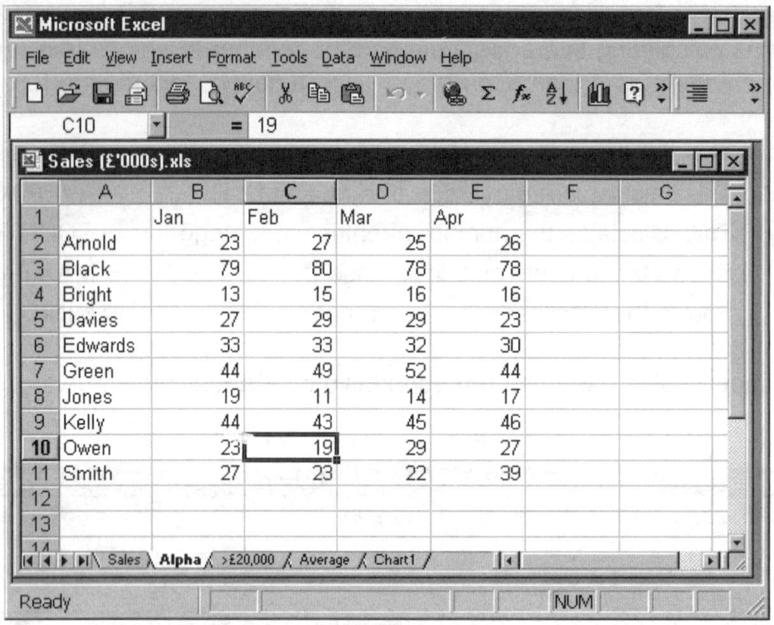

Unit 4 Gathering and analysing financial and numerical information

Figure 4.4 Sales achieved (alphabetical list of salespeople)

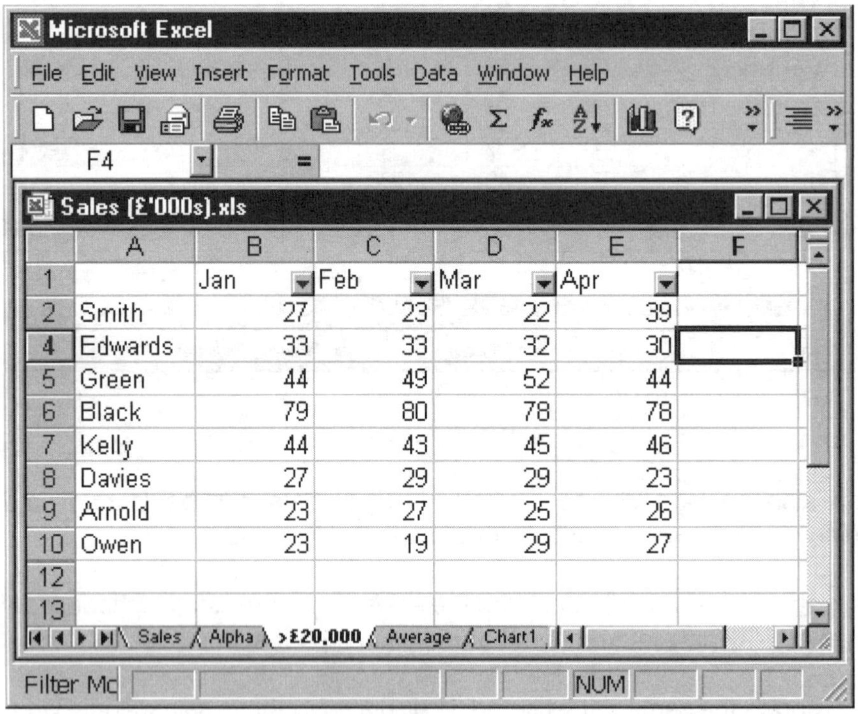

Figure 4.5 Salespeople achieving over £20,000 sales in a month during the period January–April

The examples we have looked at here represent just one of the types of numerical information you might need to manipulate in a marketing role. Others may include comparisons of competitor pricing, comparisons of prices charged for advertising by different publications, changes in profitability, comparative profitability of different products across a range, portions of promotional budget spent on different media over a period of time, etc.

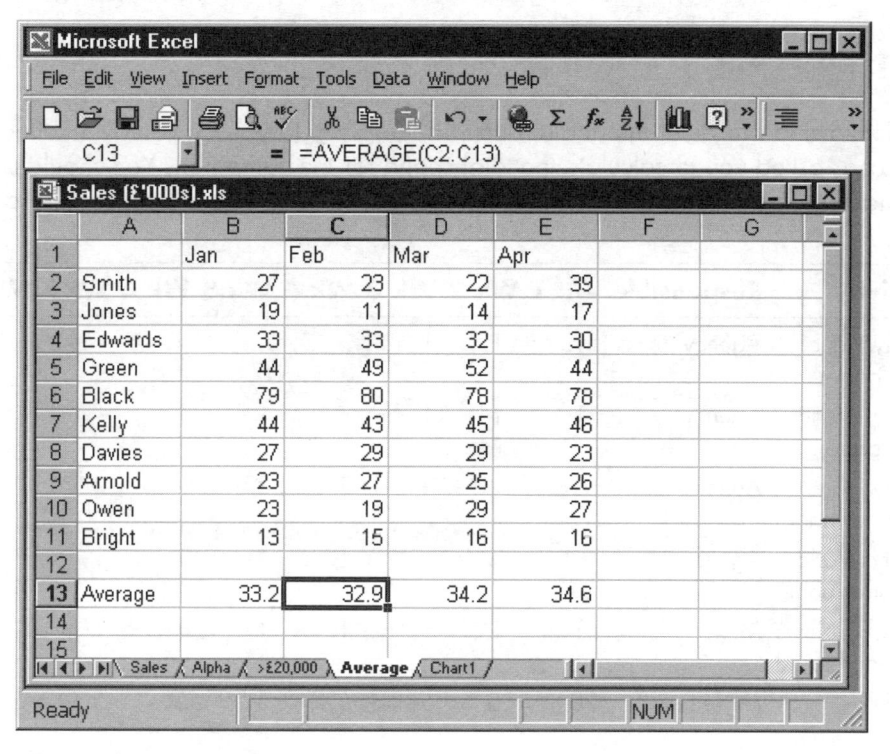

Figure 4.6 Sales figures showing average achievement for each month

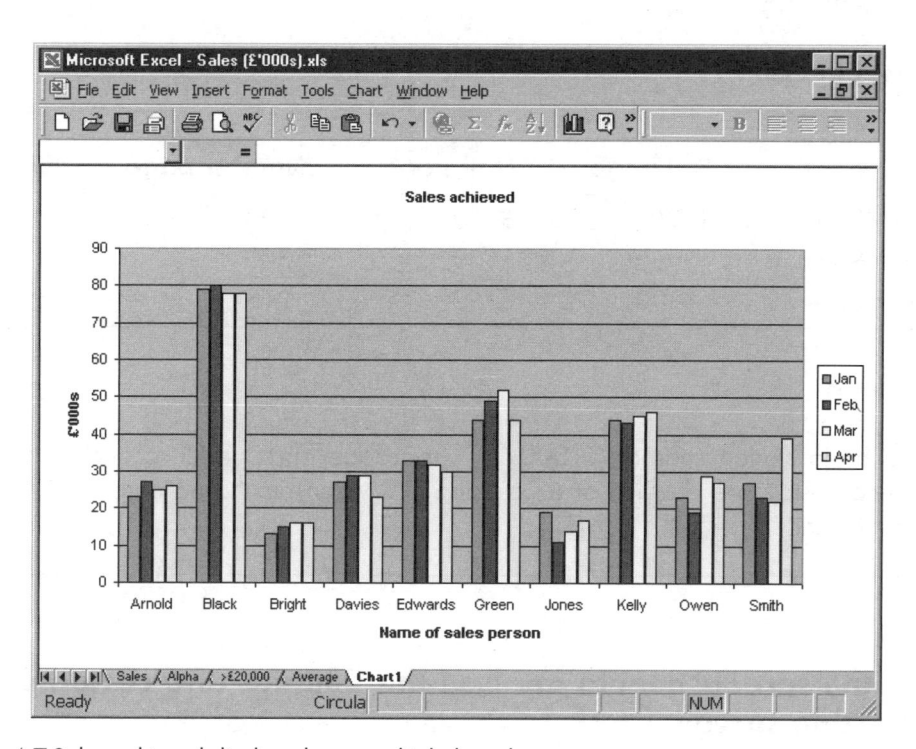

Figure 4.7 Sales achieved displayed as a multiple bar chart

Unit 4 Gathering and analysing financial and numerical information

Activity 4.2

The following pieces of information have been given to you by your Marketing Manager, who has asked you to calculate the total spend for the campaign. You should be prepared to make such a calculation in your examination – you will be allowed to use a calculator.

Activity	Responsible	Wk 1	Wk 2	Wk 3	Wk 4	Wk 5	Wk 6	Wk 7	Wk 8	Wk 9
Daily Planet (full page)	Agency	1	1	1						
Daily World (full page)	Agency	1	1	1						
Daily Planet (quarter page)	Agency				3	3	2	2	1	1
Daily World (quarter page)	Agency				1	1	1	1	1	1
Weekly News (quarter page)	MExec	1	1	1	1	1	1	1	1	1
Radio – 20-sec. slots	MExec	20	10	5	5	5	5	5	5	5

Media costings

Newspapers

	Full page	Half page	Quarter page	Eighth page
Daily Planet	$1200	$750	$400	$200
Daily World	$950	$500	$300	$150
Weekly News	$300	$150	$75	$40

Radio

Local radio station charges $1000 for a package of 10 × 20 second slots. Individual 20-second slots are charged at a cost of $120 when purchased outside of the package arrangement.

Using the spreadsheet to analyse the findings of a customer satisfaction survey

A spreadsheet can be useful in analysing completed questionnaires from a customer satisfaction survey, for example – and most spreadsheets software packages today have integrated graphic facilities, so that stored data can quickly be converted to graphs. These graphs can then be added to reports in a word processed document, or to a presentation slide.

Unit 4 Gathering and analysing financial and numerical information

'How important is the availability of parking to you?'

1. Totally unimportant
2. Unimportant
3. Neither important nor unimportant
4. Important
5. Very important.

And then you might ask:

'How satisfied are you with the availability of parking?'

1. Very dissatisfied
2. Dissatisfied
3. Neither satisfied nor dissatisfied
4. Satisfied
5. Very satisfied.

Figure 4.8 shows the data input from 50 respondents to the spreadsheet.

Figure 4.9 shows a bar chart of the findings from the question regarding the importance of parking to customers.

Figure 4.10 shows a bar chart of the findings from the question regarding the level of satisfaction about parking shown by customers.

Ten per cent of customers view parking as very important and 10 per cent are very dissatisfied with the current availability of parking. Only more detailed examination of responses will reveal whether these are the same 10 per cent of customers.

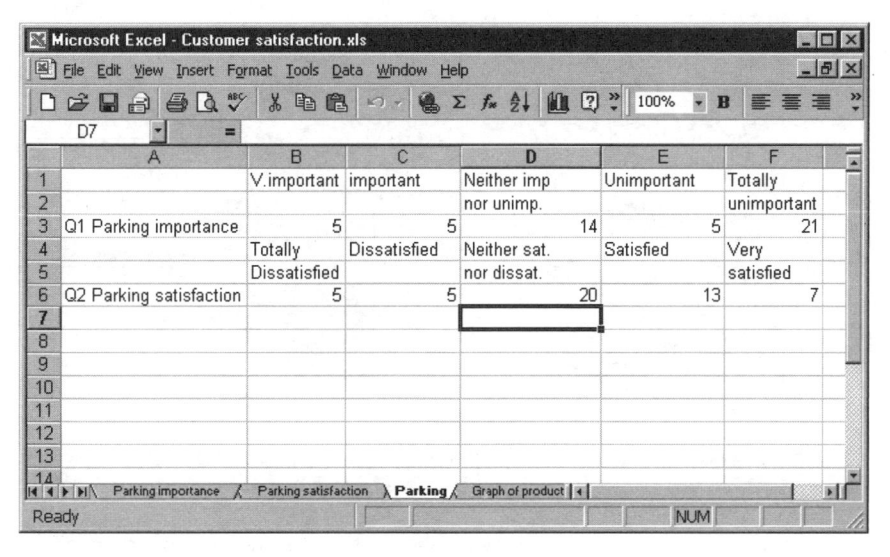

	A	B	C	D	E	F
1		V.important	important	Neither imp	Unimportant	Totally
2				nor unimp.		unimportant
3	Q1 Parking importance	5	5	14	5	21
4		Totally	Dissatisfied	Neither sat.	Satisfied	Very
5		Dissatisfied		nor dissat.		satisfied
6	Q2 Parking satisfaction	5	5	20	13	7

Figure 4.8 Data from 50 respondents

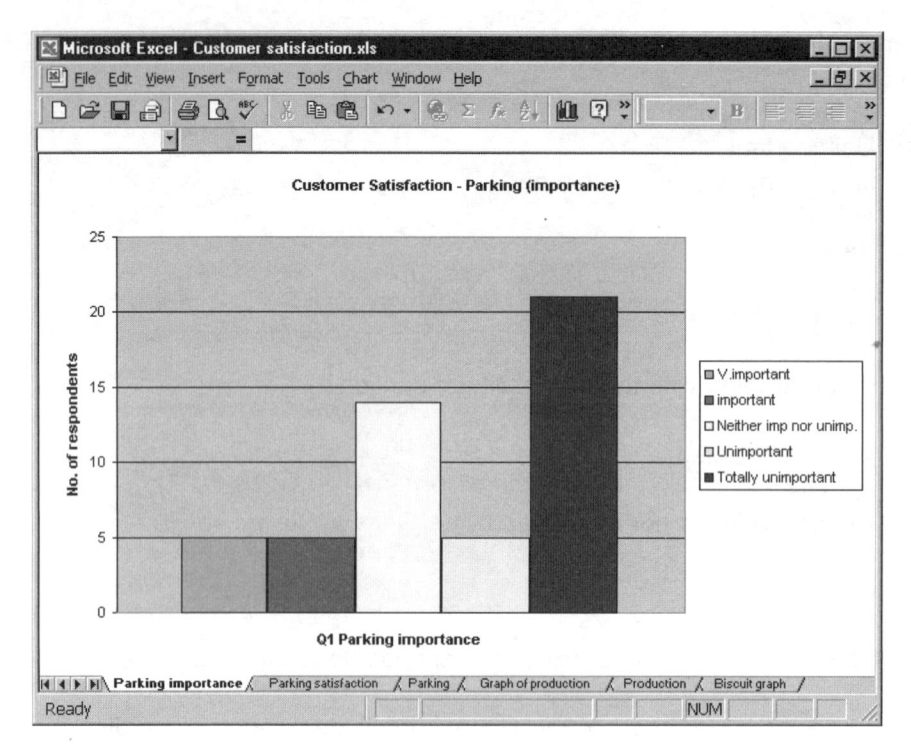

Unit 4 Gathering and analysing financial and numerical information

Figure 4.9 Bar chart showing findings on importance of parking availability

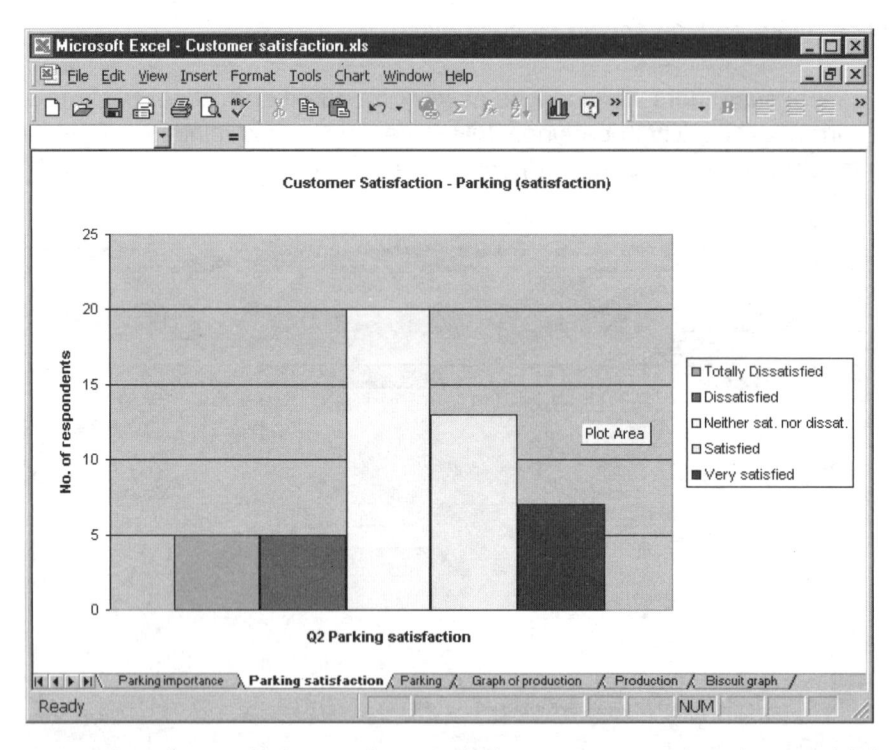

Figure 4.10 Bar chart showing findings on how satisfied customers are with parking availability

The vast majority of customers see the availability of parking as totally unimportant – again, this does not tell us why this is the case. Do most customers walk to your outlet? Are you in the area where most customers work? Is there a bus stop outside? If your objectives in sending out your questionnaire had been to find out who your customers are and where they travel from, then your questions would have to be worded differently to find appropriate data.

In this case you are interested in customer satisfaction. You may choose to carry out this type of research every three or six months, in which case you will have other questionnaire findings with which to compare. You are looking for trends – ideally, improving results which reflect action you are taking in response to previous findings.

Basic statistical techniques

Averages

As can be seen in the above sections, charts and graphs are a useful way of presenting data for comparison, and averages are another useful way of summarizing data. They are commonly used in describing business issues (e.g. 'The average consumer has spent more on leisure goods this year'; 'The average price of electrical goods has risen by seven per cent'; 'Average sales have fallen for the second month in succession'). They are useful in that they summarize a group or list of figures, smoothing out any 'abnormal' figures. However, it must be recognized that they do not provide a full picture.

An arithmetic *mean* (the average that most people refer to when they use the word 'average') is calculated by adding together the figures in a list, and then dividing the total by the number of figures in the list. It can also be represented as follows:

Arithmetic mean = total value of items/total number of items

e.g. Five different retail outlets sell the same pair of shoes for £15, £17, £18, £25 and £25 respectively.

The average price charged is £20.

Arithmetic mean = £100/5 = £20

Another form of 'average' that is widely used is the *median*. This represents the middle value of a distribution which is listed in ascending order.

In the example above, the median is £18. The median is most useful when a list has some 'extremes' in it.

For example, a region achieves the following monthly sales figures during a year:

Jan	£2000	Jul	£2500
Feb	£2750	Aug	£1000
Mar	£3000	Sept	£3250
Apr	£3000	Oct	£2500
May	£2500	Nov	£3000
Jun	£2750	Dec	£20,250

The arithmetic mean would show a value of £4042, which has only been achieved in one month of the year. The median, however, is £2750 – a value that is much closer to that regularly achieved.

Unit 4 Gathering and analysing financial and numerical information

The figure achieved in December is probably explained by a seasonal factor – this would warrant further investigation.

The final type of 'average' that you need to understand is the *mode*. The mode is the most frequently occurring figure in a list. This might be relevant in the sales of clothing, for example, when the manufacturer is interested in which sizes are the most popular when making decisions about future stocks.

Look at the example of sales of dress sizes shown below (this is obviously a reduced list):

10, 10, 10, 10, 12, 12, 12, 14, 14, 14, 14, 14, 14, 14, 14, 14, 16, 16, 16, 16, 16, 18, 18, 18, 18, 18, 18, 20, 20, 20, 20, 22, 22

The mean average size sold may show as 14.4 – not a useful figure. The median may show size 16. In this case it is the mode which is most useful, as it shows that size 14 is the size most frequently sold.

Probability

This provides a numerical measurement of the likelihood of an event occurring. In marketing it can be used in estimating the likelihood of a new product becoming profitable, or the probability of peak or seasonal demands occurring. In these examples an element of subjectivity is involved in assigning a probability to a situation – historical information is unlikely to be available, as every new product launch is different. An organization will want to take more than one opinion on the probability of a successful outcome – a number of individuals involved in the development, as well as financial advisers, will be involved in the prediction.

Simple time series and the moving average method

Definition

Time series – A set of observations measured at successive points in time or over successive points in time. Examples of time series are annual profits, monthly sales figures, etc.

This data can be used to identify a trend to assist with forecasting. Most time series data does not convert into a straight line when represented in a graphical format (see Figure 4.11). It can therefore be useful to employ the 'moving average' method of creating a trend line – this will then smooth out many fluctuations that exist in the time series. For example, Figure 4.12 shows the sales of digestive biscuits over a four-year period. Sales figures are produced quarterly. The actual data has then been transferred to the graph shown in Figure 4.13 and raises questions such as:

Unit 4 Gathering and analysing financial and numerical information

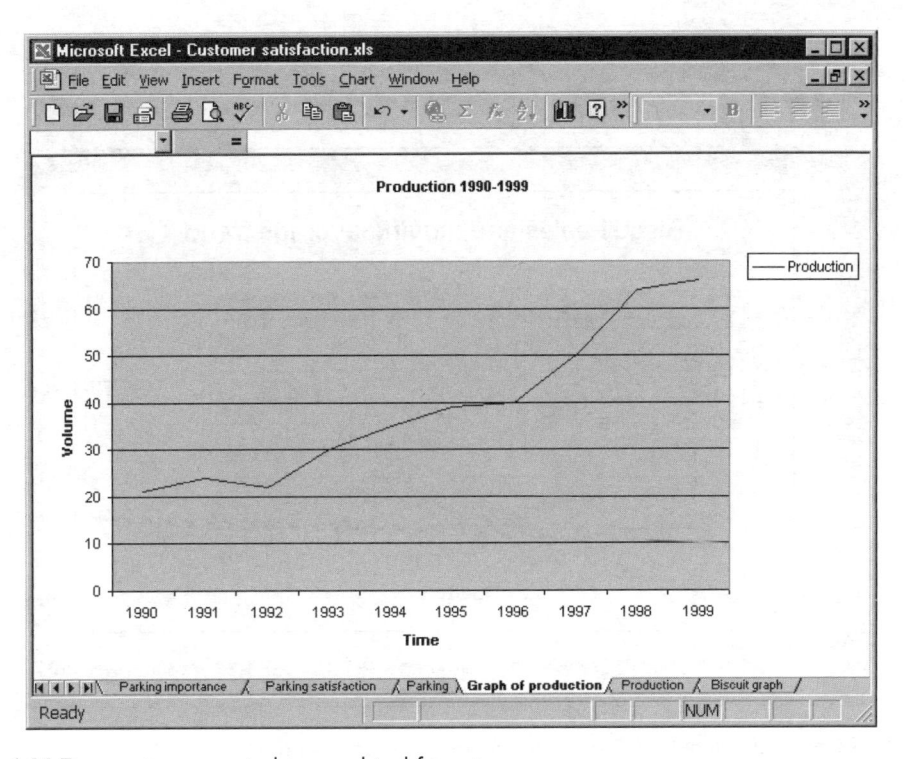

Figure 4.11 Time series presented in graphical format

- When were price increases implemented and did these have a noticeable impact on sales?
- When were advertising campaigns introduced? Did any of these have a significant impact on sales?
- Do we have any seasonal trends that might explain the fluctuations in sales? For example, there seems to be a pattern of a drop in sales in the third quarter of the year, followed by an increase in the final quarter. The year 1993 was an exception – can this be explained by a particular marketing campaign? If so, what format did it take, and can we build on the experience in the future?

Figure 4.12 shows the sales of the same biscuits, but this time the moving average trend figures have been calculated. This calculation is made by averaging four quarters' figures, and then centring these by averaging them again. These are plotted on the same graph in Figure 4.13.

Year/Quarter	Sales of biscuits 000's packets	Four-quarter moving averages	Centred moving average trend
1995 Q1	18		
Q2	22		
Q3	30	23.5	
Q4	24	24.5	24.0
1996 Q1	22	28.0	26.25
Q2	36	30.5	29.25
Q3	40	32.5	31.5
Q4	32	39.5	36.0
1997 Q1	50	45.5	42.5
Q2	60	51.5	48.5
Q3	64	58.5	55.0
Q4	60	60.0	59.25
1998 Q1	56	62.5	61.25
Q2	70	66.5	64.5
Q3	80	69.5	68.0
Q4	72		

Figure 4.12 Table of biscuit production showing four-quarter moving average trend

Unit 4 Gathering and analysing financial and numerical information

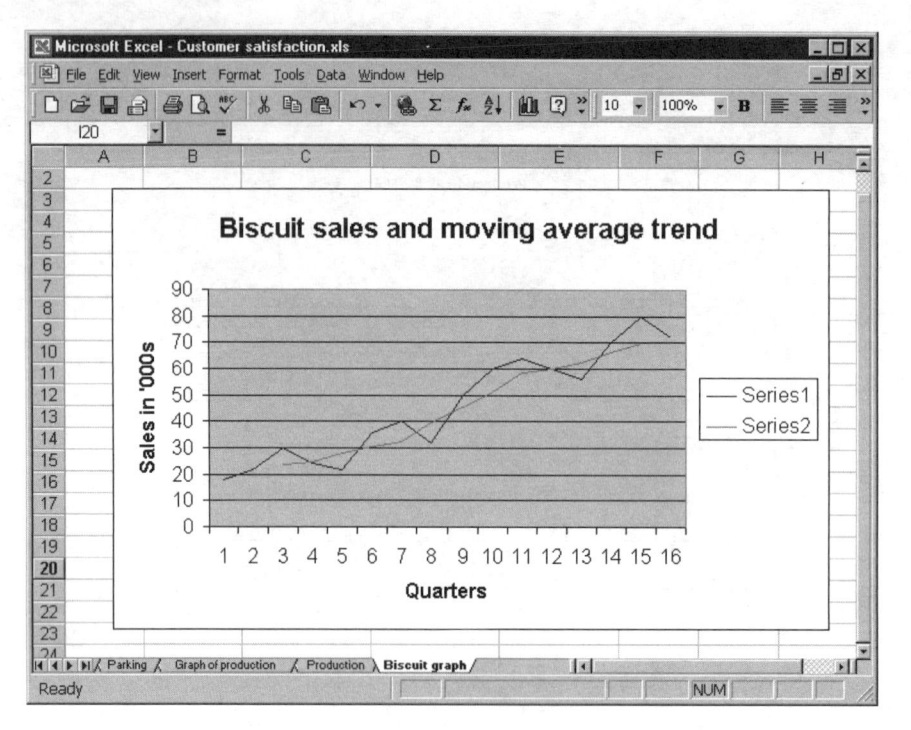

Figure 4.13 Graph of actual biscuit sales and moving average trend

A 'line of best fit' can be applied to a past time series, and trends extrapolated to try to predict the future. This does have risks attached, however, as it assumes that the same conditions will exist in the future.

Activity 4.3

Figure 4.14 shows 'the Source' table of durable goods ownership.

What do trends showing in this table tell:

1. Car manufacturers?
2. Manufacturers of 'entertainment' systems?

Unit 4 Gathering and analysing financial and numerical information

GSS The UK in Figures/Regional Statistics — Page 1 of 1

the Source
of UK Facts and Figures
Government Statistical Service
home | StatBase | UK in figures | publications | links | sitemap

the UK in Figures

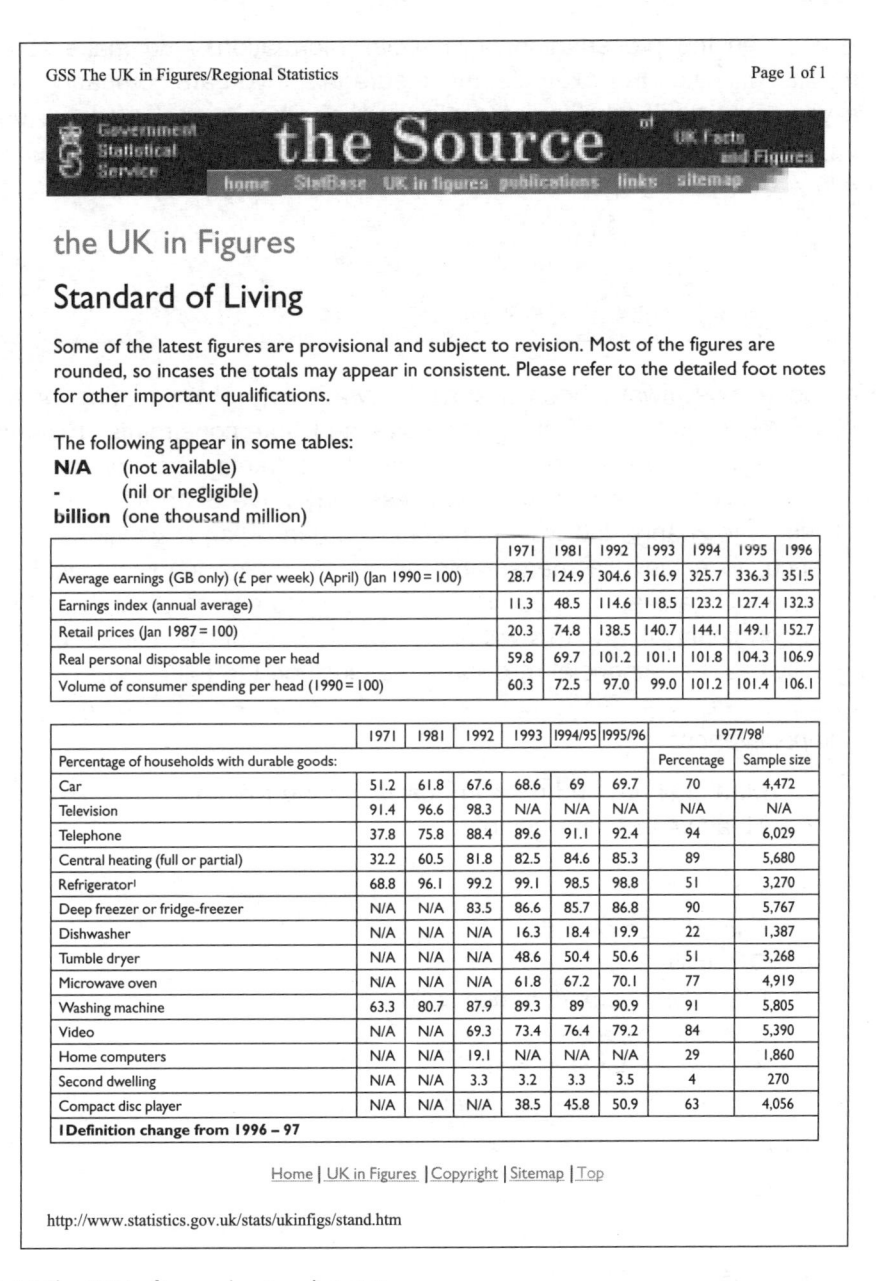

Standard of Living

Some of the latest figures are provisional and subject to revision. Most of the figures are rounded, so incases the totals may appear in consistent. Please refer to the detailed foot notes for other important qualifications.

The following appear in some tables:
N/A (not available)
- (nil or negligible)
billion (one thousand million)

	1971	1981	1992	1993	1994	1995	1996
Average earnings (GB only) (£ per week) (April) (Jan 1990=100)	28.7	124.9	304.6	316.9	325.7	336.3	351.5
Earnings index (annual average)	11.3	48.5	114.6	118.5	123.2	127.4	132.3
Retail prices (Jan 1987=100)	20.3	74.8	138.5	140.7	144.1	149.1	152.7
Real personal disposable income per head	59.8	69.7	101.2	101.1	101.8	104.3	106.9
Volume of consumer spending per head (1990=100)	60.3	72.5	97.0	99.0	101.2	101.4	106.1

	1971	1981	1992	1993	1994/95	1995/96	1977/98[1]	
Percentage of households with durable goods:							Percentage	Sample size
Car	51.2	61.8	67.6	68.6	69	69.7	70	4,472
Television	91.4	96.6	98.3	N/A	N/A	N/A	N/A	N/A
Telephone	37.8	75.8	88.4	89.6	91.1	92.4	94	6,029
Central heating (full or partial)	32.2	60.5	81.8	82.5	84.6	85.3	89	5,680
Refrigerator[1]	68.8	96.1	99.2	99.1	98.5	98.8	51	3,270
Deep freezer or fridge-freezer	N/A	N/A	83.5	86.6	85.7	86.8	90	5,767
Dishwasher	N/A	N/A	N/A	16.3	18.4	19.9	22	1,387
Tumble dryer	N/A	N/A	N/A	48.6	50.4	50.6	51	3,268
Microwave oven	N/A	N/A	N/A	61.8	67.2	70.1	77	4,919
Washing machine	63.3	80.7	87.9	89.3	89	90.9	91	5,805
Video	N/A	N/A	69.3	73.4	76.4	79.2	84	5,390
Home computers	N/A	N/A	19.1	N/A	N/A	N/A	29	1,860
Second dwelling	N/A	N/A	3.3	3.2	3.3	3.5	4	270
Compact disc player	N/A	N/A	N/A	38.5	45.8	50.9	63	4,056
1 Definition change from 1996 – 97

Home | UK in Figures | Copyright | Sitemap | Top

http://www.statistics.gov.uk/stats/ukinfigs/stand.htm

Figure 4.14 The UK in figures/regional statistics

Comparing financial information

Comparison of financial information is an essential part of financial analysis. One set of figures alone will not be very useful. If you are looking at how financially stable an organization is, then one set of financial accounts will tell you little. If you are able to obtain two or three years' figures, you are in a position to start looking for positive or negative fluctuations, and then make some decisions based on an overall picture. You may be asked to present financial data in such a way that your team or line manager can effectively base his or her decisions on it.

The basics of graphs and charts are covered above, and it is much easier to base decisions on clearly presented images than it is when faced with a page of figures. If you do not have the resources to produce graphs or charts easily, put figures into tables and separate each set of figures for consideration with 'white space' on the page.

One final point on the presentation of financial information – do make sure that you are comparing 'like with like'. For example, make sure that if you are comparing 'profit before tax' from one year, you don't take 'gross profit' from another year. If you are unsure because terminology has changed from one set of figures to another, then ask an expert – speak to someone in your finance department and ask for advice.

Balancing financial decisions with other factors

Setting a budget has always been a straightforward way of measuring whether a planned activity has been completed within given cost- and time-constraints. However, it is not a measure of cost-effectiveness. For example, has the marketing activity undertaken made any difference in terms of the objectives set? These may have been to increase awareness, to change attitudes, to change the way a product or organization is positioned in the mind of its target audience, to achieve a measurable number of sales leads, to achieve a quantified increase in sales. Organizations need to assess success across a number of measures, both financial and non-financial, and this will apply equally to your measurement of the success of marketing activities. Non-financial measures may include the following:

- *Competitiveness*
    1. Market share and relative position in the market
    2. Measures of your customer base.

- *Quality of service*
    1. Friendliness of staff
    2. Reliability
    3. Effectiveness of communication
    4. Capability of staff
    5. Knowledge level of staff
    6. Accessibility (location, opening hours, parking).

- *Flexibility*
    1. Delivery capability
    2. Volume production capability
    3. Customization potential.

All criteria for success are measured against the objectives that were originally set. For example, you may have decided to recommend that you arrange a stand at a particular exhibition. You do not expect to actually sell your products or services while you are there, but have identified that the businesses it draws in terms of attendees are, in the main, in your specific target market. One of your organization's objectives is 'To increase penetration of the UK office printer market from x per cent to x per cent within two years'. The related marketing objective is 'To increase sales of office printers in the UK by 15 per cent by the end of 2003'. Your Marketing Manager has decided that part of your strategy will be to raise awareness through attendance at trade shows throughout the UK.

You have recommended attendance at this exhibition on the basis of information you have received from the event organizers about their target market. You decide to put forward two objectives to achieve through this attendance.

Unit 4 Gathering and analysing financial and numerical information

- o *The primary objective*
  - o To improve prompted awareness of your company as a leading player in the office printer market in the north-east of the UK to 25 per cent within three months of the show.
  - o You will measure your success by including a question in your telemarketing team's script when making contact to obtain an appointment for one of your salespeople to call. They will record how many contacts answer positively when asked whether they know your company. The results will be compared to a similar exercise carried out one month before the show.
- o *The secondary objective*
  - o To obtain 200 contact names for your database from attendees at the show. The number of new contact names you obtain will measure this. However, you have decided to qualify the achievement and limit it to names obtained by your show staff in conversation with attendees. You are also running a competition that requires entrants to put their business card into a draw for a free bottle of champagne. These names will not qualify against your original objective as they will need to be followed up by the telemarketing team to assess their potential as future clients.

Sometimes, when you need to justify a proposal that is not profit- or cash-based, it will be useful to carry out a *cost/benefit analysis.* This simply takes all the other benefits (and disadvantages) of a course of action and attempts to put a monetary value on each. For example, imagine the situation of someone opening a new retail outlet or launching a new product. It is essential that marketing research is carried out before making a final decision – but how is the cost of this research to be justified?

An example of a cost/benefit analysis is shown in Figure 4.15.

Costs	£
Fee to agency for carrying out primary research	12,500
Cost of time spent on carrying out desk research	1000
Total	13,500
Benefits	
Reduction of risk of:	
Loss of rent (3–6 months)	9000–18,000
Loss of wages	2600
Cost of stock (most would transfer to other outlets)	2500
Impact on company image of failed outlet	5000
Total	19,000–28,100

Figure 4.15 Cost/benefit analysis on research before opening new outlet

Unit 4 Gathering and analysing financial and numerical information

This is relevant to the example of attendance at a trade show given above. You will see that a further assessment of your secondary objective will be needed in this case. You have sold the benefit of attending the show in terms of the fact that two new sales to new names on the database will compensate for the cost of attending. This will take longer than one month to achieve and you will therefore need to make the sales team aware of the source of all leads so that you are able to recognize when the minimum number of sales is accomplished.

Summary

This unit has considered various ways in which spreadsheets can be used in a marketing role. It has also looked at some basic statistical techniques that are relevant to marketing and how these can be used.

Finally, it has considered many factors which may affect decisions in marketing – whether to proceed with certain actions, which quote to accept, which trade show to attend, etc. A cost/benefit analysis is shown to be a useful way of proposing a course of action.

Further study and examination preparation

When you have completed this unit you will be able to answer Question 6 from the December 2002 Examination paper. Go to www.cimeduhub.com to access Specimen Answers and Senior Examiner's advice for this exam question.

unit 5
making contacts for marketing

Learning objectives

In this unit you will:

- Consider the different roles that make up the marketing department (4.2.1 & 4.2.2)

- Identify the relationship between the marketing department and other departments in the organization (4.2.1 & 4.2.2)

- Develop a practical understanding of working in a front-line role (4.2.3 & 4.2.4)

- Identify the different relationships that are appropriate to customers, suppliers and distributors. (4.2.5 & 4.2.6).

By the end of this unit you will be able to:

- Explain the role of the individuals that make up the marketing department (4.2.2)

- Receive and assist visitors in a professional manner (4.2.3)

- Recognize key relationships within and external to your organization (4.2.1, 4.2.5 & 4.2.6)

- Develop key relationships with customers, suppliers and distributors (4.2.5 & 4.2.6)

- Explain the concept and application of e-relationships (4.2.8)

- This unit covers the key skill of Working with others

- It also covers the statement of marketing practice Embrace change and modify behaviours and attitudes.

Study Guide

This unit covers a range of relationships that you may be involved in building to assist you in your marketing role. With 'Practical networking skills' (Unit 6), it covers the 20 per cent of the syllabus devoted to 'Building and Developing Relationships'. It looks at relationships with other individuals in the marketing department, other departments in the organization, and suppliers (including external agencies), customers and distributors. Completion of the unit will take approximately eight to ten hours, including the completion of all activities.

Introduction

The marketer's role is complex and will vary from organization to organization. Very large organizations may include many of the roles listed below, and, in contrast, very small family firms may not have anyone with 'marketing' in their job title. In this case marketing activities may be undertaken by one of the Directors and his or her Personal Assistant. In all cases, however, marketing involves communicating with various stakeholder and customer groups both inside and outside the organization. This unit introduces some of those relationships and how they interrelate.

Who's who in marketing?

The following terms are used in a variety of senses in different companies and different industries. The descriptions below provide a general view only of the role that various individuals play in the marketing department.

Marketing Director

The Marketing Director is often a Board member, reporting directly to the Managing Director. This person's role is to shape the organization's marketing strategy and business plans. Often responsible for large teams of people and large budgets.

Marketing Manager

The Marketing Manager usually reports to the Marketing Director and is responsible for implementing the overall marketing plan and evaluating progress against it.

Advertising Manager

This person is sometimes known as the Marketing Communications Manager, although this implies a slightly wider role. Responsibilities include planning and implementing the advertising for the organization, and often managing an advertising department.

Sales Manager

The Sales Manager is responsible for the sales force. He or she may have Field Sales Managers or Retail Managers working for him or her, depending on the size of the sales team.

Public Relations Manager

Sometimes known as the Corporate Communications Manager, this individual is responsible for planning and implementing a Public Relations programme for the organization. This role involves building relationships with all the organization's stakeholder groups and maintaining the corporate image. Sometimes required to work closely with an external PR agency.

Marketing Research Manager

This individual is responsible for the research activity for the organization. Sometimes works closely with an external agency.

Direct Marketing Manager

Manages the direct marketing function and creates an effective communication channel. Often manages a team of people and is increasingly responsible for building customer loyalty and extending the existing customer base.

New Product Development Manager

This individual takes responsibility for new product development and research & development. Often manages a team of R&D people.

Product Manager

Taking responsibility for a product or range of products, this person is responsible for communicating all marketing activity, including pricing, promotions and point-of-sale where appropriate. Also responsible for ensuring that the marketing activity stays in line with overall brand strategy.

Account Handler

This is a role within an agency. The Account Handler is the point of contact between the agency and the client. This role is that of liaison between the two parties, with a heavy responsibility for ensuring that the relationship between the two stays positive.

Account Planner

This is another agency role. The Account Planner will carry out research and put forward proposals to other members of the account team based on the research he or she has undertaken. This may involve audience research, attitude research and media research.

Brand Manager

This is usually a senior role that is responsible for building, developing and protecting a brand.

Events Manager

This individual takes responsibility for planning, organizing and project managing events such as sporting activities, exhibitions, industry/trade events, etc.

Marketing Executive/Assistant

This role usually involves a wide range of activity stretching right across the marketing mix within an organization. These activities can include writing and delivering direct mail campaigns, organizing events, promoting the organization and its products and services, copywriting, database management, and many other projects. Note that the MIP examination is usually, centred around the tasks for this role.

This is not an exhaustive list, but gives an overview of the types of roles and responsibilities that exist.

Activity 5.1

Talk to the people in your marketing department to find out their job titles and responsibilities. Set them out in a list, like this:

Role	Description

Understanding the organization

In the Marketing Fundamentals module you will have covered the differing structures that can affect the way marketing is managed within an organization. These include *functional* organization structures, *matrix* management structures, *geographically* structured organizations, and *product-based* organizational structures.

However your organization is structured, it is important to recognize that different functions within it will have different priorities to those that exist in marketing. These other functions or departments are internal customers of yours, and vice versa. It is therefore important to understand where differences in priorities may arise, so that you can work together to the benefit of your customers.

For example, if you are in a retail organization you may wish to hold large stocks of certain popular items to make sure your customers are not disappointed by items being out of stock. Your purchasing department may prefer to buy stock in smaller quantities to balance cash flow.

If you are in a manufacturing environment, then you may encourage higher production of customized products to meet customer needs. The production department prefers to produce standard items as they have fewer changeovers of machinery to undertake and fewer mistakes are made.

Your finance department may want to utilize a pricing strategy that covers costs plus an amount to contribute to profit. You may wish to price a certain product as a loss leader to improve the development of a particular market.

If you work in a technical environment, your R&D department may work more slowly than you would like and take a less commercial interest in the work that is being undertaken.

As you will see from the above examples, there are good reasons for differences which exist. However, in a truly marketing-focused organization the needs of the customer will always come first.

> ## Activity 5.2
>
> Make a note of three other internal departments that you interact with. How might their priorities differ from yours? How might this affect the business relationship that you have with them?

Marketing-orientated organizations

Whether your organization is marketing-orientated or not depends on a much bigger picture than just your activity. However, the more your organization adopts such an orientation, the more you will be affected.

The degree to which the organization is focused on the customer will also be affected by whether it chooses to operate in a centralized or decentralized way. If decision-making is centralized, then decisions tend to be made by senior management and then communicated down the organization for implementation. This means that decisions are taken a long way from the customer, and it is difficult to ensure that customer needs are met quickly.

If decision-making is decentralized, then decisions are made by people who are close to the customer, and so more flexible solutions can be found to achieve customer satisfaction. A chain of hotels in the USA 'empowers' its staff to tear up a customer's bill if the customer is dissatisfied with the service in any way (they use a sophisticated database to track customers who have stayed without paying, and if there is any suspicion that they are trying to avoid paying they are politely asked to register with another hotel).

The big advantage of this decentralized system is the degree of loyalty to the hotel chain that it creates. Satisfied customers who believe they are put first are much more likely to return. The hotel is also able to track problems with customer service and deal with them very quickly. As all staff are equally able to make these decisions, they all work together to ensure that service is second to none.

This type of organization does not happen by magic – it takes hard work and considerable time to build the type of organization where staff are sufficiently confident to make such decisions. However, once this is achieved the organization has a distinct advantage over its competitors. Think about the level of responsibility you have for taking decisions on behalf of customers – can you refund money if they have a complaint? If you do not have that power, do you know what the policy is within your organization for dealing with complaints? Who can make such a decision?

If this level of decision-making is outside your level of responsibility at the moment, think about how you would feel if the company changed its policy and asked you to start making such decisions in the future. What would you want to know before you felt confident?

E-relationships – using electronic media to communicate with customers and suppliers

Building relationships is recognized as becoming increasingly important in marketing, and this applies to relationships with both customers and suppliers. The internet and e-marketing generally are providing new ways of building these relationships, but there are some basic rules that must be applied if techniques are to be effective in this respect.

- Adopt a permission-based approach – do not bombard people with information they have not asked for. This is more likely to result in them moving to a competitor than building a relationship.
- Marketing communication should be two-way – remember the necessity for the 'feedback' loop in the basic model of communication.
- E-marketing can offer many opportunities for dialogue with customers and suppliers about products and services. E-mails (that are responded to promptly), discussion threads, and focus discussions run through 'chat' facilities can be cost effectively managed.
- Give people who 'opt-in' the opportunity to 'opt-out'.
- Don't use purchased e-mail address lists – it will be more effective to gather information that you can analyse through a dialogue with people who know you and people who are recommended to you.

Extranets can be used to develop relationships with suppliers, offering them exclusive information that facilitates easier and faster trade. This in turn will contribute positively to relationships with customers.

CRM (Customer Relationship Marketing) focuses on relationships with customers. What does CRM mean? It means different things to different people.

- To the *customer* it means that the company's representatives who talk to you know who you are and have information at their finger tips such as what you have bought in the past, what current orders remain unfulfilled, when delivery is due. It may also mean expectations of financial and other benefits.
- To the *company*, it means higher levels of business with the same customers and therefore lower marketing costs.
- To the *IT department* in the company it means large and complex information systems which are capable of updating and delivering all relevant customer information to customer-facing staff.

For CRM to work, the company has to keep potentially large amounts of information about its customers. Naturally it will want to pay most attention to its most profitable customers, often (but not always) those who spend most. This implies identifying and differentiating between customer groups. For example, supermarkets offer about one per cent discount to cardholders in return for the right to personal information about their buying behaviours. But not all customers carry store cards. So CRM does recognize the existence of different customer groups, sub-segments perhaps.

Will this discourage non-cardholders and infrequent users from shopping in these stores? If price discounts are available only to cardholders then it might. But the supermarkets use CRM as just one weapon in their marketing armoury along with, for example, an array of discounts and promotions to appeal to other groups.

This highlights the importance of identifying different customer groups for a company's goods and services and then using an appropriate customer care strategy. Its biggest contribution to business has been to focus companies on relationships with customers over time rather than just the sales transaction. CRM may be valuable but is not appropriate for all businesses or all groups of customers.

> **Activity 5.3**
>
> You work for the provider of telecommunications equipment to small businesses. List the information you might expect to keep on a customer database used to develop relationships with your customers.

Unit 2 on 'Gathering information from inside and outside the organization' introduced the growing use of intranets to share information across departments and between individuals within an organization. Large organizations such as the major supermarkets have used Electronic Data Interchange (EDI) for some time, and the improved communication it offered meant that suppliers received automatic orders for items that were running low, enabling supermarket stock levels to be maintained at an optimum level. EDI, however, has its disadvantages when compared to an extranet (which gives customers and suppliers controlled access to information from the organization's intranet). EDI is expensive to install and requires both parties to have compatible systems. It is often designed specifically to meet a single purpose, and is not as flexible as the extranet. The extranet allows easier access from any PC or laptop through a dial-up modem, and is made secure in that a unique user ID is issued only to those that the organization wishes to have access. More permanent connections can also be made available, depending on the amount of use that a link is anticipated to have.

Research has indicated that suppliers maintaining long-term relationships with their buyers enjoy greater sales, better return on investments and lower stock-holding costs. An extranet can be used to achieve competitive advantage through an improved level of customer service and communication. For example, customer feedback on new product design can be input to the NPD process before the test-marketing stage. Relationships are strengthened simply by facilitating access to up-to-date information on a 24 hours per day, 365 days per year basis.

Extranets are used for various purposes by different organizations: to receive and track orders from customers; to provide information in the form of Frequently Asked Questions (FAQ) pages, technical support bulletins, and quotations; to improve communication between a Key Account Manager and his client; to provide dealers and distributors with up-to-date information on products and prices, etc.

Dealing with external agencies

There are many types of agency that you may deal with over the course of your marketing career. These include research agencies, advertising agencies, direct marketing agencies, PR agencies and sales promotion agencies. Some provide a full range of services.

It doesn't matter what type of agency you are dealing with, the principles of selecting an appropriate partner and building a relationship with them is the same. It is important that, when first selecting an agency to work with, you look at the type of work they are doing and consider several agencies before you make your decision. Ask them to present to you generally at first, so that you are able to see whether you feel you will be able to build a relationship and work with them on a long-term basis.

Eventually, narrow down your choice to two or three agencies and ask them to make a 'pitch' for your business. Whilst a key factor involved in your decision is the type and quality of work the agency is producing, you also want them to be able to work with you as part of your team. It is also important to try to find out what level of staff turnover the agency has – you don't want to build a relationship with someone who then leaves the company. Once selected, you need to take responsibility jointly for the development of a close relationship.

Relationships are affected by lack of communication or poor communication. It is important to take responsibility for the effectiveness of the 'brief' that you give the agency to work with. It must be very clear and concise, while covering all relevant information.

'Briefs' to agencies are reference documents, and provide guidance as to what is required while a task is being carried out. There is no set format, but areas commonly covered are shown in Figure 5.1.

Briefs are not just appropriate to agencies. You may have to produce guidelines for other staff who are undertaking a task for the first time. The example shown in Figure 5.1 gives guidance to someone who is going to give part of a presentation to potential customers at a new product launch.

Product/ Brand	Brief description of background information.
Current market perception	How is the product/service currently perceived?
Objectives	What are you looking to achieve?
Previous communications	What activity has there been in the past? This is particularly important if you are briefing an agency for the first time.
Target market	Who are you looking to target? Give a brief outline. If consumer, give demographic and psychographic background.
Product/ Service benefits	What is your USP (Unique Selling Point)?
Any special offers	
Competition	Brief background to your competition
Positioning	How do you want your product/service to be perceived?
Other media activity	
Budget	
Restrictions/ Constraints	
Timing	When do you need everything completing?

Figure 5.1 Agency brief: main headings

The example shown below gives guidance to someone who is going to give part of a presentation to potential customers at a new product launch.

Brief to presenters for new product launch 29 November 2003, 11 a.m. (Presenter B)

Objective
To introduce new AS70 to press representatives and demonstrate benefits offered.

Location
New Park Hotel, London, UK

(Simultaneous presentations will take place in Madrid, Rome, Paris and Brussels).

Budget
Allocated centrally – approval granted 31 August 2002.

Audience
Invited audience. Representatives from all associated trade magazines and national press.

Content
Presenter A – Welcome and background information on company (Managing Director).

Presenter B – Information on product. USP. Benefits. Price. Target customer (Marketing Manager).

Presenter C – Technical information and demonstration (Product Manager).

Presenter D – Close and manage Question and Answer session (PR Manager).

General guidelines

1. Full rehearsal arranged at location – 7 p.m. on 28 November 2003
2. Slides pre-prepared in MS PowerPoint format. Copy attached with your slides marked
3. Please be at the venue at least 30 minutes before the presentation is due to commence
4. Dress – dark suit and white shirt/blouse. Name badges will be provided
5. Audience size will be small – no microphones will be necessary
6. Speak clearly and at an appropriate pace for the audience. They will be provided with full Press Packs at the end of the presentation
7. Personal presentation being made to add enthusiasm and dynamism to written information
8. Smile!
9. Do not be drawn into answering negative points raised by the audience – Public Relations Manager will deal with Q/A.

Activity 5.4

If you work with an agency, ask them to give you feedback on the last brief you provided. If they suggest improvements, rewrite the brief following their suggestions.

If you do not work with an agency, write a brief for another member of staff who will be attending an exhibition as part of the team on the stand for the first time.

Dealing with customers

Dealing with customers may vary depending on whether you work in business-to-business, industrial or consumer marketing. In all cases it is important to understand the buyer. In the Customer Communications module you have learned about different types of customers and how you need to shape your message differently when communicating with them. The modern consumer is sophisticated, and this applies to the business-to-business buyer also. In many cases the buyer will have been trained and will be working professionally to obtain the best quality and service for his or her organization. In getting to know the buyer you can match the way you communicate to suit. There may be a 'decision-making unit' (DMU) made up of several individuals who jointly make the decision as to whether to buy. In smaller organizations, the same person may play all of these roles! Each of them will need to be communicated with differently as they will all have different priorities. The members of the DMU are as follows.

- *The User* The individual who will use the product or service when purchased. Often, this is the person who starts the search for a new purchase
- *The Influencer* These are often technical specialists, but can include anyone who has an impact on the buying decision
- *The Decider* Sometimes the person holding the budget, or a financial accountant who is responsible for releasing the money. In smaller organizations this may be the Managing Director
- *The Buyer* This person usually has formal authority to select the supplier. This may be the person who compiles and controls the 'preferred supplier' list
- *The Gatekeeper* These are people who can control the flow of information to others in the organization. This can be a secretary or the Managing Director's Personal Assistant.

Consider the DMU of the following fictional large company that buys business travel regularly.

Joe Evans has just been promoted to the role of Buyer in the purchasing department. He has recently qualified through the Chartered Institute of Purchasing and Supply, and wants to impress his manager by making sensible decisions about purchases made.

Ellen Watkins is Business Development Manager (Europe). The company is investigating the market in South-East Asia, and, for the first time, Ellen is going to be taking long-haul flights. She knows the implications of jet lag, and is concerned not to neglect her regular customers in Europe for longer than she has to when she returns from her trips to the new market.

Alan Smith is the Marketing Director. He has extensive experience of travelling on business worldwide. He is Ellen's manager.

Anna Durant is the Receptionist/Switchboard Operator. She has been with the company for some years and feels she has extensive knowledge of all areas of the business. She can be very protective of staff when she knows the caller has something to sell.

In the above example, Ellen is the User, Alan is the Influencer and the Decider (as he holds the budget for the Marketing Department), Anna is the Gatekeeper and Joe is the Buyer. Each has different 'needs' from your service and your company – in fact, if you are the face-to-face contact with this DMU there are several key factors you need to address when making contact.

Your first point of contact will probably be Anna – you can respond to her 'need' to be recognized as a source of knowledge by asking for her help. You will also need to contact Joe – this organization has a purchasing department and therefore will have a policy on use of suppliers. There may even be a 'preferred supplier' list. You need to identify what this policy is – Joe personally has a need to 'look good' in the eyes of his new manager. Through careful questioning and effective listening skills you can establish the policy of the company, and you can then communicate the way in which your company, as a supplier, will minimize the risk to Joe of making a mistake.

Finally, you will arrange a meeting with Alan and Ellen – how can your service overcome Ellen's concerns about jet lag? And how will you convince Alan that you are as good, and better, than the companies he has used in the past?

Working in marketing, you may well be the one chosen to meet visitors to your organization, greet them when they attend events that your company is hosting, or speak to them from a stand at an exhibition. In these situations it is important to remember that you 'are' your organization. It is their memory of you that will stay with them following their visit. You want them to say 'We were met by Jane/John Smith – she/he was very friendly'.

The following are just a few hints and tips for when you are put into just such a situation – this list is extended in Unit 6, 'Practical networking skills'.

- Make sure that your appearance is suitable for the occasion
- If you are going to be on an exhibition stand all day, never wear new shoes, and take a spare pair to change into halfway through the day
- Show enthusiasm for your work at all times
- Make sure that if the press or TV are attending, your company name is displayed close to any likely photo shot. In the case of TV in particular, the scene shown may be just a short clip with their presenter speaking over it. There is no guarantee that you will be named, and if your name cannot be seen you have lost a golden opportunity.

Dealing with cultural differences when meeting people

Another important issue to remember in dealing with customers in a face-to-face situation is that different nationalities have different customs depending on the culture from which they come. It is important that you make yourself aware of some of these customs so that you do not inadvertently offend someone who may be an important client.

We are all at risk of acting ethnocentrically – that is, we judge other people by standards that are the accepted norm for our own cultural group. The main differences in culture are categorized in terms of time, space, food, acceptable dress, manners, decision-making, and verbal and non-verbal communication. The following examples demonstrate some of the issues you need to consider:

- *Time* Time and a sense of urgency are treated differently within different cultures. In the USA, UK and in Germany in particular, it is considered disrespectful to be late for an appointment. In Spain, Italy, Latin America and Buddhist cultures, a different concept of time is held – arriving late is socially acceptable.
- *Space* How comfortable do you feel if someone stands very close to you? To one culture, standing close can be taken as someone 'invading your personal space'; to others, those who do not stand close may be seen as cold and aloof.
- *Food* One way of getting an idea of customs that concern eating is to visit restaurants in your own country that serve food from other countries. If you are visiting another country on business, or have business customers from another country, it is important to research this area thoroughly. For example, pork is forbidden in the Middle East, and alcohol is forbidden for Buddhists, Muslims and Hindus.
- *Acceptable dress* Again, rather than risk a mistake, it is better to ask about the mode of dress that is appropriate for an occasion in a country you are visiting. In the West and in Eastern Europe, smart business suits are accepted dress for men and women.

In Singapore, a long-sleeved shirt and tie is accepted, and in the Middle East long cotton coats are often worn. Other issues to check are whether you should cover your head – this applies more to women than men.
- *Manners* Should you shake hands on meeting someone (UK and Germany), or bow (Japan)? Adopting the manners of a country may mean that you spend two to three hours over a business lunch in Europe.
- *Decision-making* In the USA, Germany, UK, Singapore, the Netherlands, Scandinavia and Switzerland, decisions are made quickly and (according to Western culture) in a businesslike manner. By contrast, decisions in Japan are made through consultation with others and through consensus. In some parts of the world it takes considerable time to build a relationship to the point where people are sufficiently comfortable to do business.
- *Verbal communication* When you are listening to people speaking their own language, you may think that they are angry because of the pace of their speech, the tone they are using, or how they link their speech to hand gestures, etc. In fact this is rarely the case, as other cultures and languages use tone of voice and pace as a normal part of speech to a greater extent than applies in English.
- *Non-verbal communication* Facial expressions can have very different meanings across cultures. For example, the Japanese change their facial expression very little – this is because it is thought to be unacceptable to give away your personal feelings. In the Philippines, you may become confused when individuals smile and laugh even when they are angry. Other gestures also mean different things in different countries.

This section deals with just some aspects of international culture that may impact on your marketing activities. The important message is that we are all different, and we need to recognize those differences in order to build effective and lasting business relationships.

Activity 5.5

Find out whether your organization deals internationally. If so, choose one of the countries where you do business and list aspects of culture that affect the relationship between your country and theirs.

Personal selling

You may also be involved in selling to customers, either over the telephone or face-to-face. This area is covered in detail in many supporting textbooks. However, the basic process is briefly covered below.

In the past, selling was perceived negatively as a high-pressure process which looked to persuade people to buy products, whether they needed them or not. Major efforts have been made to change this perception, and effective salespeople play a key role in their relationship with the marketing department. They can feed back information about competitor activity, and about customer reactions to products and services, promotional activity and prices. In business-to-business and industrial marketing, they can play an important role in promoting products in ways that traditional promotional activity would not achieve. Imagine trying to sell a very complex piece of machinery, which can offer different benefits to different industries, by simply placing an advertisement on the 'flat' page. Far better to send a salesperson who can demonstrate specific benefits and answer questions from a particular customer.

The sales process includes several key stages that are outlined below.

Prospecting and planning

Personal selling is the most expensive part of the promotional mix. Salespeople need to make their activity as efficient and effective as possible, so planning their call and finding the right prospect is important. Part of planning involves finding out as much as possible about the prospect's company, background, industry and needs. You also need to find out whether the person you are planning to see is the decision-maker (see the DMU above).

You may be contacting existing customers from the company's database, or you may be looking for new customers in the same marketplace. Alternatively, you may be investigating the possibility of a new market. There are numerous sources of leads for sales. You may have a support team that makes contact for you, or you may be part of that support team. Leads can come from coupon response from advertising, records of ex-customers, national press, regional and local press, trade directories, referrals given by existing customers, etc.

Establishing a rapport with the customer

When an appointment is made with the right person, it is important to remember the phrase 'You never get a second chance to make a first impression'. Arrive on time, look the part, smile and make every effort to establish a relationship with your prospect.

A cheerful greeting or business-like manner can set the tone of the meeting that follows. It is up to you to recognize which is most appropriate for the situation. The research you have undertaken before the visit will help you establish your credibility with the customer. You can also gain by being observant – what can you tell about the interests of the individual from the office? Try to make an opening comment that the customer will agree with. A positive start helps lead to a positive conclusion.

Fact-finding

If your main aim is to meet the customer's needs, then the first thing you need to do is to find out what they are. Excellent questioning and listening skills are important here – using open questions to encourage the prospect to talk about their business, and listening carefully to see how your product or service can best meet those needs.

You should look to guide and control the conversation as much as possible, but be prepared for the unexpected. Do not 'dive-in' too quickly. Be yourself and try to keep your questioning conversational. No customer wants to feel that they are being interrogated – it should flow as naturally as possible. This is a skill that needs practice.

Making the presentation

When you have found out all you need to present your product or service, then you need to confirm that you have understood everything correctly. A quick summary of the discussion is all that is needed – before moving on to demonstrate or state how you can help the prospect.

The key to this stage is not to confuse your listener with too much detail. You do not need to tell him or her all about your product or service – just the parts that are of clear benefit to him or her.

Imagine trying to sell an investment account to someone from a range of six or seven different products. If you begin by saying 'We have six products that we can offer – one needs a minimum investment of £25,000 and can only be accessed after three years, but offers the highest rate of interest – the next needs £10,000 to open, can be withdrawn from once per year, and has a slightly lower interest rate – the third . . .', you can imagine how the potential customer will feel by the time you have covered all six! If you have asked the right questions earlier, for example:

- 'How much will you need to withdraw from the account?'
- 'How much were you looking to invest?'
- 'How often will you need to withdraw from the account?'

then you will have all the information you need to present appropriate benefits to the customer.

'In that case, Mr Jones, the best account for you is our Easi-flex Account. It allows two withdrawals per year, which means that you will be able to take money out in an emergency without losing any interest, and you will still get a high return on your investment.'

Overcoming objections

If there is a misunderstanding about the product or service, the salesperson can handle it as the sales presentation progresses.

Many people fear objections from the customer. In fact, they are usually an expression of interest and so give you opportunities to sell. When dealing with objections:

- Do not become argumentative
- Think ahead and try to anticipate any objections your customer might have
- Do not change your manner – stay positive, and don't become defensive
- Do not 'put down' the competition – have a clear knowledge of their products and yours, and use benefits to counter objections
- Be firm and confident in your approach
- Take responsibility – even if the customer has misunderstood, remember it is your communication that has caused the misunderstanding.

Closing or gaining customer commitment

This is the point where the salesperson tries to secure the business. You may try to 'close' at points during the presentation, and it is important to watch for signals through body language or what the customer says that indicate that he or she is ready to buy. The 'close' may also uncover further objections that you need to overcome before you can secure the business.

The big advantage a salesperson has over other forms of promotion is that he or she is able to adjust his or her message to the needs of the buyer immediately. A more personal approach helps to get complex information across and build a long-term relationship.

Follow-up

In relationship marketing, this stage can be key to moving the customer up the 'loyalty ladder' from customer to client. You should follow up a successful sale to ensure that the customer is satisfied with delivery, knows how to use the product, and whether any other points have arisen. In the buying process this can help to overcome the buyer's post-purchase cognitive dissonance. This contact can also help you find out whether the customer has future needs you can help with.

Unit 5 Making contacts for marketing

Dealing with contacts up and down your supply chain – suppliers and distribution channels

Over recent years there has been a move towards building relationships with the whole of a supply chain, as organizations see the benefits that such co-operation can have on the end relationship with the customer. Whereas in the past organizations might try to play one supplier off against another to try to knock prices down, the value of having a good supplier relationship to ensure quality, and extra efforts to supply something slightly different when needed to satisfy customer need, is now being recognized.

Case history

Robert Horne Paper

Figure 5.2 shows the five channels of communication within the supply chain of Robert Horne Paper. In each case, there are different communication goals, different individuals involved, and different communication tools used. These are all important to the business of the company.

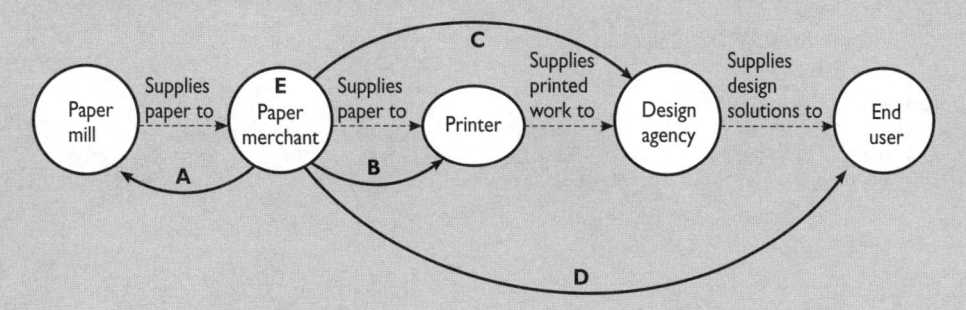

Figure 5.2

Channel A: Paper merchant to paper mill

Communication goals

- To attract and retain the best suppliers in the industry
- To build Robert Horne's reputation as the best merchant to trade with
- To gain marketing sponsorship for individual marketing campaigns.

Key communicators

- Marketing department
- Buying department.

Communication tools

- Face-to-face meetings and relationship building
- Supplier surveys
- Direct mail – to inform them of current campaigns.

Channel B: Paper merchant to printer

Communication goals

- To increase sales volume, value and market share
- To increase the number of buying customers.

Key communicators

- Sales force
- Office-based salespeople
- Marketing department.

Communication tools

- Salespeople building relationships
- Quality of product and service
- Price and value for money
- Packaging of goods
- Direct mail
- Newsletters
- Trade press advertisements (e.g. *Printweek*)
- Public Relations
- Corporate events and entertaining
- Trade exhibitions
- Website.

Channel C: Paper merchant to design agency

Communication goals

- To increase specified orders for specialist, value added products
- To build the Robert Horne brand.

Unit 5 Making contacts for marketing

Key communicators

- Paperlink – Robert Horne's 'backselling' team
- Marketing department.

Communication tools

- Backselling team (for face-to-face meetings)
- Telemarketers
- Direct mail
- Newsletters
- Trade press advertising (e.g. *Design Week*, etc.)
- Public Relations
- Exhibitions (e.g. The Creative Show)
- Corporate events and entertaining
- Website.

Channel D: Paper merchant to end-user

Communication goals

- To encourage end-users to source all paper from Robert Horne – from photocopying paper, to Annual Reports, to Chairman's invitations
- To achieve increased sales through these customers.

Key communicators

- Specialist 'Corporate Accounts' team
- 'Paperlink' to provide support activities
- Marketing department.

Communication tools

- Face-to-face meetings and relationship building
- Project management.

Channel E: Paper merchant internal marketing

Communications goals

- To encourage high levels of involvement and motivation in all employees
- To ensure that all employees understand and are working to achieve corporate goals
- To ensure that each employee understands and can 'sell' the features and benefits of all products and services relevant to them.

Key communicators

- Senior management team
- Training department
- Marketing department
- Divisional heads of departments.

Communication tools

- Team briefings
- Direct mail
- Employee newsletter
- Sales conference
- Training courses
- Employee satisfaction surveys
- Suggestion scheme
- Intranet
- Incentive schemes
- Presentations
- Bulletin boards.

As the case study demonstrates, there is value in the relationships built in all channels. Some of the communication tools overlap, and, in all cases, it is important that the message communicated is consistent and does not detract from the image of the company.

It is important to keep up communications with all distributors. For example, when your organization introduces a new product, your distributors need time in which to plan for the change. They may need to arrange further warehousing space or change the transportation arrangements for getting products to end-users. It is also important to understand the roles that members of your distribution channel play. Again, this will vary from industry to industry. They may be a useful source of information about what is going on in the marketplace, they may take responsibility for promoting your products further down the chain, or they may fulfil a storage and transportation role. Their different and often very complex roles will affect the support they need and expect from you.

In the Marketing Fundamentals module you learned about relationship marketing, and the importance of establishing good relationships with all stakeholders of your organization. If you gain a large new order, it may be as a result of a recommendation by an existing customer (your referral market). You will then rely on your suppliers for increased components of the quality that you are used to, and possibly on your financial stakeholders (influence markets) to provide funds for new equipment to fulfil the order. You will also rely on your employees to provide the skills and effort to fulfil the order.

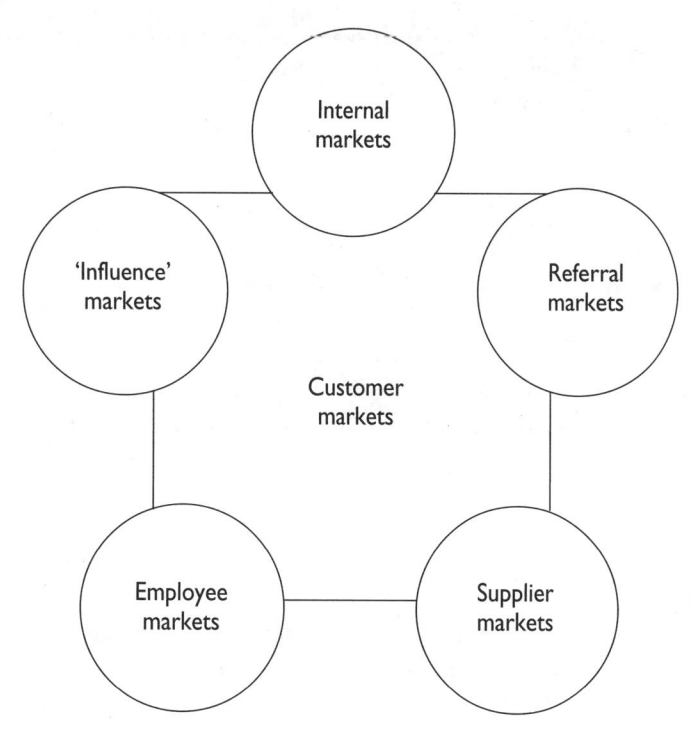

Figure 5.3 Relationship marketing – a wider view
Adapted from Christopher, Payne and Ballantyne, *Relationship Marketing*

You will not gain the confidence or assistance you need unless your communication is effective. Figure 5.3 shows this wider view of marketing in terms of 'the six markets model'.

Activity 5.6

Draw your supply chain and identify how your organization communicates with each member.

Unit 5 Making contacts for marketing

Summary

In this unit we have considered many different contacts that you may need to make within your marketing role. In addition to this, aspects of international culture are explored, and how these must be managed to build effective relationships over time. One of these key relationships is that between yourself and your manager.

There are, of course, many other people you will need to deal with – in organizing events you may be dealing with hotel or conference centre staff, or the organizers of exhibitions. Remember that they are all suppliers of services to your organization – you are paying for that service. It is important to set out your expectations clearly at the outset of the relationship and then monitor progress to your brief on an ongoing basis.

Increasingly, marketing people are using electronic media to assist in developing relationships with their suppliers, customers and others within their own organization. We have looked at ways in which this can be achieved.

Further study and examination preparation

When you have completed this unit you will be able to answer Questions 3 from the December 2002 examination paper and also question 7 from the same paper. Go to www.cimeduhub.com to access Specimen Answers and Senior Examiner's advice for these exam questions.

Extending knowledge

Publications such as *Marketing*, *Marketing Week* and *Campaign* can give you an idea of the activities organizations are involved in, and the personalities that are involved in successful campaigns. These are published weekly and are available online through subscription.

unit 6
practical networking skills

Learning objectives

In this unit you will:

- Consider the importance of networking in building your marketing role (4.2.7)
- Think about how others see you (4.2.2)
- Explore personal communication skills that work (4.2.3 & 4.2.4)
- Consider techniques for dealing with the press (4.2.4)
- Consider ways of managing your manager (4.2.9).

By the end of this unit you will be able to:

- Present yourself positively within your work role (4.2.3)
- Describe techniques available to assist in managing your manager (4.2.9)
- Use communication effectively to build a useful network of contacts (4.2.2 & 4.2.7)
- Use your network of contacts to help you achieve your goals (4.2.7)
- Use recognized techniques for dealing with the press (4.2.4)
- Use techniques for dealing with your manager
- This unit covers the key skill Working with others
- It also covers the statements of marketing practice Embrace change and modify behaviours and Review and develop one's skills and competences.

Unit 6 Practical networking skills

Study Guide

This unit covers the skills that you, as an individual, will use to make contact and develop relationships with the people introduced in Unit 5, 'Making contacts for marketing'. With this it covers the 20 per cent of the syllabus devoted to 'Building and Developing Relationships'. Completion of the unit will take approximately three hours, including the completion of all activities.

Why networking is important

There is an old saying: 'It is not what you know, but who you know'. In this unit we aim to turn this saying into: 'It is both what you know and who you know', and show that it is a combination of these two areas that leads to success for individuals and organizations.

> **Definition**
>
> **Network** – A *network* is an interconnected or interrelated chain, group or system. This can be a system of co-operating individuals, and it is in this context that we consider networks in this unit.

Networking has become a buzzword in recent years, but here it is used in the sense that it simply relates to your ability to make contacts to help you in your work. There are several actions you can take to improve your networking ability, and these are covered below.

The first thing you need to do is to think about all the people within your existing network. Who do you know now? We all have a huge number of contacts that we have made over the years and that we take for granted. Try writing them down (see 'Building your list of contacts' below), and you may be surprised at the size of your existing network.

Once you have identified your network, think about how you can extend it using the people already in it.

You can also expand your network of contacts through developing three 'habits': collecting business cards; joining organizations or attending events; and learning to introduce yourself to other people. This last topic is covered in 'Personal skills for building relationships' later in this unit.

Collect business cards proactively when you attend an event or meeting, or are introduced to someone whose area of expertise may be of use to you in the future. We are often given cards which we later find in a pocket, and we cannot remember anything about the person who passed them to us. When you take a card, as soon as you can without making it very obvious, make a brief note on the back of the card about the conversation you had with the individual, and where you met him or her. The simplest way to file them is to use an index card box containing sections that relate to the main areas of your job, e.g. 'Events', 'Research', 'Promotional literature', 'Print' and 'Meeting venues'. File cards alphabetically in the relevant section, and they will be easier to find when you need them.

Joining organizations or societies can also extend your network of contacts considerably. You are probably already a student member of the Chartered Institute of Marketing, and you will receive a programme of events organized by a local branch of the CIM that you can attend on a monthly basis. These branch meetings are usually organized in such a way that it is possible to meet people before or after the formal session, and the people attending will be working in marketing or sales, so you will have an immediate area of common interest. There are many other organizations that exist locally or nationally and may be relevant to your work. Look for them in the local and trade press, mailings that are sent to you, or contact the local Chamber of Commerce, who also organize local events for their members.

You may be asked to greet guests at an event, or be on a stand at an exhibition. The hints and tips that follow will act as a reminder when you are preparing to take on a role which involves meeting and greeting people. This can be adapted depending on the role you are asked to play.

- Arrive at least 15 minutes before the start time each day.
- Make sure you know your organization's objective for attending or holding the event. It is important that you work towards this objective and not against it.
- Wear appropriate business dress, even if the guests or people attending may be informally dressed.
- Wear older, more comfortable shoes – and take a spare pair to change into halfway through the day. It is very difficult to smile and be pleasant for long periods of time when your feet are being pinched by new shoes!
- Do not carry out conversations with other stand staff – stay alert, at the edge of the stand, showing your willingness to help and answer questions.
- Body language is also important. Try to appear relaxed and open. Think about how you will appear to others – for example, standing with your hands in your pockets can imply that you don't care and looks casual rather than professional.
- Speak clearly – exhibitions can be noisy places.
- Use the first part of your conversation to 'qualify' your prospect. Is this person a genuine prospect? If not, don't waste valuable time. Remain pleasant, but give your attention to visitors who are customers or prospective customers.
- Use 'open' questions. Have a plan in mind, but stay conversational.
- Remain professional and businesslike.
- Make notes – do not rely on your memory.
- Unless your main aim is to promote awareness, do not give out promotional literature indiscriminately. Many people put all they have gathered into the bin as they leave.
- Wear a name badge on your right so that it can be seen when you are shaking hands.
- Keep coats and personal belongings out of public view.
- Do not eat, drink or smoke on the stand – and try to avoid interruptions from mobile phones.
- Smile! And enjoy your experience.

Building your list of contacts

Think broadly about all the people you know and list them in order to identify your existing network. They will include family, friends, other students from your course, colleagues from work, customers, suppliers, people you have met at CIM meetings, etc. The list grows and grows. Don't dismiss contacts because they do not appear to be of use to you in your marketing role. You may wish you had kept their details when things change and you need a new source of information.

Find a way of recording their details that suits you – this might be in a written format as shown in Figure 6.1. Alternatively, you might keep a record of your contacts in an electronic organizer, or in a database.

Name	Address	Phone	Other details

Figure 6.1 A simple record of your contacts

Another list of contacts that you will need to develop is a press list. This should include local press and any relevant trade press. Building relationships with the press can help you to present a positive image of your company or organization over a period of time. If you are sending out press releases on a regular basis, then get to know the names of the contacts. As you establish a reputation for quality communication you will find that they contact you during a quiet time, to provide them with information they can use to fill space. Use British Rate and Data (BRAD) or the *Writers' and Artists' Yearbook* to check that your list is complete, but a first source of information will be *Yellow Pages*, followed by a phone call to the switchboard to obtain names of contacts.

Personal skills for building relationships

People like to deal with positive people. You only have to think about the last time you were faced with repeated negativity to realize why. We are all different, and the first step in developing your interpersonal skills is to identify where your own strengths and weaknesses lie. How do others see you? We sometimes think that we are behaving in a way that is acceptable to other people, but it is their perception of us that matters. So how can you find out how others see you? The only really effective way is to ask them. However, you may already have been given some feedback in the past in the form of a performance appraisal or review. You may also have been given 'unspoken' clues in meetings or in one-to-one situations at work. Think about others' body language and what it might be giving away. You may feel that you are behaving confidently, while others see you as brash. On the other hand, you may think that you talk too much in meetings, while others think that you make valuable contributions which help decisions to be reached.

The way people see you is coloured by a combination of the way you dress, the way you speak and act, your attitude, your body language, your skills and experience and the people you mix with. You will have heard the phrase 'You never get a second chance to make a first impression', and this is often true – people make up their minds about you within three minutes of meeting you, based on the above. Once someone forms this impression, it is difficult to shake off. A useful starting point is to think about what you like to see in other people. What is it about them that makes you feel that you can trust them? What is it about their appearance or the way they speak that you admire? What is their attitude towards their work? For example, are they ever late or always punctual? Do they always seem to be moaning about work, or do they display a positive attitude towards their job and are enthusiastic about it? How do they get on with other people? When you have decided on the way in which you would like to be seen, make a list of the characteristics, and rate yourself against the list. Identify areas that you will need to work on. We all have some weaknesses, and it is in our own hands to change them. Start work on yours now.

When you are attending events or meeting new people, you may initially feel self-conscious and therefore hold back from speaking to people. If you are trying to build up your network of contacts and feel a little shy, as most of us have at one time or another, it can be quite daunting to be on your own in a room full of strangers. One way of overcoming this problem is to take a friend or colleague with you. However, there is now a danger that because you both have company, you won't speak to anyone else. Plan in advance that you will introduce him or her to at least one other person, and that he or she will do the same for you. Once you start talking to people, it is not as difficult as it seems.

It is not always possible to attend events with others, and, if you have to attend on your own, having a definite objective in mind will help you feel less awkward. This is part of your job, and you are setting yourself a challenging goal to work towards. Start realistically, and build up your target until you no longer need it. You will soon find that many other people who are attending feel the same way as you do, and are pleased that you have made the first move.

Developing assertive behaviour will help you in this and in many work situations. Many people confuse assertive behaviour with aggression. Assertiveness is based on personal responsibility and an awareness of the rights of other people. Being assertive means being honest with yourself and others. It means having the ability to say directly what it is you want, need or feel, but not at the expense of other people. It means having confidence in yourself and being positive, while at the same time understanding other people's points of view. It also means being able to behave in a rational and adult way. There are many useful techniques that can be learned to help you behave assertively, and a few of the most common are detailed below.

The three steps to assertiveness

Step 1
Actively listen to what is being said, then show the other person that you both hear and understand him or her.

Step 2
Say what you think or what you feel.

Step 3
Say what you want to happen.

Step 1 means you have to focus on the other person and not use the time he or she is talking to build up a defence or attack. By really listening you are able to demonstrate some understanding and empathy for his or her situation or point of view, even if you do not wholly agree with it.

Step 2 enables you to state directly your thoughts or feelings without insistence or apology. The word 'however' is a good linking word between steps 1 and 2. 'But' tends to contradict your first statement, and can therefore be unhelpful. The word 'however' can become routine, so it is worth thinking of a number of reasonable alternatives like: on the other hand; nonetheless; in addition; even so; nevertheless; alternatively, etc. The words you use should be ones you are comfortable with.

Step 3 is essential so that you can indicate in a clear and straightforward way what action or outcome you want.

Once the three basic steps to assertiveness have been mastered, there are a number of key assertive techniques which will add to the competence and confidence of people working with assertiveness.

Positive inner dialogue

All of us talk to ourselves regularly, usually inwardly, and often before a difficult or undesirable happening. We can persuade ourselves 'into' the most dreadful situations in advance and if we do it well enough we can almost guarantee a self-fulfilling prophecy of a real disaster. If we have a difficult meeting on our agenda, our 'inner conversations' could go like this:

'It's Friday... the management meeting is today... it's a difficult enough meeting at the best of times and today I'm going to have to look for extra money... it won't go down well... they'll tell me I didn't do my forward planning well... it's not my fault. I monitored my progress against the budget... they won't accept that... now they'll have a go at me about expenses in general... I know I won't get the extra money... I wish I was off sick today.'

All of this is, of course, negative, and these downward-spiralling thoughts leave little room for assertive behaviour.

The sports world discovered a way to use this kind of inner thinking in a positive way quite a few years ago, and there are lots of books about the 'inner game' of tennis/golf/squash/football and so on. The positive inner dialogue technique is very useful before a crisis or tricky situation to coach yourself into doing your best in the given circumstances. It is not a question of thinking rosy thoughts so that you can pretend it will be all right with false optimism – it is a way of stopping the downward spiral with positive but realistic options.

In the example shown above, your thoughts could go as follows:

'It's Friday... the management meeting is today... it is not going to be an easy meeting as I am going to ask for extra money... I do have a good case and I can demonstrate that it is valid... not everyone will be helpful... if there is any problem I know how to be assertive... I believe my case is a good one... I'll do my best to see my department has a fair hearing.'

As you can see from this example, with a positive inner dialogue it is so much easier to move on to the next thing than remain trapped in a difficult situation.

The broken record technique

Children are experts in the use of the broken record technique and use it very effectively. It is useful to help make sure that you are listened to and that your message is received. Sometimes when people are actively involved in their own concerns or needs they pay little attention to what you have to say or to your situation. Broken record makes sure that your message gets through without you appearing to nag or whine.

With the broken record technique it is important to keep on repeating the message until it can no longer be ignored. It is also important to use some of the words over again in different sentences. This reinforces the main part of your message and prevents your listener raising red herrings or diverting you from your central message.

Example

'We won't be able to complete the report by the 15th. I understand it causes you problems, but the hard facts are it won't be possible to put it all together by the 15th. However, we can promise to let you have a copy of the draft, but what we can't do is let you have a complete report by the 15th.'

Assertive behaviour is essential when dealing with the press (see the section that follows). In all cases, whether face-to-face or on the telephone, it pays to keep calm and take a few seconds to ensure that you respond, rather than react, to what you are asked. Responding requires consideration of the question, whereas reacting tends to be a defence mechanism – you answer quickly and allow yourself to be pushed into putting across the wrong message.

Assertive behaviour can be useful when dealing with difficult situations, whether they involve customers, your manager, and people in other departments of the organization. One final useful thing to remember in making your job easier and more enjoyable is 'Do favours'. If you are able to help someone out in a way that does not take you too much time, but saves them a great deal of time, they will be extremely grateful. You don't know when you may need them to return the favour, and you will have a useful contact in another department when you do. Having a knowledge of the 'right' person to speak to is worth a great deal in your work role.

It is also worth thinking about the way in which you communicate with people. Do you keep your standards high? How is your spelling and grammar? When talking to people who 'ruffle your feathers', do you retain your calm manner or do you adopt a manner that could be construed as rude or condescending? Do you speak clearly so that you cannot be misheard – especially on the phone? Do you check your work to make sure that it says exactly what you intended it to say? We are all very busy at work – more to do and fewer people to do it – and it is when we are working under pressure and to tight deadlines that we are most likely to let things slip.

Keeping the conversation relevant

You are an interesting person, and easy to talk to. You have a good, open style of communication that encourages people to talk, so that you learn from them. You are a good listener. However, how do you make sure that the conversation stays 'on track', so that you get the most from the time you have allowed for networking?

The answer to this question starts before you attend an event – what is your objective? What is your reason for attending? Even if it is just to meet new people to build your network of contacts, you can apply the SMART technique (see 'Planning events'). How many people would you like to meet on this occasion? Are you looking to meet people with a particular background because you have a current project in mind? How many people are likely to attend, and is it therefore realistic to expect to add x to your list?

With this objective in mind every time you introduce yourself to someone, you are more likely to keep the conversation brief and to the point and give yourself the opportunity to move on as necessary. You can learn to pull a conversation back on track through careful questioning techniques. Listening for an opportunity to ask an *open* question which relates to the conversation and links back to your area of interest is the best way.

What if this opportunity does not arise? *Closed* questions – those which require just a one-word answer – are your most useful ally. They temporarily close the conversation and stop the flow of words – this creates an opportunity for you to turn the topic back to a work-related issue.

Activity 6.1

Practice these techniques in a social situation first if you can. Explain to a friend what you are trying to achieve so that he or she can give you feedback on how it feels from the other side.

Unit 6 Practical networking skills

Promoting yourself at work

If you are not yet in marketing, or are relatively new to the role, you can use your study to 'heighten your profile' at work. You will need to ask questions and find out more about how things are done within your own working environment. Other students will share their experiences with you and will expect you to do the same. If you are studying this module on the continuous assessment route, you will be basing your assignments around your own organization and activities at work, and this will also demonstrate your interest in marketing to others.

Think of yourself as a 'product' which needs marketing in the same way as any other. Just as, in the Marketing Environment module, you identified an organization's stakeholder groups, think about your own. In your work situation there are several different groups of people that you will need to communicate with. These will include:

- Your work colleagues
- Your managers
- Your own team (if you are in a role which involves managing people)
- Your customers or clients
- Your suppliers
- The staff at your advertising, sales promotion or research agency
- The general public
- The local community
- Other departments in your organization.

Activity 6.2

Think about the work you do, and your strengths and weaknesses. Do you behave in the same way when you are dealing with different groups of people? Thinking about all your stakeholder groups as 'customers', how does customer need differ from group to group?

Some groups of people will expect you to behave in a more formal manner than others; all will expect you to be enthusiastic and reliable. Your own team will expect you to be a good listener, as will your customers and your managers. When you know what is expected of you, it is easier to work on your strengths and weaknesses to improve your overall image.

Do you have a curriculum vitae (CV) – and if you have, is it up to date? Does it do a good job of marketing you? Would you be ready if an opportunity to move into a much-wanted role presented itself? If you are studying this module and being continuously assessed, rather than by taking the exam, you will need to put a CV into your Portfolio (go to www.marketingonline.co.uk or www.bh.com/marketing). One of the first things to think about is your 'Profile'. What is it about you that will make you invaluable to an employer? What skills do you have? What are your key strengths? What is it about your personality or character that makes you suitable for this position?

Activity 6.3

Profile preparation

Imagine you are talking to an interviewer, a person who wants to know your skills, strengths and character.

Write down, in a maximum of 100 words, what you would tell the interviewer in order to impress. Use this information when putting together your CV.

Your CV should be concise, clear, positive and well presented.

- *Concise* Ideally, your CV should not exceed two to three pages of A4 paper. When you use it you want someone to read it, and if it is too long they may be reluctant.
- *Clear* Like any marketing document, it needs to be written without jargon and in easily understandable language.
- *Positive* The reader is more interested in what you have achieved than what you have done.
- *Well presented* A well-thought-out layout. The content should show the reader common threads running through your experience.

It should contain personal information about you and how you can be contacted, your career history and details about your educational background.

- *Contact information* Start with your name, address and contact numbers.
- *Career history* This should start with your current or last role and go backwards in chronological order.
- *Job title* Remember to explain this if it may be difficult to understand outside your own industry – and then outline your responsibilities and key achievements. Remember that you need to tell the reader what you have achieved (e.g. 'Exceeded sales targets by x per cent'; 'Designed and introduced new sales lead tracking systems which are now contributing to the success of the department').

Give full information on your current or most recent role, and limit the information you give on previous roles, highlighting key elements which may be relevant to your current situation.

- *Education* List all schools and educational establishments you have attended, together with your qualifications. This should again be in reverse chronological order.
- *Personal information* Finally, give your date of birth, your marital status, details of your dependent children, and your hobbies and interests. In this section, think about how the information will be perceived by the reader. If you are using the CV to apply for a job, your prospective employer may wonder how you will balance your busy social life with work. Interviewers also like to ask questions about your areas of interest to encourage you to talk. If you list 'reading', be prepared for questions on the last book you read and what you liked or disliked about it. If you list particular sports, be prepared for questions from someone who plays the same sport regularly. If the first and last time you played badminton was 12 years ago and your interviewer plays for the county team, you are in danger of giving an immediate poor impression of yourself! When you have finished writing your CV, ask someone who knows you well for their comments.

Unit 6 Practical networking skills

Handling the press

There are two kinds of publicity that your organization may receive – that which is planned and that which is unplanned. Organizations communicate with the general public whether or not they make a positive decision to do so, and the more you have been involved with planning the communication, the more control you will have over its content. This applies to spoken communication as well as written.

The press cannot obtain an accurate news story about your organization unless someone is prepared to talk to them about it. Your organization may have a Press Officer or Public Relations Officer whose job it is to deal with the press. Alternatively, if you work in a small organization, you may take on a combination of both roles.

For examples of different styles of press information look at the following websites:

- www.j-sainsbury.co.uk Click on 'Media Centre'
- www.fedex.com Select your own country and then look at the 'News' section
- www.hilton.com Click on 'Press & Media'
- www.shell.com Click on 'Media Relations'.

Activity 6.4

Find out who, within your organization, deals with the press. If someone holds this role, ask if you can 'shadow' them at a press briefing or press conference, and observe their behaviour when handling the press. Make notes of how they deal with difficult questions from the press.

The person selected to deal with the press is often singled out because he or she has excellent communication skills and his or her personality and interpersonal skills are suitable. Even in a highly specialized or technical environment, technical expertise tends to be secondary to an ability to communicate.

Contact with the press may take one of many forms.

It may be through a *press release* (for writing press releases, see your 'Customer Communications' coursebook). If the press wish to follow up on the story, they may telephone you as the named contact for that communication. On the telephone it is always more difficult to be fully prepared, but there are certain actions you can take to help with this situation:

- Always have a copy of the press release, together with the names of relevant people, close at hand
- Take a few seconds to think before you speak – this time will seem longer to you than it will to your listener, and the end result will be a more professional statement, rather than a garbled response
- One final point – you can hear a smile on the phone. Try not to fall into the trap of thinking that, because you cannot be seen, your appearance does not matter.

Contact might also take the form of a *press briefing*. This is usually a short, one-way statement to the press to announce a particular piece of news. It is important that the statement is clear, concise and contains all the relevant facts. These statements are often backed up by written copy.

If you are asked to 'brief' the press, you need to be clear whether you are allowed to answer questions, and, if so, how far you can go with those answers. Often questions are not welcome, and in this case it is best to make a quick exit after your statement, or answer 'No comment' if questions are posed.

Finally, you may be asked to organize or attend a *press conference.* These are usually much larger events, and questions are usually welcomed. Press conferences are planned in advance to maximize the number of attendees, and may involve more than one speaker on behalf of the organization.

If you are asked to represent the organization, it is essential that you are clear as to where your 'boundaries' lie. Larger organizations often have written procedures on dealing with the press, and it is important that you make yourself aware of these. Most importantly, you should be able to keep calm under pressure. This is one of the characteristics of a good press or public relations officer. The press are trained to try to uncover information which you are not revealing – their pressure is not directed at you personally, but at the organization. Be assertive and keep calm.

Meeting your goals through networking

Now that you have identified and started to develop your network of contacts, you can start to make it work for you. When you have to take on a new project at work, think about what you need to know, how you are going to source this information, and who can help you either through their existing experience or their knowledge of someone who has this experience.

Who was it you were talking to at college last week who said that they had just had to arrange three presentations by software houses to find a suitable database for their company? They will have the contact numbers to hand.

Who did you meet at a CIM branch meeting who told you about a local company that specialized in digital printing and was highly recommended? You did not note the name of the company then, as you did not have an immediate need for it – but it is surprising how quickly things change at work today.

First you need to identify what your 'goals' are. If you work for a company that undertakes 'performance reviews' or appraisals, then you probably have set objectives that were agreed by you and your manager at your last review. These will be work related and directly relevant to the job you are doing – they may also include 'development' objectives, linked to skills and knowledge that you need to obtain to move forward in your role. The following tables show the 'Objectives' section of appraisal forms for two individuals.

Alice Bell	Objectives	Date
Communication	To set up a system of regular communication between field staff and office to update database on a weekly basis	31 December 2000
Data input	To improve rate of input from 76 per cent accuracy to 85 per cent accuracy within three months of review	30 September 2000

Nik Spivac	Objectives	Date
Sales	To improve performance to target (sales value) from 80 per cent to 100 per cent by the end of the financial year	31 March 2001
Communication	To submit monthly reports on time. To improve quality of report writing (remove waffle as discussed)	Immediate

How can Alice and Nik use networking to help them meet their goals?

Alice knows that Lorraine at college has set up a similar system for updating a database, because she used it as an area for her Learning Log and has talked about it several times. She will ask her about it next week, and this will save her time in planning her system. She has also decided to talk to Sheila in the accounts department, who has worked for the company for over ten years. Alice has developed quite a speed of data input since she joined the company, but her accuracy has dropped as she has become faster. Sheila may have some hints to help her achieve this objective.

Nik has decided to talk to his manager about techniques he might use to improve his sales performance. He will also talk to his cousin, who is also in sales, although he doesn't sell the same products. He is very successful in his company and won a 'Salesperson of the Year' award last year. Last month at his CIM branch meeting he heard a group of people talking about training courses they had attended. He has decided to look for them at the next meeting to find out details – there may be a course on report writing. He will also contact his training department, as they have a Learning Resource Centre that may have materials on the subject. If he can improve the quality of his reports he feels he will be able to do them quicker, which, in turn, will help him submit them on time.

Other goals may relate to specific projects that you take on from time to time. When you take on a project, how long do you take wondering where to start? Ask yourself who, in your network, may be able to provide guidance by telephone, by e-mail or face-to-face?

Managing your manager

Management is usually viewed as a downwards function, or possibly laterally in an organization. Management can also refer to management of projects or budgets and not necessarily to the management of people working for you.

One definition of management is 'achieving objectives through others', and if we take this definition, we can see how this might then apply to 'managing your manager'. You know your objectives in the organization; does your manager help you achieve them? If not there may be a variety of reasons.

Bullying

Here a manager uses his superior status unfairly. This can be very serious indeed; there are still those working in marketing who feel this is acceptable and makes for better performance. Thankfully, the vast majority are more enlightened. Often, the best advice here is to leave the organization or seek help from higher up.

Poor delegation

Many managers have had little training on management, being promoted because they were good at their last job (which might be the one you hold now). Seek clarification on what exactly you are to do, by when and for what purpose. Explain that you also need some of the 'bigger picture' so that you can appreciate the context and constraints in which you are working.

Ineffective communication

Again, do not be afraid to seek clarification, and ask open questions of your manager so that you are clear on what needs doing. Instigate a regular time for meetings/briefings so that you are never left drifting.

Your manager does not know what you are doing

To you, the latest request is totally unreasonable – you are so busy already! Tell your manager if you are too busy and actively seek their advice on prioritizing your workload. Remember, your tasks are within your manager's objectives so they have an interest in ensuring things are done in the right priority order.

Summary

This unit has covered the personal skills you need to build your network of contacts, including assertiveness techniques and questioning skills. It has looked at ways in which you can identify your existing network of contacts and widen this network. It has also considered you as a marketable commodity, and ways in which you can build your image within your marketing role.

Further study and examination preparation

When you have completed this unit you will be able to answer Question 5 from the June 2002 paper. Go to www.cimeduhub.com to access Specimen Answers and Senior Examiner's advice for these exam questions.

Extending knowledge

The Institute of Professional Selling provides a range of services to individuals involved in the sales process. They can be contacted at Moor Hall, Cookham, Berks SL6 9QH, UK.

unit 7
planning events

Learning objectives

In this unit you will:

- Develop an appreciation of the need for planning and see how simple planning tools can be applied to managing events in marketing

- Identify factors which are conducive to success

- Consider the importance of venue

- Look at events from the angle of customer needs

- Develop a practical understanding of the realities of event management

- Examine ways of measuring success.

By the end of this unit you will be able to:

- Employ a disciplined planning-based approach to event organization

- Undertake an objective appraisal of possible venues

- Anticipate and respond to pressures, incidents and problems surrounding event management

- Devise mechanisms for evaluating success and cost-effectiveness of decisions.

This unit covers sections 4.3.2, 4.3.3, and 4.3.4 of the syllabus.

This unit also relates to the key skill for marketers Problem solving and the statements of marketing practice

- Contribute to project planning and budget preparation

- Monitor and report on project activities

- Complete and close down project activities on time and within budget.

Study Guide

In this unit, we will be looking at the planning of events. We will explore the stages of a typical planning process and begin applying it in our specific context. We shall consider the importance of objective setting prior to the event, and the subsequent, often forgotten, task of measuring results afterwards. There is scope for the student to carry out local research into venues that may be used for marketing purposes, and a total of three to four hours should be allowed for this and other activities, whilst it should take around two hours to work your way through the unit itself. The practical nature of this unit cannot be over-emphasized, and your real-life experiences and those of fellow students are a valuable additional resource for the satisfactory completion of this and other units.

The contents of Units 7 and 8 are interdependent and linked to each other, so it is advised that you treat them as an entity, covering Section 4 of the syllabus. This unit 'Planning events' focuses on *planning*, while 'Marketing activities and events – exploring their diversity and application' focuses on *context*. Having said that, the planning aspects of the unit 'Planning events' are to some extent placed into context to make the planning process more real. Similarly when examining the different types of activity in 'Planning events', there are specific mentions of detailed planning.

Approaches to planning

'Nobody plans to fail, they just fail to plan.' How true is this statement? In this unit, we will see how a planning-based approach can pay dividends when organizing a marketing event.

> **Definition**
>
> **Planning** – Is the detailed drawing up of schemes and methods in order to achieve an objective.

If we look at the definition of planning, a key word is 'objective' – i.e. what you wish to achieve by the particular course of action. This, then, would seem an appropriate moment to examine what objectives may be set for various marketing events.

> **Definition**
>
> **Marketing event** – Is a generic term to cover a wide range of activities undertaken whose purpose is a marketing one. As such, it would cover store or product launches, exhibitions, conferences, roadshows and sponsorship packages.

Unit 7 Planning events

> ### Activity 7.1
>
> What objectives are behind various marketing events? Take, for example, a new store launch. Objectives here may be to sell a certain amount of stock on the first day, the second day, first week, month, etc. There may be an objective concerning the number of customer visits; there could even be objectives concerning customers' attitudes to the new store. What objectives may be behind the following?
>
> - Sponsoring a local football team
> - Having a stand at a trade show
> - Showing your products in a shopping mall
> - A series of seminars with salespeople in different locations.

There are a number of different planning frameworks that may be used. One that particularly lends itself to the planning of marketing events is SOST + 6Ms – situation, objectives, strategy, tactics, men, money, machines, materials, minutes and measurement (see Figure 7.1).

We now need to apply this planning framework to the context of planning marketing events.

Situation　　　　　　　　　　**M**en

Objectives　　　　　　　　　　**M**oney

　　　　　　　　+ 6 M's　　　　**M**achines

Strategy　　　　　　　　　　　**M**aterials

Tactics　　　　　　　　　　　　**M**inutes

　　　　　　　　　　　　　　　　Measurement

Figure 7.1 A planning framework

Situation

Here we need to consider what situation we find ourselves in. For instance, if we are launching a new product, is this an exciting innovation or a response to competitors? Is the company buoyant and optimistic or has it been through a tough time? These and other factors will have a great deal of influence on how much budget is available, and hence the size and format of subsequent marketing activities. Depending on the circumstances, it may even be necessary to use a tool such as LEPEST & CO to gain a structured understanding of the situation.

> ### Exam hint
>
> At first it may appear that the use of models such as SOST + 6Ms, LEPEST & CO, etc. is making life more difficult for the student and providing an additional obstacle to surmount. This is not the case. Using such models as a checklist enables more valid points to be made and prevents the omission of critical stages in an answer. Put bluntly, using models and frameworks will allow you to gain more marks.

Objectives

We have already looked at how objectives lay behind the event in Activity 7.1. Now we need to take a closer look at the business of objective *setting.* The most important point to remember about objectives is that they are concerned with what you want to achieve, not merely descriptions of what you intend to do.

Case Study

Renault the French car manufacturer along with many industry rivals, is committed to a presence at county shows, and its products are to be seen at over 200 such events annually in the UK, plus at Grand Prix and other motor sport events throughout the world.

The situation car manufacturers find themselves in is that many potential customers are reticent about entering a car showroom. One strand of strategy to overcome this is to take the cars to the public in 'neutral territory', hence the comprehensive show programme. However, the true objective is not to attend shows and motor racing events.

Objectives would instead be centred around exposure, visibility, customer enquiries, test drives booked and even, ultimately, sales generated. These objectives would be very similar to DAGMAR based objectives which concern themselves with moving customers or potential customers along a continuum as follows:

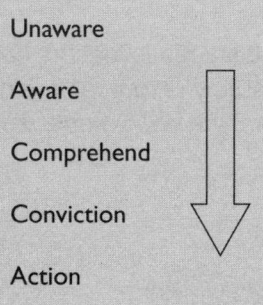

Unaware

Aware

Comprehend

Conviction

Action

Activity 7.2

We have seen above how a well-known multinational car manufacturer utilizes a presence at shows in the UK as a major part of its promotional armoury. For this activity, you are now a marketing assistant for Tata, the Indian vehicle manufacturer who is not well known in Europe. You have been approached by the organizers of the Royal Agricultural show who are offering a stand which can contain five vehicles for the duration of the show which attracts over 200,000 visitors per year. The stand costs £10,000. What would you propose as your objectives for participating?

Exam hint

Make them SMART! If you find yourself writing objectives, remember the acronym SMART, which stands for specific, measurable, agreed, realistic and timed. For example, on a store launch 'To generate customers' would be a very poor objective. 'To generate 5000 customer visits in week 1 of trading' is much better, fulfilling the SMART test.

Strategy

Strategy concerns itself with how a particular objective is to be achieved. As an example, we might have as our objective 'To equip our 200-strong sales force with details of our new product line by June 2004'. So we have a clear indication of what needs to be achieved. Strategy concerns itself with how we might achieve this, and clearly there are a number of ways. One possibility may be to gather the entire sales force together in one location for a large, impressive, conference-style presentation. Alternatively, regional presentations could take place at ten locations, allowing greater participation. But do we need to see all the salespeople? Could details be cascaded by regional managers to their teams, and product manuals distributed by post or even electronically? There are always a number of strategies, or combinations of strategies, that could be employed to fulfil a given objective, and part of a marketer's role is to make appropriate decisions concerning such options in the light of the organization's situation and available resources.

Tactics

Tactics are very much about the detail, once our strategy has been decided. Referring back to the example of Renault's outside show programme, the tactical details here would centre around exactly which events to attend, what cars to show, and the logistics of moving stand materials, vehicles and personnel around the country. At an even more detailed level, such matters as food, sleeping accommodation, site access, supplies of brochures, leaflets and other give-aways would all need consideration if the event is to be successful.

So now, having examined the four stages, situation, objectives, strategy and tactics, we have in place the skeleton of a plan, but surely resources are needed to carry out the plan, and we also need some way of evaluating what we do. So now we need to examine in turn the 6Ms of our planning framework.

Men

Or perhaps we should talk in terms of human resources. At this stage we need to consider what human resources need to be devoted to the event in question, be it a conference, exhibition, roadshow or some other activity.

First, the marketer needs to estimate what is needed in terms of skill and expertise, ascertaining whether this is available in-house or needs to be contracted out to a third party supplier. If this is a conference, it is almost certain that venues will need to be visited (see later in this unit), and it may well be necessary to liaise with a conference production company.

What input is needed from others? Perhaps the speakers at the conference need to produce scripts and rehearse in good time. Is extra help needed on the day to greet delegates and act as ushers? It is a good idea at this stage to produce a plan detailing who does what and by when. This should then be circulated to all concerned, and be amended periodically in line with developments.

A wide range of interpersonal skills may be needed by the typical conference co-ordinator, who has to deal with people inside the organization, often from different departments and often of higher status, in addition to dealing with a variety of suppliers on a contractual basis.

Money

The prime starting point here has to be the initial budget allocated for the task in hand, and there are a number of ways of initially setting a budget (see Unit 11, 'Introduction to budgeting'). Assuming that a budget has been set, this has a great bearing on what can and cannot be done. If we have an important message to get across to our 100 salespeople, but have a budget of only £5000, then clearly we are not in a position to fly them with their partners to an exotic location for a full-blown presentation, followed by a dinner dance and overnight stay! Here, a convenient, medium-sized venue with simple presentations would be more realistic. An important point to stress is the likelihood of extra or hidden costs occurring, so it is always advisable to work with a contingency of around 10 per cent.

Machines

In marketing events there can be a great reliance on machines. For instance, even a relatively small conference would have speaker support, either as slides or PowerPoint, there would be lights, autocue and public address systems. There may well be video or other audio-visual support. All of these are vital to the smooth running of the conference. For a roadshow, vehicles may need to be hired, and machinery physically moved around. Increasingly when we talk of machines we are talking of IT, software, and increasingly sophisticated machinery which may prove vulnerable to the rigours of constant use (or abuse) in a different environment.

Materials

What is physically needed to fulfil our plan? Again, this would vary according to the type of marketing event. If we are looking at a new store launch, then adequate stocks of product, especially traffic-generating special offers, is very much a necessity. We would also need promotional materials, whether leaflets, brochures or advertising. A typical conference would also need support materials for delegates, which may comprise anything from badges through presentation packs to videos for future reference.

Minutes

Minutes or time can often prove to be the most precious and scarce resource in the busy world of marketing. Realistic estimates need to be made regarding the time needed to fulfil the necessary tasks. At a conference it is often alleged that each minute of a speech may require half an hour of preparation, writing, editing and rehearsing. Similarly, the production of a five-minute video insert may take a day! It can greatly help to produce a timing plan, showing critical dates and times, and this is detailed later in the unit.

Measurement

If we have set clear objectives for our activity, then it follows that we can measure the success of what we do against those objectives. For instance, our store opening objective may concern store visits – easily measurable in a store fitted with a turnstile or other measuring device, but otherwise impractical if a person is needed to be employed to count customers as they enter the store.

Although it may appear a little threatening to some marketers, measuring against objectives is very much needed in today's environment, and it is better that you do it and take corrective action or make alternative recommendations than someone else.

Unit 7 Planning events

Activity 7.3

Monopharm plc

You have recently been appointed as Conference and Exhibitions Assistant to Monopharm plc, a pharmaceuticals company whose head office is in Amersham, Buckinghamshire. Although the future looks bright thanks to a revolutionary cold remedy about to be launched, there are still problems due to the fact that Monopharm is a company formed by a recent merger of two companies. A total of 300 staff were made redundant as a result of the merger, mainly due to the closure of a factory in the north-east of England. The company now employs 220 staff at a manufacturing base in Belgium, 170 at its UK-based head office and research and development facility in the UK. Additionally, there is a pan-European sales force of 120, comprising the former sales teams of the two former companies. Rumours are rife within the company that the sales team is to undergo a 20 per cent reduction. There is still a deep mistrust and cultural divide between the partners in this business marriage.

The Marketing Manager, to whom you report, and who is also a recent appointment, has asked for your thoughts on how the new product may be used as a vehicle not just for future success, but also as a means of healing old wounds. She is keen that the budget of £100,000 allocated for conferences be used for this rebuilding purpose. You are keen to impress your new manager, and wish to show how the structured approaches you are learning on your CIM course can be applied.

Task

Prepare a brief presentation using SOST + 6Ms as a framework to give your initial thoughts.

An alternative approach to planning

Whilst SOST and the 6Ms is a perfectly valid and acceptable framework for planning, you may have come across other planning tools and subsequently be feeling confused about which to use.

One very user-friendly planning tool is one which uses the analogy of a journey, and which poses a series of questions a would-be traveller may ask.

> Where are we now?
>
> Where do we want to be?
>
> How might we get there?
>
> ... and which way is best?
>
> How do we ensure arrival?

It is easy to see how the above fits journey planning. You need to know where you are at the moment before deciding where you want to be, too ambitious a destination may be impossible if you are not in the right place. There are always a number of options for travel: rail, air, sea, car, bus etc. and which is best would vary according to your own criteria. You may need speed, or economy may be a driver. You may seek flexibility, or reliability of transport mode. Ensuring arrival may entail checking timetables, or even setting your alarm clock to catch the early flight.

Transferring the above to marketing, we need to start out with an audit and analysis of our present situation – that is where we are now.

Where we want to be involves the setting of mission statements, aims and clear objectives.

How we get there and which way is best brings us to looking at the many different options available to us.

How we ensure arrival involves the control and measurement of our plans.

Case Study

MG Rover was bought out from the BMW group three years ago, and is an independent, but tiny car manufacturer with an ageing product line-up and little money to invest.

That is where they are now.

They need to ensure survival.

At the present time, this objective surpasses all others, where they want to be is, quite simply, still in existence in 5 years time.

How to get there and which way is best is what MG Rover is currently attempting to resolve. It appears that a link with Chinese manufacturer Brilliance may be one way forward. Another strand of their strategy is to build an alliance with Tata, the Indian conglomerate and build a new, small Rover car based on the Indica, a new Tata model.

Meanwhile, they have revitalised their line-up with increased application of the MG brand.

Ensuring arrival will need constant monitoring and re-appraisal of plans.

Watch for this story unfolding as you study for MIP over the next few months.

A checklist for success

Now that we have already used one planning framework, you may like to consider using a different one, which also exerts a rigour and discipline on the planning process but which is framed as a set of questions rather than as a linear process. The questions we have to ask ourselves are: why, what, where, who, when, how much?

- *Why?* The first question to ask before embarking on a course of action is why are we about to do this? This question prompts us to think about objectives. We are not doing something for its own sake, we are doing it in order to achieve something. For instance, we may be exhibiting our product range in a public location. The reason why we are doing this is to gain exposure among xxx members of our target audience, to generate xx sales enquiries and x actual sales. The question 'Why?' should also be asked in conjunction with the other questions, as we shall see.
- *What?* So what is it that we intend to do? Or perhaps we need to ask ourselves what else could we do, what other ways are there of fulfilling our objectives? If our objective is to communicate a new programme to the field sales network, what alternative ways are

Unit 7 Planning events

there of doing this? This then leads us again to ask the question 'Why?', in the sense of why are we doing what we are doing and why have we decided against another course of action?

o *Where?* This question makes us consider location in all its aspects. (This is examined more thoroughly in the next section of this unit.) Just as before, the question 'Why?' needs to be asked in parallel with 'Where?', so we need to be able to justify our selection of venue and argue against other possibilities. A clearly established range of criteria would be a great help here.

o *Who?* The human aspect is vital, and two basic questions need to be asked. First, who is this marketing event aimed at, i.e. the target audience? Secondly, who is to do what in connection with our marketing event? This leads on to further questions surrounding contracting out work, and who should be selected. It is hardly necessary to mention that at this stage the question 'Why?' again needs asking – why are we inviting a particular group and why are we using a particular production company?

o *When?* Time is always a critical factor, and you will be asked this question most often – 'When will the MD's slides be ready?' 'When are the vehicles due to arrive, shouldn't they be here now?', etc. A useful tip here is to draw up a timing plan which is agreed and circulated to all parties. On a large project, plans may well need updating on a daily basis. Again, be prepared to justify timings by having already asked the question 'Why?'

o *How much?* Budgets, and in particular variances from budget, will always be a focus of attention, and a full unit of this coursebook is dedicated to the subject. Again, 'Why?' prompts the marketer into an examination of costs, which at worst can pacify others in the organization and at best may result in substantial savings.

Activity 7.4

If you work in a marketing role, try applying the framework of why, what, where, who, when and how much. Be sure to answer the question 'Why?' throughout the exercise. How useful/usable do you find this?

Alternatively, try applying this to something outside work that you have helped organize, such as a wedding, holiday or some other trip.

Venue selection

In this section we will examine the process of venue selection. We will look specifically at organizing a conference, although much of what applies here would also apply to another kind of marketing event.

Activity 7.5

Imagine that you have been charged with finding a suitable venue for a conference for your organization. What criteria would you use to draw up a shortlist of suitable venues? Compare your list with the one on p. 95.

Criteria for venue selection

A useful acronym is ASFAB: access, size, facilities, appropriateness, budget.

Access
Access is one of the main criteria in selecting a suitable venue for a conference. Is the venue easily accessible for the delegates by various means of transport, i.e. road, rail or even air? Even if it is accessible, is it in an area prone to problems with traffic congestion? Assuming road is the main method of transport, the conference organizer needs to check on the availability of parking spaces. Also to consider is whether you wish the location to be near where the majority of delegates live, or feel there would be a benefit in choosing somewhere further away to physically separate your conference and its important message from their day-to-day lives. Indeed, the conference industry is a truly international one, especially where attendance is seen as a reward or motivational tool.

Whilst we have considered access from a geographical standpoint, it also needs to be considered from a physical viewpoint; for instance, a manufacturer of trucks may need special access to display its products. From a human angle, most venues have adequate access for people with disabilities, but it is well worth checking on this.

Size
Size is another important criterion. We need to ensure that the delegates can be catered for in comfort, and it is well worth checking the conference room for its height and also for any pillars or other limiting obstructions. It is also necessary to consider whether the venue is used to handling events of the size you propose. It is possible that your event is rather small and you may not receive the service and attention you need, whereas on the other hand it could be that the venue does not have the experience of dealing with events on such a grand scale as yours.

Facilities
Here you need to make a list of what you need, especially if it is not commonplace. For instance, you may require bedrooms for all the delegates for an overnight event, you may need sporting or recreational facilities, for the conference itself you may need video projection facilities, staging, special lighting effects, lifting gear, ramps or other equipment, depending on the scale and content of the conference production.

Appropriateness
There are three broad categories of venue for a conference. There are special conference venues, such as the GMEX in Manchester; then there are a vast number of hotels throughout the world which have suitable conference suites, such as the Hilton chain which is truly global; or alternatively there is a range of 'unusual' locations – examples of this being Whitbread's old brewery in London or the National Motorcycle Museum, both of which are not immediately obvious as venues but host conferences and other events on a large scale.

Budget
Last, but not least, budget – or can we afford this particular venue? Indeed, for many organizations, budget is the starting point when drawing up a shortlist of venues. Remember to see this in terms of total budget; it would be a false economy to hire a venue which involved a great deal more expenditure on travel or other expenses.

Conference and event costings and budgets

The costs of holding an event can vary from a few hundred pounds for a small meeting to millions of pounds for a major conference or event presence. Activity 7.6 will ask you to check out some costings. This is a vital exercise for you to undertake in your part of the world as costs vary so much. Once you have a feel of costs this may prove extremely useful in an exam situation as you will be able to make better judgements based on some outside real-life knowledge.

A marketing assistant is likely to be responsible for reporting and advising on expenditure to their manager, although it is unlikely that a marketing assistant would be responsible for major decisions involving substantial capital outlay.

Areas of costing

It may be useful to split the costs into different areas for clarity of presentation. These could be as follows.

Venue costs
These would include some or all of the list below:

- Room hire/stand space
- Service costs, e.g. cleaning, maintenance, telephone installation, power
- Food and drink.

Accommodation and transport costs
These would include:

- Hotel costs for staff/delegates
- Transport to the event (by air, rail, car).

Staging costs
This covers the 'physical' set up, comprising:

- Set, staging or stand design and build
- Technical support, equipment hire.

Production costs
This would include the following:

- A/V (audio/visual) materials such as video filming
- Script writing (for a conference).

Staff costs
Some organizations would take into account the management cost of organizing an event or conference, others would not show this cost as being separate from the normal wage bill for the company.

Support materials costs
This would usually comprise printed materials such as:

- Brochures
- Information packs
- Posters.

But could cover other 'give-aways' such as:

- Balloons
- Badges, etc.

Other costs
This covers miscellaneous items not included in the above.

> ### Exam hint
>
> The above list of costs and the previous mnemonic ASFAB are the key to answering questions on this paper, and have been used by many candidates over the last three years. Have they done well? Not necessarily. The key to a really good answer is not just to reproduce a list you have remembered but to actually use and contextualize it. For instance, the facilities needed may differ if you are putting on an exhibition and conference about military aircraft, as indeed may size, access and budget. Costs would also be very different.
>
> Other considerations are those of a cultural nature. It will always be important to ensure that conference venues can meet the various needs of customers including dietary related requirements either due to health needs or of cultural orientation.

Activity 7.6

So just how much does it cost to hire a suitable venue for a conference? Try obtaining some information from a local hotel or conference centre. Alternatively, there is a lot of information on the internet. Try searching 'conference AND venue' or check out the sites of hotel chains such as Holiday Inn. Alternatively search by location. Best of luck.........

Activity 7.7

Budget status

You have been asked by your manager for an update on the costs for the annual sales conference. You are to present this in a clear format.

The information you have to date is that 150 people will be attending for the day. The cost of invitations and other printing is estimated at $10,000. The venue costs $5000 to hire with a daily delegate rate of $50. Yourself and five colleagues will be staying at the venue the night before at a cost of $75 each. Production is estimated at $15,000 and set design and build has been estimated at $12,000.

Prepare an estimate of costs.

Event evaluation and selection

Imagine you work in a marketing department and you have been asked to sponsor a local football team, but on the other hand there exists an opportunity to become involved in a tennis tournament where there are corporate hospitality facilities. You know that the nearby air show attracts large crowds, but you have just been offered a chance to display your range of products in a local shopping mall. How do you compare and evaluate such a diverse range of marketing opportunities? It makes sense to draw up a list of criteria by which a fair evaluation can take place.

Cost

This time we start with cost, as this will immediately screen out many courses of action (although if the other criteria are fulfilled, it may be possible to make a business case for more money).

Customers

Is this a viable, effective and efficient way to reach either our customers or our target audience? If we are very much a local business there would be merit in sponsoring a local football team or some other sport, but we would need to ascertain whether the spectators formed part of our target audience. If we represented a high-class department store, or a budget supermarket, our choice of sport may well be very different. As regards efficiency, an air display may well attract a large crowd, but this may be wasteful if it is from a large geographical area. Also to be considered under this criterion is what opportunities are there for providing corporate hospitality for major customers or clients?

Competitors

We always need to know what our competitors are doing. For instance, if all our competitors are attending a major trade show, there is a strong argument to say that we also should attend. But then, on the other hand, we may wish to stand out from our competitors by becoming involved in something new and different.

Activity 7.8

Consider two companies in the same sector who demonstrate involvement in very different types of activity, for instance Ford, who sponsor the European Champions League (football), and Volvo (owned by Ford), who are heavily involved in golf sponsorship. Why do you think they do things so differently, and what do you think they achieve?

Synergy

Here we need to consider whether a particular activity fits with our company mission and image, whether real, perceived or desired. For instance, Land Rover display their off-road vehicles at large agricultural shows and have off-road trials as this fits their image, despite the fact that most vehicles are bought by urban dwellers who keep their vehicles very much on the road.

Meeting customer needs

When organizing a conference or other type of marketing event, it is always important to consider customer needs rather than to plan purely from the standpoint of an organization's objectives. 'The food was poor and we had to wait so long for it that it was cold' is typical of comments received about a conference. Never mind about the quality of the production or the clarity of the speeches, this delegate will only remember the event for one thing – poor food. One way in which we can begin to understand this and plan accordingly is to look at Maslow's hierarchy of needs and apply it to our audience (see Figure 7.2).

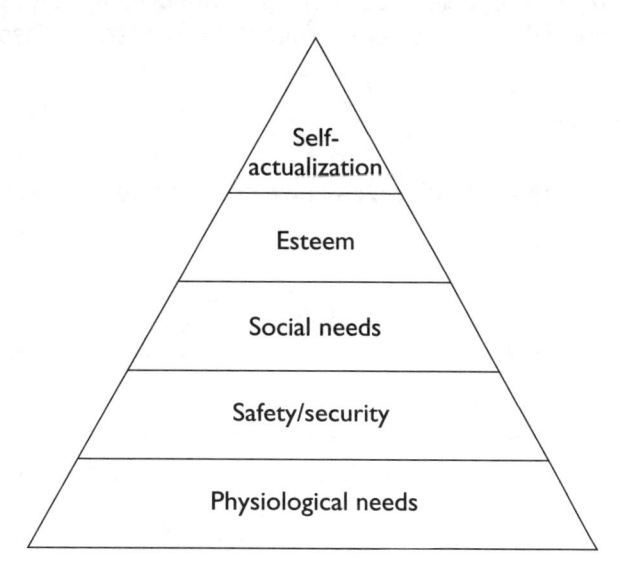

Figure 7.2 Maslow's hierarchy of needs

You may recall from Marketing Fundamentals that a person's needs have to be fulfilled at the lower levels before we can communicate at the higher levels, so it is no wonder that our hungry delegate missed out on the important message of the day. Let us examine these needs and apply them to our conference.

Basic needs

Food, drink and shelter are the most basic human needs. So we make sure that coffee, tea and biscuits are provided on arrival, especially if delegates have travelled a long distance. Delivery of food needs to be carefully timed, and special attention needs to be paid to dietary requirements, whether because of religion (e.g. a Muslim or Jew cannot eat pork), personal choice (e.g. varying degrees of vegetarianism), or for health reasons (e.g. nut and dairy allergies). As regards shelter, any overnight stays need to be booked well in advance. Also, if car parking is at some distance from the venue and rain is forecast, a supply of umbrellas will prevent a lot of complaints.

Safety and security needs

On a physical level, it is necessary to ensure that there are no worries about the security and safety of people or their belongings, so we need to check on cloakroom and left luggage facilities where appropriate. On another level, we may need to consider the requirement for a 'safe environment' for a delegate to express his or her views without fear of either ridicule or retribution, and this can sometimes be difficult to provide.

Social needs

Often a conference might be the only occasion when people see each other, and they enjoy the opportunity to socialize and network. There can also be a very valuable exchange of ideas and this can add to the value of the conference itself, so it pays to timetable a period of informal mixing.

Self-esteem needs

Here we need to make the delegates feel good about themselves, and this can often be achieved by the tone and motivational aspects of the conference itself.

Self-actualization

Once the other needs are satisfied, we can now concentrate on the important messages of the conference itself.

Detail planning, anticipating and on-the-day management

While we have examined the planning concept and employed various planning tools earlier in this unit, we now need to look at detailed planning. An excellent way to undertake detailed planning of a complex marketing event is to use a Gantt chart, which shows what happens when, how long it takes and who is responsible for making things happen. A sample chart is shown in Figure 7.3.

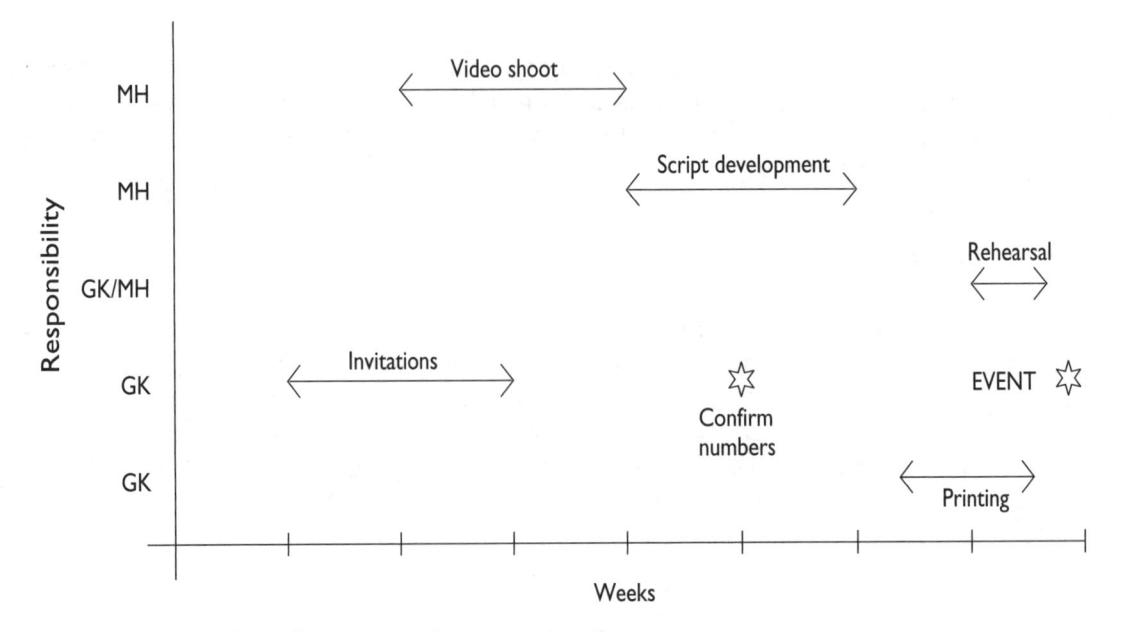

Figure 7.3 Gantt chart, showing tasks for a typical conference

How to construct a chart

First, insert the date(s) of the marketing event(s). Obviously, everything has to happen before this date, with the probable exception of measurement, which can only take place afterwards (more of this later in the unit). Next, divide what needs to be done into broad areas of activity, e.g. printing requirements, food, invitations, video production, scripts, logistics, as appropriate. Now work backwards from the date of the event. For example, you need printed leaflets two days before the event, and it takes five working days to produce them at the printers; artwork takes two days, and internal approval takes a week; your agency takes four days to produce a visual, and approval for this takes a day. Using a chart as follows (Figure 7.4), we can work out the latest date on which the ad agency needs to be briefed.

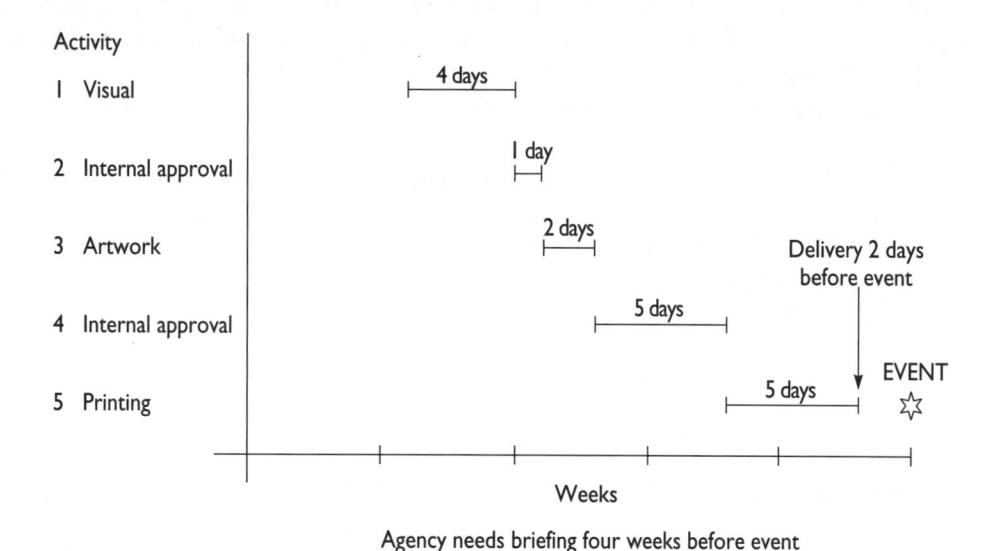

Figure 7.4 Gantt chart, showing stages of printing and necessary tasks

However, the above assumes that the first visual is approved immediately, and you have checked the Marketing Director's diary to find that he is on holiday abroad when final approval is needed. This then gives a revised schedule (Figure 7.5).

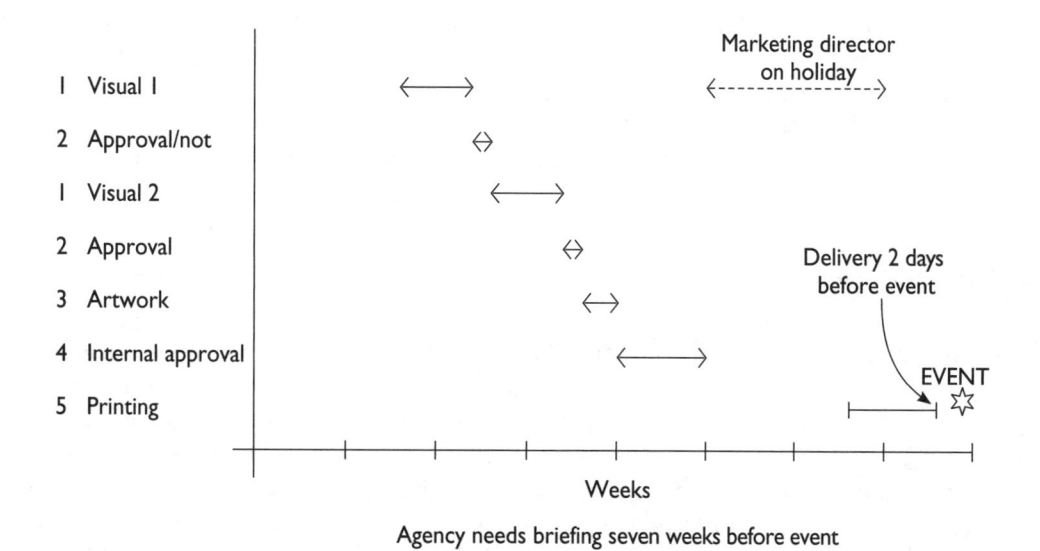

Figure 7.5 Gantt chart, showing revised schedule

Unit 7 Planning events

Activity 7.9

The sales conference

This is due to take place on 1 August, and 100 of your distributors are to be invited. Replies are usually received within a week, but around 20 need to be contacted by telephone to ascertain their attendance.

The venue has accepted your provisional booking, but needs to know exact numbers of attendees a week in advance, and any overnight stays as soon as possible.

The intention is to provide packs for delegates to take away. The printer normally takes a week to deliver, but has warned you that the works are shut down during the last week in July. The agency you use can provide visuals within 24 hours, and takes three days to produce the artwork for a typical pack.

The four speakers at the conference have requested that their presentations be produced on PowerPoint, but none of them can do this for themselves, and a speech usually requires three hours' work to put into the required format, whilst checking this can take up to two days according to the availability of staff.

Technical set-up takes a day, and a day is also set aside for rehearsals.

Task

Produce a planning chart for the above sales conference.

Daily management of the project

A complex task such as organizing a conference, exhibition or roadshow involves many people. All the individuals rely on everyone else, yet probably only really know about their own limited input. For instance, a printer may know that some leaflets are needed for a conference, but may not realize that they are actually needed two days before and that the Sales Director is likely to make some changes in a week's time. Similarly, the Sales Director is so involved in the changes to the sales programme that he or she is unaware of the deadlines that others have to work to. For this reason the Gantt chart may not be sufficiently detailed. So that all players are fully briefed, a status report or call sheet should be produced at agreed times.

Definition

Status report – Details the current situation of a project. It shows what has been done, what needs doing, who needs to do it and by when. It can also be used to highlight problems that need resolving and decisions that have to be made. In appearance it may resemble the minutes of a meeting, except that those mentioned may never have met each other. A status report can be produced to effectively delegate upwards and outside the organization by a comparatively junior marketer. A *call sheet* is similar and is typically used on the day of a conference to give precise timings and other instructions and information.

Example of a status report
Status report

Date of issue: 23/2/00

Circulation: J. SMITH, M. JONES, K. HARVEY, A. PATEL, F. REED, G. MOULTON (Moulprint), F. JENNINGS (Advantage), S. WALTERS (Video productions), T. HEMMING (Grand Hotel)

March sales conference

Activity	Complete by	Responsibility
Finalize attendance numbers	28/2	JS
Finalize costings	3/3	JS, TH
Scripts due	28/2 urgent	MJ, KH
Video shoot	10/3	SW
Products needed for shoot	7/3	MJ
Support materials dispatched to print	5/3	MJ, KH, AP
Media support schedule	9/3	FJ

Depending upon the complexity of the project the status report could be issued weekly or, as the time draws near, even more frequently, and should be the prime document by which all parties plan. Changes can be specifically highlighted as can problem areas and the documentation of events in such a way can greatly reduce the stress on the organizer.

Measurement

This is very much connected with the initial setting of objectives for our marketing event at the beginning of the unit. A useful framework for measuring success (and for devising objectives in the first instance) is the DAGMAR model, more usually associated with the world of advertising. But it is useful in the way it takes the customer or prospect through clearly defined and hence measurable phases: unawareness, awareness, comprehension, conviction, action, or, put another way, not knowing, knowing, understanding, believing, doing. So, for our event, we may have an awareness-raising objective and subsequent measurement.

Case Study

Briefing the distributor network

Events for distributors, dealers and sales agents are held regularly, across all sectors. Let us imagine that there is a major change to the product line-up of a company producing business stationery, and that we are looking at setting objectives.

Our first objective may be about making the distributor network AWARE of the changes. This may happen with the initial mailing of invitations as it may be assumed that not all may attend. A subsequent ACTION may be no more than attendance at the event. We now need distributors to understand (COMPREHEND) the changes in product. More importantly we need to CONVINCE them that the changes are worthwhile and will bring increased profits. Finally, further ACTION is needed, with distributors agreeing to stock the new product range.

Methods of measurement

Thought needs to be given to exactly how the measurement is to take place. Questionnaires may be one method of gathering information, although we need to consider how many we should get completed for a meaningful measurement – but more of that in 'Gathering information from inside and outside the organization'. If we have set ourselves a sales objective for our activity, it should be possible to track ensuing sales, although again this may not be accurate if other factors come into play. Always remember that the purpose of measurement is to improve what you do next time.

Analysis of the results of a marketing event

The conference is over. The long hours you have put in to make it a success appear to have been worthwhile and the delegates seem to have gone away happy. But is that just because it is over and they can go home to their families? You are left wondering just how much of the new product knowledge they have absorbed. A lot of money was spent on the conference and your company is eager to know if the investment worked before planning for next year. How then can we measure the effectiveness of such an event?

At the event

Attendance is easy to measure numerically. If 200 attended the event which cost £40,000, then it cost the organization £200 per person to get across its messages. This could then be compared to other methods.

Satisfaction could be measured using a suitable questionnaire and it may even be possible to check the delegates' retention of the information passed on by way of a simple test.

Also it is possible to gain feedback by observing the delegates' behaviour and attitudes displayed.

Post event

Perhaps a truer indication of the longer-term effectiveness could be obtained by having questionnaires filled in some time later.

Also, harder numerical information will become available such as the number of sales or enquiries.

The difficulties of measurement

As in any marketing activity it is difficult to make wholly accurate judgements. The delegates may give poor feedback, is that really about the conference or about their feelings towards the company? Are their comments about the food and catering or about the conference content? And the soaring sales afterwards, is that as a result of the conference or the advertising campaign and introductory pricing?

Even though measurement is difficult, we should still undertake it as an integral part of our planning and working.

Summary

In this unit you have seen that:

- Planning frameworks assist in planning marketing events. Two such frameworks are SOST + 6Ms, and why, what, who, when, where and how much

- There is a need for clear criteria when evaluating alternatives and making decisions

- The customer's needs have to be met

- Detail planning is greatly aided by using Gantt charts

- Measurement needs to take place against clear objectives.

Further study and examination preparation

When you have completed this unit you will be able to answer Question 7 from the June 2002 paper and Question 2 from the December 2002 paper. Go to www.cimeduhub.com to access Specimen Answers and Senior Examiner's advice for these exam questions.

Extending knowledge

You may also like to visit the websites of some venues

www.hilton.com

www.conferencevenuescountrywide.co.uk

There are periodicals that specifically relate to exhibitions and conferences. These include:

- *Exhibition Bulletin* (published monthly)
- *Exhibition Management* (six issues per year)
- *Conference and Exhibition Fact Finder* (published monthly).

You might also refer to O'Connor, R. (1994) *The Complete Conference Organiser's Handbook*, Piatkus.

unit 8
marketing activities and events – exploring their diversity and application

Learning objectives

In this unit you will:

- Examine the scope of marketing activities and events
- Consider the target audience for chosen events
- Explore the process of staging a conference
- Assess the role of exhibitions and shows
- Explore outdoor and roadshow opportunities
- Examine the process of launching a new outlet.

By the end of this unit you will be able to:

- Appreciate the wide scope of marketing activities and events
- Select appropriate activities/events for different organizations in different circumstances
- Understand how to apply your understanding of conferences, exhibitions, outdoor events, roadshows, new outlet launches.

This unit covers sections 4.3.1, 4.3.3, 4.3.5 and 4.3.6 of the syllabus

This unit covers the key skill for marketers' problem solving. It also relates to the statements of marketing practice:

- Contribute to project planning and budget preparation
- Monitor and report on activities
- Complete and close down activities on time and within budget.

Study Guide

The scope of marketing has increased and a conference once organized by personnel is just as likely to be the responsibility of marketing, as is the new outlet launch which may have been the province of operations. Indeed job roles and demarcation lines have become blurred as marketing follows information technology in becoming a pan-company responsibility rather than the name of a small department. Conferences, sponsorship and corporate hospitality in particular have grown into major industries in their own right and are now very much part of mainstream below-the-line activity.

This unit looks at these different areas of activity and how they are used for marketing purposes. The previous unit provides various frameworks and underpinning material for further use in this section.

You will need around two hours to read this unit. Fully engaging in the activities should take at least another 3 hours and best be achieved over a time span of several weeks.

Conferences and events – a truly international business

There is an increasingly international aspect to these areas of marketing activity. This has been influenced by a number of factors, including:

- Globalization – the world increasingly becoming one marketplace
- Cross-border ownership and investment – many companies operating within a particular company are actually owned by a company whose base is in another country
- Easier and cheaper travel and hotel accommodation – once expensive, most of us now routinely travel overseas for holidays and business.

This internationalization can manifest itself in several ways. If we take, for example, Premier Brands of the UK, who are currently planning a new product launch conference for their sales staff and customers, they could:

- Hold the event in the UK, but have delegates flying in from operations in other countries, such as France, Germany, India and Sri Lanka
- Hold the event at an overseas destination, and charter planes to take all staff to a destination such as Gambia or the Caribbean.

Unit 8 Marketing activities and events

> ### Activity 8.1
>
> Both the above approaches have advantages and disadvantages. What are they?

The scope of marketing events and activities

> ### Study tip
>
> In this unit, it is well worth drawing on your own experience, whether as a marketer planning events or as a consumer or potential customer attending a show, conference or exhibition. As you are now studying the subject, why not look out for events near where you live and visit them in order to evaluate them?

In Unit 7, 'Planning events' we defined a marketing event as something undertaken for a marketing purpose. As such this would be directed at customers, which might seem to imply people who buy a product or service from our organization. This is rather narrow, so we need to be clear exactly who could be classed as a customer.

> ### Definition
>
> **Customer** – is anyone to whom you owe a product or service. This can be someone inside the organization (an internal customer) just as much as it could be someone outside (an external customer).

Taking the above definition, for our annual sales conference the customers are our sales force and the 'products' we supply at the conference are information about results, incentive schemes, new products, etc. The company may also feel it owes rewards, either as praise or as tangible benefits. The transaction is two-way as in any customer interface, and something is expected from the sales force in return.

At a hospitality event for an organization's distributors or dealers there is a similar exchange, although the relationship is obviously different with external customers for a variety of reasons: their business is independent from yours, you may need them more than they need you (or vice versa); they may also buy from your rivals; their motivation also differs from end-customers or consumers in that intermediaries seek benefits such as profit margin and marketing support rather than the features and benefits of the product itself.

When planning a consumer exhibition or show, it is tempting to think of it being aimed at 'the general public', or if it were a motor show it might be aimed at 'motorists'. Such vague thinking would not be tolerated in any other marketing initiative, such as a new advertising campaign, so we need to be more precise as to whom we are targeting. For instance, an air display might attract a huge crowd and it might be tempting to show our product on a stand, but if our target audience is 'mothers with small children' a carnival might prove more cost-effective, as there may be much less wastage. It is also worth considering which different members of a family may be involved in a decision, so the offering may have different aspects to it to broaden the appeal. Again, if we are aiming at families, it is well worth considering putting on an attraction for children (e.g. crèche facilities, face painting, competitions), as bored children will only drag the adults away from your stand.

> **Definition**
>
> **Target audience** – Is who we wish to hear and see our message. As such, this is usually the person who buys the product or service. This needs clarification using market segmentation (e.g. AB males aged 35–45). This may also help in deciding whether an event is worthwhile.

Sometimes an activity may be aimed at more than just the obvious consumers or customers, and we need to think in terms of stakeholders or 'publics' in order to clarify what we are trying to achieve.

> **Definition**
>
> **Public** – Is defined as a group of people who have an opinion of our company or organization, and whose opinion we wish to influence. In the world of public relations (or publics relations), this is often represented as a wheel diagram (see Figure 8.1).

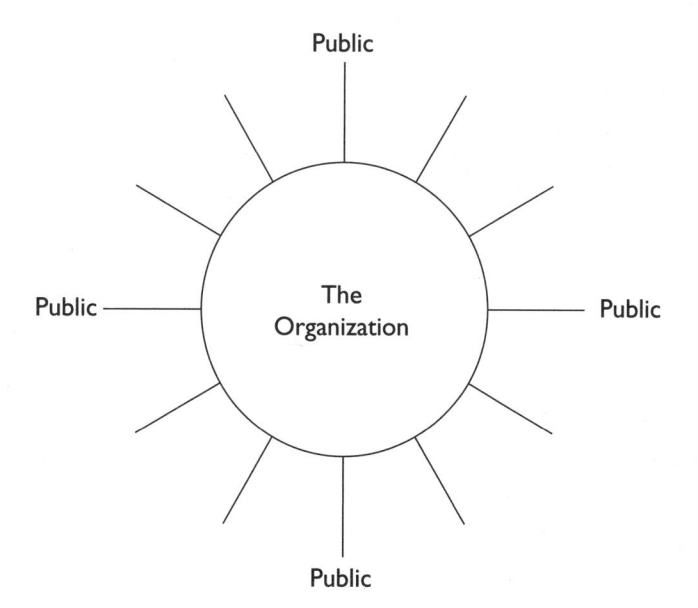

Figure 8.1

Having defined our publics, we need to consider what we wish the various groups to think. As an example, let us look at a large engineering factory having its annual open day. The publics may be identified as follows:

- Employees
- Managers
- Their families
- The local community
- Shareholders
- Politicians
- Former employees
- The media
- Suppliers
- Customers
- Prospective customers.

A planning framework for our publics

A useful tool for planning for our publics or stakeholders is as follows:

- Who are our publics? (involves identification of interested parties)
- What do they think of us now? (may involve research)
- What do we want them to think of us? (identify the gap)
- How will we alter their opinions? (what we are to do)
- How do we measure the change? (self explanatory, but worth stressing).

Activity 8.2

Can you add to the above list? Why exactly are the identified groups important to the factory, what opinion do we wish them to have (this may differ or even contradict in some instances), and how might we put on different activities to appeal to the groups and put our message(s) across?

Question 8.1

Anytown Children's Hospital

The hospital's annual fun day is due to happen in the summer, and the hospital's senior management, who know you are studying for a CIM qualification, have asked you to prepare a brief paper on the event. In particular they wish to see clear objectives, who the event is aimed at and how it can be evaluated. (30 minutes)

Exhibitions and shows

There has been a massive increase in the number of exhibitions and shows offering stand or display space to organizations. This growth has not been well documented in the marketing press, and many companies are sceptical about such a fragmented industry, which often employs high-pressure selling techniques to sell its products. Advertising agencies would also consider this to be very much below the line, and the case for shows and exhibitions to be given full recognition as a medium in its own right is not helped by the difficulty in evaluating effectiveness.

Activity 8.3

What shows or exhibitions do you have experience of, either as an exhibitor or as a consumer? If your organization had a stand, how successful was the exercise? If you know the budget, how does this compare with other activities such as press advertising? Do you know the reasons why your company was represented, and were there clear objectives? Alternatively, if you attended as a consumer, what did you think of the event? Who was there and why were they there? And did any company's stand make a lasting impression on you, and if so, how?

The scope of exhibitions and shows

There are a massive number of different exhibitions and shows available for the marketer to display the product or service. The first and most obvious split is between trade and public events.

Trade events are aimed at a specific sector. For example, the Spring Fair is aimed at retailers, and attracts in excess of 100,000 visitors over four days, all looking for new product lines to stock. Some trade shows are more specific and hence more closely targeted.

Public events can range in size and scope, from a local carnival to major events such as the Millennium celebrations throughout the world. A further major distinction amongst public shows is between specialist and general interest events, although distinctions can become blurred as show organizers seek to increase attendance by providing something for everyone.

Target audiences and objectives

Both have been mentioned previously, but are again key to deciding if attending a particular show or exhibition is to be judged worthwhile. So, is a particular show likely to attract your target audience in viable numbers? Also worth considering at this stage is wastage. You may have to pay more at a large event to have your product in front of a lot of people who are never to become your customers. We also need to consider the expectation of customers. Will they be in a buying mood, or will they consider the presence of company stands an unwelcome commercial intrusion?

Having ascertained the likely audience, we need to start setting objectives and making sure that the necessary mechanisms are in place to fulfil them. Objectives can be derived from the DAGMAR model. As regards fulfilling the objectives, we need to examine each stage of the DAGMAR model and use it as a checklist.

Awareness

Does our stand have sufficient size and presence, and if we are launching or promoting a particular product, is it given sufficient prominence? Merely having a stand may not be sufficient – we may need to reach out from the stand either by advertising or having staff handing out leaflets at the entrance or other busy location (see 'Promotional support and tactics' below).

Comprehension

If there is an objective set around understanding our offer, does our display explain sufficiently, and is it informative and couched in language appropriate for the target audience? Also worth investigating is the potential for making displays interactive. To aid understanding, leaflets or brochures need to be available in sufficient quantities, although some companies prefer to mail out information to genuinely interested enquirers, thereby building up a database of prospects in the process, and therefore deliberately do not stock expensive brochures for the benefit of time-wasters.

Conviction

At this stage, stand staff may need to interact, or even sell, to the prospect (see 'People staffing the show' below). Alternatively, some kind of product trial may be possible, whether this be touching or even eating the product!

Action

This can take various guises. If an objective is to have the customer actually make a purchase, then stock and the means of transaction are prerequisites. Alternatively, the show presence may be a tool for lining up appointments, or building a database of prospects, in which case there could be a need for a competition, prize draw or other incentive to maximize results.

Activity 8.4

How might the approach of Airbus Industries (the European aircraft manufacturing consortium), who are participating in the forthcoming Dubai International Airshow, differ from that of Proton (the Malaysian car manufacturer) at the Malaysian Grand Prix?

Consider objectives, activities, target audiences, staffing and logistics.

People staffing the show

Who is to represent our organization can be answered in two ways: our own staff, whether from the sales department or other parts of the company; or alternatively temporary staff can be hired, usually through a specialist agency. There are advantages and disadvantages to both. Attending a show may be regarded as either a reward or punishment by employees, and although product knowledge may be assumed to be higher, meaning less training required, there could be a hidden cost in employees being absent from their primary role for several days. On the other hand, agency promotional staff are very much the show professionals, and highly skilled and experienced at dealing with customers. However, they would lack product knowledge, and even after training may be unable to answer questions, especially with technical or more complex products.

Question 8.2

MDIS is a specialist software company offering a variety of software solutions to local authorities, utilities and hospitals. They have a strong base in the UK, but are now looking to expand throughout the EU. With this in mind, the Marketing Manager has booked stand space at EUR-IT2003, a major trade exhibition in Frankfurt which lasts a full week. It has been estimated that a total of ten staff are needed to cover adequately, including rest periods. Members of the sales team (who earn on average €52k per year) could be used, but would need accommodation and food at a cost of €150 per day, and the return flight at a cost of €250. Alternatively, graduate recruits could be utilized, especially as their wage costs are half those of experienced staff. The other option is to hire in promotional staff (who live locally) from an agency, at an all-in cost of €250 per day. However, a day's product training would be needed, at a cost of €800.

Task

Give your recommendations on staffing, keeping within a budget of €12,000.

Promotional support and tactics

Stand design

Whether you are hiring a simple 'shell' or having an elaborate structure specially constructed, stand design contractors will be required. A full brief may be needed, including specific requirements such as private staff or hospitality sections. Very much like in a brief for an advertising campaign, objectives need to be clearly expressed, messages and important points highlighted, and a budget agreed. The design contractors can then advise on layout, materials used, and in many cases provide a scale model of the proposed stand.

Worth considering at this stage is whether the stand, or elements of the stand, is to be re-used or destroyed at the end of the show. Then there are the other components of the display, including the product itself, but not forgetting details such as staff uniforms and everything which contributes to the overall impression.

Advertising

Most shows and exhibitions offer a range of additional opportunities for companies attending. There could well be a show guide or programme, or poster sites around the event or at its entrance. There may even be sponsorship opportunities (e.g. sponsoring crèche facilities), which generate goodwill, although additional costs need careful evaluation. Magazines and newspapers invariably run special features on shows, but again these need evaluating in their own right. An alternative, and much less expensive, way to generate extra interest in your show presence is to utilize PR techniques, particularly press releases, or even a specific press reception or preview (Advertising and PR are both covered in 'Co-ordinating the promotional effort').

Give-aways

These could comprise product brochures and literature, but a whole industry exists supplying pens, key rings and other items. One cost-effective technique often employed to gain extra visibility at an event is to hand out plastic shopping bags carrying the company logo. An increasingly common give-away is now a CD-ROM, with which the prospect has to interact at home or in the office.

Hospitality

Another variant on the give-away theme is to offer food and drink to customers and prospects who visit your stand. To avoid abuse, this would normally be by invitation only. There may also exist a PR opportunity to entertain the press, and major shows often have specific press preview days.

Outdoor events and roadshows

Much of what has been discussed so far can apply to all shows and exhibitions. However, there are additional points to consider with these variants. The most obvious difference with an outdoor event is, of course, the weather. It is also obvious that this is out of our control. This means that there can be a strong element of risk with outdoor events – heavy rain might suppress the attendance at an event, yet conversely may have the effect of driving people towards stands and displays where there is shelter. Hot weather may increase crowds, but too hot might send them to the coast or lakeside. On a practical level, the day's weather forecast may help the stand manager determine what additional items are needed. The prime consideration with road shows is *logistics* – actually moving equipment, products and people into the right place at the right time.

Information and communication technology (ICT)

ICT is having a big impact on the conference and event industry. Some observers may once have thought that the ease with which communication at a distance now happens would render the whole concept of face-to-face business obsolete. There would be no need to go to an expensive conference when you could sit in the office (or even at home) and participate. There would be no need to display your goods at a show or exhibition when a virtual show could take place globally.

Whilst the above statements have some truth in them, we are social beings who need contact, and have five senses to appeal to, and the reality is that the new technology is assisting and complementing current methods of interaction.

Earlier technology and conferences
There has long been a technical aspect to delivering conferences. Slides, invariably computer generated, have long been a part of business presentations. Video also found a natural home, especially as the cost of production has fallen in real terms. In this case the medium may be used during the conference and also be used as a means of reference for delegates to take away.

Satellite technology
BMW are amongst the growing number of users of digital satellite technology as a means of communicating with outlets throughout Europe. Presentations are made and information given using this method on a regular basis in addition to the Dealer Conferences, which are retained.

Other users include the World Bank, hotel companies and many others.

Video conferencing
The internet can also be used in conjunction with other tools at conferences and events.

Now the CEO of IBM in the USA can address a convention of African salespeople meeting in Accra, without the very great cost in time of having to travel there and back. However, there may be technical difficulties in making sure all channels remain open at the same time for the duration of the conference, and genuine two-way communication can be facilitated.

Interactive and virtual displays

These can be utilized to enhance and complement a physical presence at a conference, show or other event. Technology tends to have a stronger appeal to the young so computer-driven attractions can be used to occupy children and teenagers while the staff on an exhibition stand can deal with genuine enquiries.

Meetings and conferences

As we have already ascertained in Unit 7, 'Planning events', many of the principles, processes and planning requirements are common to a wide range of marketing activities. In this section we will focus on the task of putting a conference together. However, much of what will be explored can apply to meetings, briefings, seminars and conventions.

Whilst recognizing that the distinctions are blurred and subject to interpretation, it is useful to draw the following distinctions.

Definitions

Meeting – Is any coming together of two or more people. There should always be a purpose for a meeting. UK business culture would expect an agenda, everyone to attend the full meeting, and minutes to be circulated afterwards. This is not universally applicable, however; in France someone may attend only for what they feel is relevant, and individuals would take their own notes.

Briefing – Is where information about a particular topic is to be given to those attending. The scale of this may vary, from an informal small group setting to a large, formal gathering backed by a full production. The flow of information is predominantly one-way, although there may be time allowed for questions.

Seminar – Is a more equal sharing and pooling of knowledge and information, with contributions coming from different parties. More common in the academic world, the seminar concept still has a role in other industries.

Conference – Implies a much larger scale of event. Strictly speaking, attendees should all play a role, but most conferences are again predominantly one-way and some would actively discourage questions as this may become confrontational or demotivating!

Convention – Means coming together, and is much the same as a conference, but is a term more widely used in American business culture.

So, let us assume that we are responsible for organizing the company's annual conference and are now involved with the detailed planning. We should already have objectives in place (see 'Planning events') and should have decided on our audience. The following is a checklist specific to a typical conference: concept, venue and layout, scripts, set design, technical support, production, rehearsal, materials.

Concept

Closely allied to the setting of objectives, concept relates to what is the conference all about? It may be that a theme is chosen for the conference, e.g. 'Building the future' or 'Millennium vision', and if so this theme needs integrating across speeches, printing on support materials and applying throughout any communications concerning the conference. On the other hand, maybe the conference has as its focal point a new product, an important message from the Managing Director, or even a special appearance by a celebrity – in which case the rest of the conference needs careful construction so as not to clutter the focus.

Venue and layout

At the advanced planning stage the venue will have been chosen according to set criteria, but more detailed work still needs to be done. The layout of the room needs to be decided – this could be theatre-style, horseshoe, classroom or even 'cabaret' style, if it is necessary for delegates to have tables (see Figure 8.2). Also, it has to be remembered that the delegates need directing to the room at a larger venue. Smaller additional rooms may also be needed for syndicate work, and it is likely that any food, whether on arrival or during a break, will be served outside the main presentation arena. It is well worth while tracing the route of a delegate, and ensuring that directional signs are clear.

1) Theatre

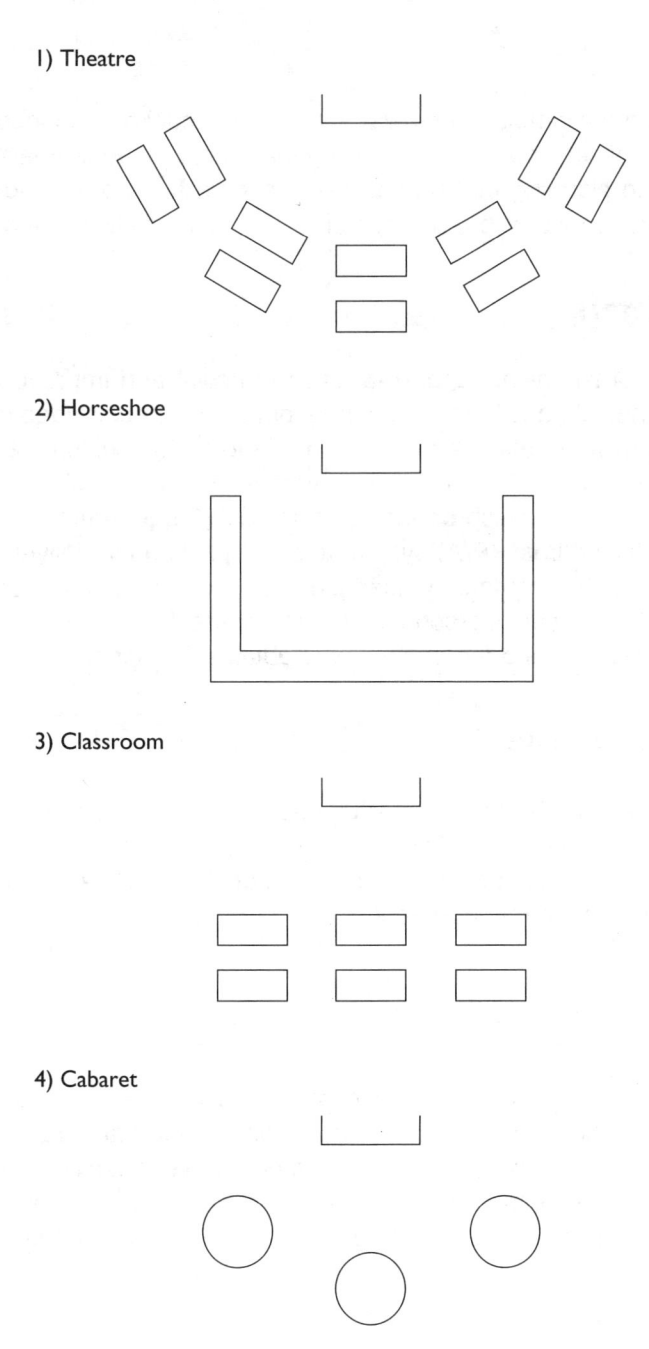

2) Horseshoe

3) Classroom

4) Cabaret

Figure 8.2 Room layout

Script writing

Here several potentially sensitive decisions need to be made. First, who is to write the script(s) for the speaker(s)? An individual speaker may wish to write his or her own, but is this a particular skill of theirs or would it take an undue amount of time? A better alternative may be to hire a professional script writer, who may be freelance or work for the company producing the conference, but then he or she will need to be briefed, and will never have such an intimate knowledge of an organization as an employee. It is also necessary for someone to have an overview of all speeches and other content and to tactfully advise on length and interest value of the contents, and this task may well fall on the marketer. Usually speeches are supported by PowerPoint and this also needs an overview to ensure that the main points are communicated clearly.

Unit 8 Marketing activities and events

Set design

This may range from a simple pack-away – a portable background incorporating a screen – to a complex theatrical set incorporating moving features, product reveals and elaborate staging. It is at this point in planning that budget may become a major consideration. There are also timing plan considerations with more complex sets, especially if rehearsals are also needed.

Technical matters

There is a range of technical support facilities to assist and improve conference production. Speaker support has already been mentioned, but some special video footage may be needed, and a shoot may have to take place some time beforehand, which may prove expensive (see Unit 11, 'Introduction to budgeting'). Other support may be required in the form of an audio-visual (A/V) presentation, which brings us on to sound requirements. Again, these may range from a simple public address (P/A) system to a complex sound delivery system managed by a sound engineer. Another commonly used piece of equipment is an Autocue or QTV. This is a simple device which projects the script onto a transparent screen in front of the speaker, and is operated by a person behind the scenes who adjusts the speed accordingly.

Working with people

Organizing a conference is likely to involve dealing with a wide variety of people, all of whom may be specialists in their own field, be they hotel staff, technical experts or people from different departments and functions within the organization. As such, a lot of 'people skills' are needed as well as project management.

Hosting international visitors

As mentioned previously in this unit, we are in an increasingly international business and a front-line marketer hosting an exhibition or staffing a stand at a trade fair may be called upon to receive a delegation of foreign visitors. This can be very exciting yet fraught with problems as the difference in customs and cultures may cause embarrassment or even offence. Even in an increasingly globalized environment there are major differences between people of different nations and cultures, centred around the following.

Food

Pork is forbidden to both Jews and Muslims, and Hindus do not eat beef, so when deciding on the menu for a business lunch, this could cause problems. Ramadan is a period of fasting during daylight hours for Muslims.

Alcohol consumption

Although many business people enjoy this, it is totally forbidden by law in Islamic countries. Also, many companies find it harmful for employees and have made it a dismissible offence to drink during work hours.

Dress

The human body is viewed differently throughout the world, and bare female flesh is most likely to cause upset even if by Western European standards nothing appears wrong.

Language

An obvious area for problems. We are all aware of misunderstandings across languages, but misunderstandings can occur within a language and this is common in English as spoken outside of the UK. For instance, take the question 'You do not want those do you?'. An English person who did not want them would say 'no' but an overseas speaker who did not want them would say 'yes', meaning that they agreed with the statement. So if 'yes' can mean 'no' to people who are speaking the same language, then we really do have a problem!

Culture

Best described as 'how we do things over here', this is a complex subject and is studied in depth at diploma level in International Marketing. Culture is not just about nationality, but about religion, and increasingly there is the phenomenon of company culture which crosses international boundaries. So a UK-born employee of IBM with Indian parents might have Hindu, British and IBM culture for us to consider.

> IF IN ANY DOUBT...ASK

With the blurring of cultures and the increase in multi-culturalism, no list of do's and dont's is definitive. In the UK, the DTI (Department of Trade and Industry) produce cultural briefing papers. However, to gain real current knowledge, simply ask overseas guests beforehand to avoid embarrassing incidents during a visit.

New outlet launches

New outlet launches could cover a variety of different circumstances, and could refer to business-to-business outlet launches where the 'trade' is the target audience, and being more tightly defined allows, or even necessitates, a different approach to media and promotional activity. More commonly, new outlet launches are directed at the end-consumer, but could be in very different circumstances. The outlet could be wholly owned; alternatively, it could be operated by a third party, possibly under a franchise or other agreement. Also, the nature of the outlet offering could be perceived differently, depending on whether you are totally new to the area, are offering something new (possibly a store revamp), or are relocating to a different site. Indeed, as marketing becomes increasingly international, the new outlet may even be in another country, bringing with it a whole range of new challenges. All outlet launches are different, even for the same organization, as the history and current circumstances vary in each case.

Activity 8.5

Look out for evidence of outlet launches for the duration of your study, perhaps keeping a file to compare different approaches. New store openings occur on a regular basis, particularly for 'edge of town' sites in the UK. Also, branded pub/restaurants are constantly being launched (or re-launched). If possible, visit the opening and witness first hand the promotional tools being utilized. If you know the area, what is the strength of the competition, and what other LEPEST factors (see the *Marketing Environment* coursebook) lie behind the launch? It would be useful to compare and contrast approaches, particularly if one of them is in a business-to-business situation.

The launch period

It is very tempting to think of an outlet launch as being on a specific day, a weekend or at best a week. However, this might not prove successful in the long run – customers attracted by special offers on launch day may be the type who only respond to offers and are unlikely to become loyal customers, even if you wanted them. The product life cycle (PLC) is studied in the Marketing Fundamentals module, and individual outlets could be seen as following the same pattern, so a build-up of business is better than a frantic opening event where it is often difficult to give customers individual attention and proper levels of service. A variant of the PLC is the *customer adoption process,* which examines matters from the customer's viewpoint, and plots when individuals first start using a product or service (or outlet in this case). (See Figure 8.3.)

Product life cycle

[Bell curve showing stages: Introduction, Growth, Maturity, Decline, plotted against Time]

Customer adoption process

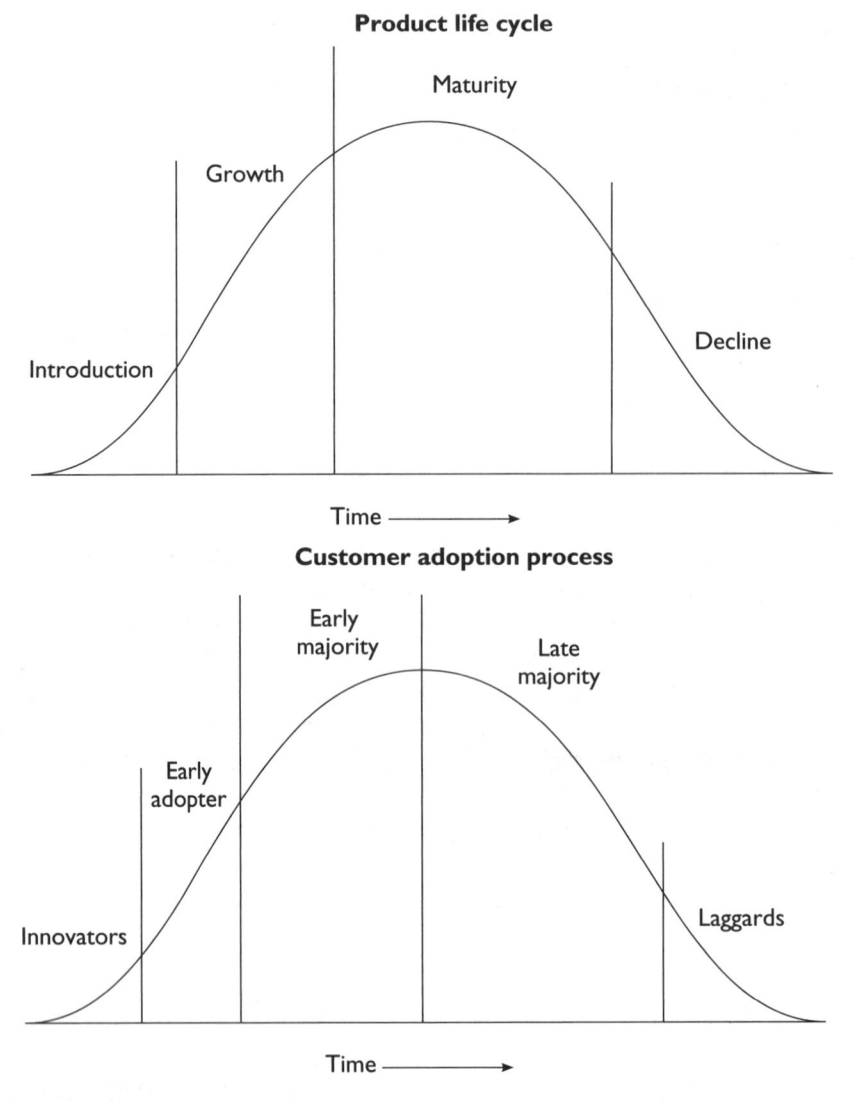

[Bell curve showing stages: Innovators, Early adopter, Early majority, Late majority, Laggards, plotted against Time]

Figure 8.3

- *Innovators* are the first to try something new, usually because it is new, and as such are an unreliable guide to a venture's long-term prospects. The bar and restaurant sectors are particularly prone to attracting novelty-seekers.
- *Early adopters* are far more reliable as longer-term customers, but may not be immediately attracted, so it is well worth prolonging the launch period to attract this segment, especially as they can bring on the next two sets of customers.

- *Early and late majority* Most of us fall into these categories, which correspond to the mature phase of the product life cycle, which is usually its most profitable phase.
- *Laggards* A new outlet launch may not seem the place to see these conservative and cautious types. However, if this is a revamp, re-branding or relocation, it could be that there are some 'old' customers not wanted in the new outlet and this may require careful handling.

Planning an outlet launch

This is much the same as anything else we might plan in marketing, and could be tackled using the framework of situation, objectives, strategy, tactics plus men, money, machines, materials, minutes and measurement (SOST + 6Ms). Alternatively, or even in addition to this, we could use the 7Ps as our checklist for action. As a reminder, these are product, place, price, promotion (often referred to as the 4Ps or the marketing mix) and also the service Ps, people, processes and physical evidence (also known as the extended marketing mix).

Product
Here it is necessary to ensure that the right products (or services) are available in sufficient quantities for the launch. This may entail special deliveries or arrangements with suppliers. If this is retail, then consideration needs to be given to the positioning of products within the store.

Place
This is the prime issue in launching a new outlet, and we have to assume the right choice has been made, but what are the implications of this P? How far are customers expected to travel, are directional posters or signs needed, does advertising and promotional material need to include a map? Also to be considered in tandem with place is time, so what will be the opening times and will these be extended for the launch period?

Price
Pricing decisions will already have been made, but if this is a totally new location, what prices do competitors charge and how are they likely to respond to a newcomer? Special opening offers could be considered under sales promotion, but very often these will be deep price cuts on selected lines.

Promotion
The next unit examines promotional matters in some detail, but it is worth stressing that this encompasses more than just advertising. Advertising is just one of the four elements of the promotional mix, the others being personal selling, sales promotion, and public relations. All of these have a role to play in a successful launch.

People
Staff may need training, or, if a busy launch is expected, may need drafting in from other locations. Promotional staff could also be hired in from an agency to allow more knowledgeable personnel to deal with genuine enquiries.

Processes
These may already be in place from elsewhere, but the process experienced by a customer will have a determining effect on whether the customer returns. So if a new restaurant is so busy in its launch period that customers are kept waiting, this may well prove counter-productive.

Physical evidence
This refers to all that surrounds the delivery of a service, and can range from written guarantees to directional signage, and interior décor to corporate identity. All of these give messages to the customer as powerfully as any advertising, so it is worth paying attention to detail to ensure that everything is 'all right on the night'.

Unit 8 Marketing activities and events

> ### Activity 8.6
>
> **Manchester United Megastore – coming to your town soon...**
>
> Manchester United are more than just a football team, they are a global brand. More income is raised from promotions, sponsorship and merchandising than in match ticket sales.
>
> They have recently announced a strategic alliance with the US baseball team the New York Yankees to promote each other's brands and products.
>
> They are shortly to introduce websites in both Malay and Chinese to communicate with their vast following in South-East Asia.
>
> Additionally they have retail outlets not just in the UK, but are expanding their retail chain throughout the Pacific Rim.
>
> A new outlet is opening in your town shortly. How can the success of this new venture be measured?

Summary

In this unit, we have taken a more detailed look at some of the specifics of marketing events. We have seen how exhibitions, conferences, shows and launches all have a role to play in the marketing mix. Although the events have been tackled separately, there is a great deal of commonality, especially at the planning stage. The process from idea to execution remains the same.

Further study and examination preparation

When you have completed this unit you will be able to answer Question 2 from the June 2002 examination paper. Go to www.cimeduhub.com to access Specimen Answers and Senior Examiner's advice for these exam questions.

Extending knowledge

Publications such as *Marketing*, *Marketing Week* and *Campaign* can give you an idea of the activities and events organizations are involved in. These are published weekly and are available online through subscription. You may also wish to visit the following websites:

> www.dti.gov.uk to find helpful sources of information
>
> www.manutd.com to see a successful 'brand' website and store offering

unit 9
co-ordinating the promotional effort

Learning objectives

In this unit you will:

- Explore different media opportunities and applications
- Analyse the benefits and drawbacks of different media
- Gain a working knowledge of advertising and media terminology
- Consider the role of printed materials in the promotional mix
- Examine a range of sales promotion techniques
- Develop an understanding of public relations activities
- Examine the interface with the selling function.

By the end of this unit you will:

- Be conversant with a range of media
- Be able to prepare basic media schedules
- Be able to appreciate the roles of sales promotion, public relations and personal selling within the promotional mix
- Be able to evaluate activities and make recommendations on courses of action.

This unit covers sections 4.4.1, 4.4.2, 4.4.3 and 4.4.8 of the syllabus.

The unit also covers the key skills Working with others and Problem solving. It also relates to the statements of marketing practice Collect, synthesize, analyse and report measurement data, Participate in reviews of marketing activities using measurement data.

Unit 9 Co-ordinating the promotional effort

Study Guide

In this unit we shall examine the different components of the promotional mix, namely advertising, sales promotion, public relations and personal selling. (Be careful not to confuse this with the marketing mix, of which promotion is but one of the 7Ps, the other six of which are examined in 'Co-ordinating the marketing mix'.) This unit should take around two hours to work through, but there are various activities involving local research and answering questions for which a further three hours should be planned into your workload.

The promotional mix introduced

Definition

Promotional mix – (or sub-mix, as it is often referred to) comprises advertising, sales promotion, public relations and personal selling.

Exam hint

Think mix. It is all too easy to give so much emphasis to advertising that the other components of the mix are neglected. So find ways of demonstrating the breadth of your marketing toolkit by at least considering possible applications for the full mix.

Advertising is not only viewed as the major part of the promotional mix, but as the major manifestation of marketing itself. This is understandable, as it is easily the most visible and we are constantly subject to all its different forms. The world of advertising is changing rapidly, with new media constantly being introduced, and it can pay to keep an open mind, evaluating opportunities with clear criteria. Distinctions are becoming increasingly blurred; information technology and marketing were once quite separate, but put the two together and database marketing allows personalized, highly targeted communications with our customers. As websites and e-commerce grow in credibility, IT, promotion and place become the same thing.

Sales promotion has become a big business, and has increased its stature from 'special offers' to being an important element of the promotional mix. The most obvious example of this is the growth of loyalty cards, but again this crosses over into information technology, and allows an intimate knowledge of individual customers to be obtained.

Public relations is another element of the sub-mix, and is often grossly misunderstood and neglected. However, in some organizations public relations has such stature that it stands alongside marketing as a fully fledged business discipline, not just a part of promotion, which in turn is just a part of the full marketing mix.

There has been a long-standing (and not always friendly) rivalry between sales and marketing, and different organizations would take different views on their relative importance. However, from our marketing perspective, there is no point having everything else right if the person who actually deals with the end-customer is not properly 'on message'.

Advertising

Advertising is the most visible of the elements of the promotional sub-mix, if not the most noticed part of the entire marketing function. There is no doubting the influence of advertising on all our lives, but at what cost does this happen? Advertising forms the biggest single source of expenditure of most marketing departments, but is not necessarily the best or only tool needed to solve a business problem or take advantage of an opportunity. The other three elements – sales promotion, public relations and personal selling – all have a role to play and can often be more cost-effective.

Simple communications models

Advertising is a means of communication, and a much used communications model is illustrated in Figure 9.1. Here we see the sender of the message on the left and the recipient of the message on the right, with the message being sent between them. In our case the medium is an advertising medium. Feedback is received by the sender – in the case of advertising this feedback may be in the form of enquiries, sales or some other measurable. However, all is not necessarily so straightforward – the message may be encoded so as to appeal to a particular market (i.e. teenagers), who in turn decode it, as they can understand what is going on. Other segments may not understand the message – indeed, they may thus be specifically excluded. Sometimes, though, things go wrong, and the message is totally misunderstood. Also, our advertising is not happening in isolation – other advertising and other distractions are taking place all around; and this is called 'noise' or 'clutter'.

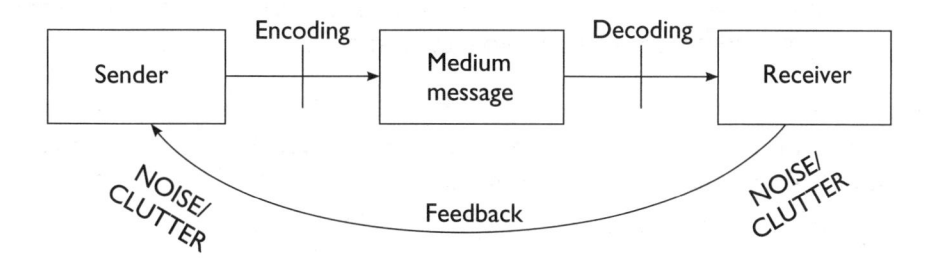

Figure 9.1 Communications

Activity 9.1

Ford are better than Mercedes (if you can decode their advertising)

Recent television advertising for the Ford Focus showed a car going along a country road in Scandinavia. A reindeer suddenly ran out in front of the car. The car comes to a safe standstill and nobody is hurt and the reindeer is also safe and runs off into the forest.

What messages do you receive from this?

AIDA: how advertising works

Another simple model which has an extremely practical application is the AIDA model, which stands for Attention, Interest, Desire, Action. These are the four stages a customer or receiver of our communication hopefully goes through (see Figure 9.2).

```
Attention
   ↓
Interest
   ↓
Desire
   ↓
Action
```

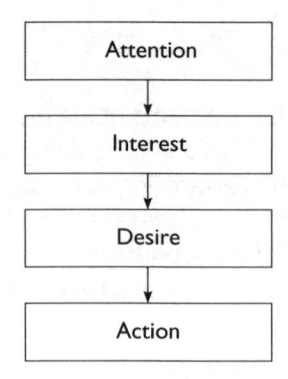

Figure 9.2 AIDA

Attention
This is the first stage. The advertising, whether TV, poster, radio or printed, has to gain the person's attention. There is a variety of ways of doing this, but it can be achieved via a headline in a press ad, by graphics in visual media, or by creative use of sounds in radio. With so much advertising competing for our attention, unless attention is achieved, our message will fall by the wayside.

Interest
Now we need to draw the customer in, and gain his or her interest. Again, there are numerous ways of doing this. Advertising copy (the text) could start selling off the page in a press ad or conveying benefits in other media. Visual appeal may also be utilized to create more interest.

Desire
The next stage is to make the customer really want something, and the best way of achieving this is to stress the advantages of the product or service.

Action
This is the final and most important stage. But we need to be clear what action or response we really need. Do we want customers to visit our store, call for a brochure, book a test drive, send a cheque as payment or some other course of action?

Activity 9.2

Monster.com using AIDA

Monster.com is an online jobsearch company which operates throughout the world and has websites for the UK, Hong Kong, Singapore, Australia and New Zealand. They have recently launched a new site, Monsterindia.com, targeted at the Indian subcontinent, in particular the large skilled professional labour pool in India. How could AIDA be used to construct an advertisement for a business magazine in Delhi?

Activity 9.3

Search out a selection of newspaper or magazine ads and examine them carefully. Do they take the reader through the various stages, or do they only go so far? Do some of them fail to gain your attention – in which case, are they really meant for you? (It could be that they are deliberately encoded to appeal specifically to different target audiences.) If your attention has been gained, are you drawn further and is there a clear 'call to action' (are you clear what you are meant to do next?).

AIDA in action

To move someone into action with a single ad is a difficult task unless this is something very special, and this illustrates how the elements of the promotional sub-mix (and the rest of the mix) work together. *Attention* could be achieved with a TV advertising campaign, backed up with PR activity. *Interest* could be gained via a more detailed press campaign, whilst *desire* could be stimulated with a sales promotional device. *Action* is further prompted by personal selling. Here we can see the elements adopting different roles, but all working together. This is the beginning of the concept of Integrated Marketing Communications, which is studied at CIM Diploma level.

Objective setting

Here we can use the DAGMAR model for setting the objectives for our advertising and this is explained earlier, but to recap, the stages of DAGMAR are unawareness, awareness, comprehension, conviction.

Use of advertising agencies, and alternative methods of sourcing

Dealing with advertising agencies, from initial selection through briefing to building long-term relationships, has already been discussed in Unit 5, 'Making contacts for marketing'. There are alternatives: namely in-house production and buying, or, for the execution of design or creative work, using the media's own facilities.

> **Definitions**
>
> **In-house facilities** – In this context this refers to having an advertising production studio actually based within the organization, and employing designers/artists/script writers to work solely for the organization.
>
> **Media production facilities** – As a service to advertisers who do not use an advertising agency, many newspapers, magazines, radio and TV stations will design and produce advertisements, often at a nominal cost. They can do this because they are not paying commission to ad agencies, and because there is no agency involvement they remain in closer contact with the advertiser.

> **Activity 9.4**
>
> What are the advantages/disadvantages of the following three methods of advertising production: using an agency, producing in-house, using media's production facilities? Would the most favoured approach differ according to the size and market sector the organization is operating in? What might be the best for a multinational confectioner (e.g. Nestlé), a business-to-business concern (such as Alstom, the train manufacturer), a retailer with two branches close together (e.g. IKEA, who have two branches in BUDAPEST), or a charity (e.g. PDSA, an animal charity)?

Unit 9 Co-ordinating the promotional effort

> **Activity 9.5**
>
> **Briefing the advertising agency**
>
> Write out a brief for the advertising agency who are working for either Monster.com (see Activity 9.2) or another organization, either your own or one with which you are familiar.
>
> If you are working with others on this module, try exchanging your briefs. How clear does the receiver find your instructions? Do you feel that verbal briefing is also needed? Would this best be accomplished by telephone, video conferencing or a face-to-face meeting?
>
> (See also the form in 'Making contacts for marketing', Figure 5.1, p. 60.

Media selection

A key task is making decisions regarding what media to use, and the choice is becoming ever wider. Even if an ad agency is employed, or a media consultancy, it pays the marketer to have a working knowledge of media characteristics, developments, advantages and disadvantages. However, before looking at the world of media we need to look at the organization itself, as this will have the biggest influence on media selection. A full marketing audit could be undertaken, but the main factors would most likely be markets, money, place and product.

Markets
Are we engaged in communicating to a large population of end-consumers, or is ours a business-to-business proposition with a finite target audience? The former may move our decision towards TV, or other mass media, whilst a trade message is better conveyed in a specialist magazine.

Money
Size of marketing/advertising budget, however derived (see 'Introduction to budgeting'), will rule out certain media if it is not sufficient to obtain meaningful coverage in those media. For example, a single radio ad would be pointless.

Place
Geographical considerations include locations of outlets, distance customers travel and area of trading. Local media may suit an advertiser with outlets in specific towns, but would actually work out more expensive if true national coverage were the objective. Of course media can reach and speak to customers anywhere, beyond reasonable travelling distance, and work in tandem with a field sales force.

Product
The medium chosen has to present the product offering, so visual, aural and moving media are better suited to different situations, although this can to some extent be overcome with effective creative work.

Planning the campaign

The advantages of different media are shown in Figure 9.3, as are the disadvantages, and as we have seen there are other considerations before making a decision and actually planning a campaign.

	Advantages	Disadvantages	Costings	Unit of sales	Unit of measurement	Developments
Newspapers	Very flexible, can be national or local. Allow targeting by geography or type of reader. Allows detail.	Usually disposed of very quickly. No movement or sound.	Varies enormously between local free papers and expensive national media.	The page, or single column centimetre (s.c.c.) which is measured to give sizes such as 25 × 4 (25cm × 4 columns) = 100 s.c.c.	Circulation – how many copies are produced/sold. Readership – how many people read the publication. (N.B.: Readership is always much higher than circulation.)	Number of titles continues to grow.
Magazines	Titles reflect jobs, attitudes and interests of readers. Allows details.	Proliferation of titles makes media choice difficult.	Likely to be much less than newspapers.	As above.	As above.	Number of titles continues to grow.
Radio	Can reach people on the move in their cars and at home.	Cannot show the product.		Timed slots, e.g. 20, 30 seconds, often sold in packages.	Audience reach. This can be for an individual ad or for a campaign (cumulative).	Special interest (e.g. Jazz) stations allow better targeting.
TV	Has sound and vision in people's homes.	Advertising increasingly ignored as viewers change channels.	Often very expensive, but local and cable TV within reach of small companies.	As above.	Viewing figures. This can be for an individual ad or for a campaign (cumulative).	Becoming more of a narrowcast than broadcast medium.
Posters	High impact, difficult to ignore.	Cannot show movement, sound or detail.	Varies according to site.	The site. Size of site also measured, e.g. 4-sheet. This refers to the area of the site.	OTS (opportunities to see). This varies according to how busy the traffic is for a site.	A truly international medium.
Leaflets	Can be precisely targeted and distributed.	Immediately binned as 'junk mail'.	Varies enormously according to complexity and quantity ordered.	Size of print run, e.g. 20000.	Reach/response.	Direct marketing/IT allows greater personalization of message.
Website	Can reach worldwide audience.	Fledgling medium.	Can be inexpensive for basic set-up, but probably not effective.	Set-up charges can be by page/facility.	Hits – how many visit the site.	Still in infancy.
Fringe	A host of opportunities.	Difficult to evaluate and measure.	There can be bargains from media trying to establish themselves.	Varies.	Varies.	Always a variety of opportunities, some great value, some bizarre.
Cinema	Increasing in popularity. Useful for targeting the young.	Cannot reach older (25+) people in quantity	Production costs could be high, or very low for local users.	Timed slots × frequency.	Audience reach.	New cinemas being built.

Figure 9.3 Media selection

Given the same brief and the same budget it is highly unlikely that two experienced media planners who work in advertising agencies would recommend the same schedule. This is a very subjective area of marketing; however there are broadly similar types of campaign and these are outlined in Figure 9.4. A burst campaign would be sudden and highly visible but not sustained. By contrast a drip campaign is sustained over a longer period, but would use smaller spaces in a newspaper or shorter times on TV or radio.

A multimedia campaign is where different media are used to support each other. A layered campaign is a variant on this, but may use different media for different purposes. For instance, the launch of a new car may start with a TV campaign. More details about the car could follow in press advertising in national newspapers and car magazines, then closer still to the customer, radio and local press could be used to give details of dealerships where the car can be seen. You may notice that this is a practical application of models such as AIDA and DAGMAR.

Week	1	2	3	4	5	6
a) Burst campaign						
Daily Planet (full pages)	X	X				
Daily World (full pages)	X	X				
b) Drip campaign						
Daily Planet (quarter pages)	X		X		X	
Daily World (quarter pages)		X		X		X
c) Multimedia campaign						
Sky Television (20sec. slots)	X	X		X	X	
Daily Planet (quarter pages)		X		X	X	
Radio (20sec. slots)		X		X	X	
d) Layered campaign						
Sky Television (20sec. slots)	X	X	X			
Daily World			X	X		
London Evening Post				X	X	X
Manchester Mail				X	X	X

Figure 9.4 Alternative media schedules

Unit 9 Co-ordinating the promotional effort

Classified Advertising Rates

Birmingham Evening Mail

	LINEAGE	SEMI DISPLAY	FULL DISPLAY
Standard Rate	5.35	28.93	30.55
Recruitment	7.60	40.95	44.80
Comm & Ind Property	5.46	29.53	31.04
Public Notices/Contracts & Tenders	8.87	47.15	49.10
Personal/Finance	9.13	48.72	50.78
Dial Messages/ Personal Services	10.80	57.89	60.32
Private Rate	2.51	13.79	25.85
Family Notices	2.40	12.85	24.17
Theatres/Cinema	3.20	17.26	26.77
Property Guide	One Zone		6.75
	Two Zones		11.55
	Three Zones		16.54
Motors	ROP		27.30
	Classified Zone		10.20
	ROP Zone		10.20
	Classified 2 Zones		16.22
	ROP 2 Zones		16.22

All rates effective from 1st January 2000

Mechanical Data

Evening Mail/Sunday Mercury
Page Area   340mm × 272mm (34cms × 9cols.)
Half Page   170mm × 272mm (17cms × 9cols.)
Column Length 340mm
No. of Advertising Columns 9 per page
Column Widths (mm) 1–28   2–58   3–89
                    4–119 5–150 6–180
                    7–211 8–241 9–272
Screen Size   32 (82 DPI)
Characters to a line   22

Birmingham Post
Page Area   560mm × 393mm (56cms × 11cols.)
Half Page   280mm × 393mm (28cms × 11cols.)
Column Lengths 560mm
No. of Advertising Columns 11 per page
Column Widths(mm) 1–28   2–58   3–89
                   4–119 5–150 6–180
                   7–211 8–241 9–272
                   10–302 11–312
Screen Size   32 (52 DPI)

COPY VIA ADVERT DELIVERY SERVICE (ADS)

Mail   0121 625 5801
Post & Mercury   0121 625 5802
All Weekly Publications
                    0121 626 8803

Artworks
Scans
All supplied scans should be scanned to fit at 100%
200 DPI (Dots per inch)
100 LPI (Lines per inch)

The Birmingham Post

	LINEAGE	SEMI DISPLAY	FULL DISPLAY
Standard Rate	2.05	10.70	11.13
Recruitment	2.35	11.66	12.60
Comm & Ind Property	2.16	10.81	11.14
Public Notices/ Contracts & Tenders	3.03	18.98	22.50
Personal/Finance	3.95	19.58	23.41
Dial Messages/ Personal Services	4.70	23.27	27.81
Private Rate	1.25	5.46	6.62
Family Notices	2.40	-	-
Theatres/Cinema	1.25	6.30	10.86

Sunday Mercury

	LINEAGE	SEMI DISPLAY	FULL DISPLAY
Standard Rate	2.16	12.11	14.43
Recruitment	2.50	13.60	15.20
Comm & Ind Property	2.20	12.27	14.60
Public Notices/ Contracts & Tenders	3.95	21.41	24.06
Personal/Finance Dial Messages/	2.60	13.62	16.32
Personal Services	3.08	16.17	19.38
Private Rate	1.16	5.90	11.65
Family Notices	1.51	7.24	10.97
Theatres/Cinema	2.14	11.93	14.25

Software:
We accept the following formats:
Quarkexpress 4
Adobe Illustrator 7
Adobe Photoshop 4
These are Apple Macintosh based applications.
We do not accept Freehand files unless sent via ADS
Disks:
CD, 100MB Zip disks
Colour:
Premium for full colour +33%,
Spot Colour +20%
We use 4 process colours: Black, Cyan, Magenta & Yellow. We do not use Pantone or any other colourmatch system.

Figure 9.5 Rate card from Birmingham Post and Mail

Unit 9 Co-ordinating the promotional effort

Activity 9.6

Using the rate card

Using the rate card, work out the following:

1. How much does a single-column centimetre cost at full display rate in the *Birmingham Evening Mail*?
2. How much would a 25 × 4 advertisement cost Virgin Cinemas in the *Sunday Mercury*?
3. Tattersfield Property Holdings have £3000 to spend across the three titles to promote rental of their shop units. Devise a suitable schedule.
4. You work for a group of franchised car dealerships in the West Midlands. How would you spend a £250,000 local press budget throughout a year?

Evaluating media opportunities

Throughout the world, the number of media opportunities grows by the hour, whether press, magazines, radio, or other new media such as portals on the internet. For instance in India there are now over 50 satellite TV channels, where there used to be just one state owned service. For mainstream media, there are recognized means of measurement and **cost**, so evaluations can be made both within and across different types of media. Sometimes a new opportunity may emerge, such as advertising on supermarket trolleys as masterminded by Trolleymedia. The advertisements are small but are now seen by everyone who shops in a given supermarket. We can thus build an **estimate** of how many will see an ad. We know in this case that these are the right target **audience**, so this seems a good idea. However, we need to consider the **environment** in which the ads are seen. It is very busy and thousands of products with their packaging, plus the supermarkerts own messages are continually confronting the shopper, but then the **timing** is such that it is right next to the point of sale. We also need to consider the mood and **receptiveness** of the audience. Is a busy woman with two small children likely to take time out to read your ad?

There is thus a great deal of subjectivity in making judgements on media, helped by the acronym CREATE

Cost

Receptiveness

Environment

Audience

Timing

Estimate.

But then of course we need to consider what we are going to say in the media, and as is often quoted to media sales people, 'there is no such thing as bad media, only bad advertising!'

www.intelligencia.com is an extremely useful website used by professionals in ad agencies to find media that may be suitable. The site is accessible to students, who can find much useful information without incurring any cost. Try exploring this site.

Managing the print production process

The management of the print process is substantially the same as managing the advertising process, both entailing the production of a finished communication. Put simply it is as follows:

- Identification of need for printing
- Briefing of the requirements
- Liaison with printers and others involved in the project
- Developing copy (words) and subsequent typesetting
- Developing visually (design aspects, illustrations and photography)
- Production and checking of proofs
- Printing (plus additional processes such as collating, stapling and packing)
- Delivery (to yourself)
- Distribution (to where the printing is needed).

A briefing document can be used in the initial setting up of the printing so that all parties can agree on what they need. Whereas an organization typically has an ongoing relationship with an advertising agency and places all their advertising through them, there may not be such a relationship with a printer. It is often a practice to obtain quotes from two or three printers before commissioning work as prices vary according to the printers' capacity, stockholding order bank and specialization according to the type of job.

A particularly important stage is proof checking, before actual printing takes place. Any mistakes that are not corrected or any alterations not specified can lead to the entire print run being wasted. If an advertisement in the press (or TV or radio) is wrong it can at least be changed for subsequent occasions. A mistake in one catalogue means a mistake in the entire print run of maybe five million!

Delivery and distribution of a catalogue or other printed materials is entirely different from the final stages of advertising where the ad merely appears. With printing we have a physical entity to get to the right place at the right time. For Marketing in Practice, technical knowledge of the printing process is not required, but an overview of the processes involved is useful, and was examined in December 2000, and this paper is included at the end of this coursebook.

Public relations

This element of the promotional sub-mix can prove highly effective, but on the other hand the benefits of public relations activity can be very difficult to measure and quantify. This often leads to PR not being viewed as seriously as above-the-line advertising. A further misunderstanding arises due to the confusion between press relations and public relations. To make matters worse, PR activity is sometimes undertaken only as a belated defence against adversity or bad publicity, whereas good, sustained PR builds such a powerful image in the minds of the publics that an organization can withstand problems or even elicit sympathy rather than blame or other negative reaction.

Unit 9 Co-ordinating the promotional effort

Public relations activities

Typical PR activities include:

- Press releases
- Press launches
- Media briefings
- Stakeholder briefings
- Corporate hospitality
- Open days.

There is a strong crossover between PR and the types of activities detailed in the units on 'Planning events' and 'Marketing activities and events – exploring their diversity and application'. A possible differentiation factor of PR activities is that PR typically concerns itself with more than just customers who are, of course, the main focus of marketing activity.

Definition

Press relations – Are a part of public relations – the press being a particular public or set of publics who you want to have a favourable view of your organization. What is important about press relations is that press is the medium primarily used to reach other publics (Figure 9.6). Public relations has already been mentioned in 'Practical networking skills'.

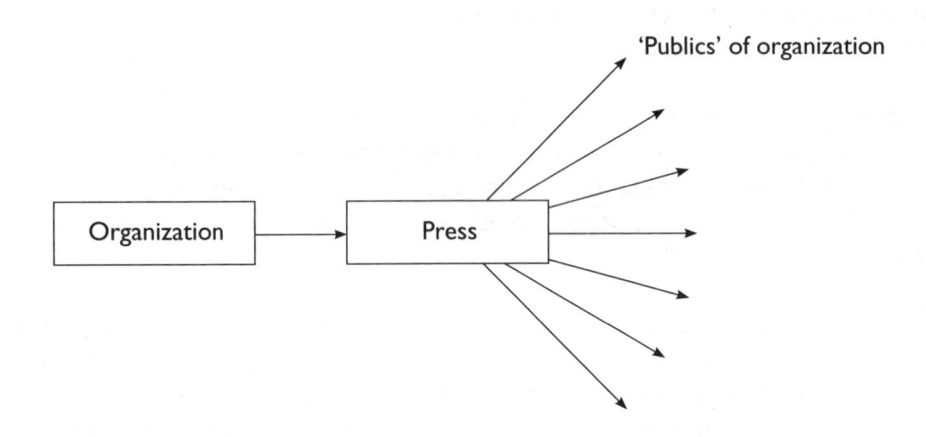

Figure 9.6

Identifying the publics

Working with the idea that publics are groups whose opinion you wish to influence leads us into a broader range of target audiences than marketing (for instance, shareholders, institutional investors and the City itself). The publics for a typical organization are shown in Figure 9.7.

```
                    Staff
       Shareholders      Government (local)
   Press                        Government (national)
   Opinion          The         Pressure
   formers      organization    groups
       Rivals                   Neighbours
         Old customers    Prospects
                Customers
```

Figure 9.7

Activity 9.7

For your organization (or one of your choice), make a list of its publics. Having identified the various publics, what does each one think of the organization now, how do you know that is what they think, why does their opinion matter and what would we like them to think?

Definition

Opinion formers – Are influential individuals who command respect and whose opinions are passed on and believed by many more people. By targeting opinion formers, a message reaches far more people and as it is passed on by the opinion former rather than by your organization it is generally more likely to be believed. A similar effect takes place using the media, as in Figure 9.8.

Activity 9.8

Who are the opinion formers for your organization to target? For each of the publics you can identify, are there specific individuals whose opinion really matters?

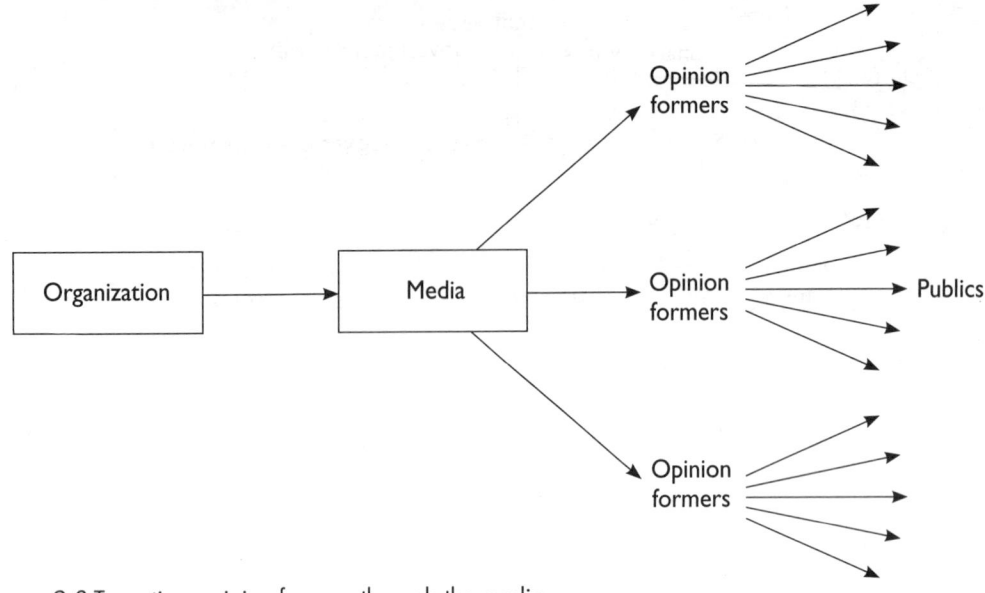

Figure 9.8 Targeting opinion formers through the media

Having successfully defined our publics, identified opinion formers and attempted to ascertain what views are currently held, the rest of the PR effort can now take place with the clear objective of moving these opinions, or at least maintaining them in the case of any future adverse publicity.

Building relations with the press

Business relationships are fully covered in 'Making contacts for marketing', but a good starting point in developing good relationships with journalists is to make their lives and jobs easier. This holds true for radio and TV journalists as much as for those who write for newspapers and magazines. There are several ways in which to do this:

- Supply interesting, usable articles or news stories
- Make the press contact feel special by sharing information on an exclusive basis
- Be ready and willing to provide quotes or other assistance when it is needed
- Use of hospitality and other promotional techniques, where appropriate, supplying free samples or trials.

All the above need careful judgement; people generally do not like being pestered or appearing to take 'bribes'.

Press releases

The most frequently used tool in PR is the press release, sent in the hope of receiving free and advantageous press coverage. It must always be remembered that there is no guarantee of coverage or publication and, even where this does happen, there is a possibility that the message will be distorted. Press relations activity is often measured by the editorial space occupied. The cost per single column centimetre (s.c.c.) is applied as if it were advertising space to give a value to what has been obtained. It is generally accepted that we are more willing to believe what we read in the news than in advertising copy, so a premium could be put on this. Likewise with news coverage gained in other media.

Constructing a media hit list

There are three broad categories of target media.

1. *Geographic* Here we would choose media using criteria based around where the organization, its outlets or its customers are located (e.g. Solihull College targets the *Solihull Times, Solihull News, Birmingham Post* and *Mail,* plus the local radio and TV station).

2. *Subject/trade* Here, media would be targeted which specifically cover the industry (e.g. IVECO trucks would target *Trucking International, Truck and Driver,* and *Commercial Motor Magazine*).

3. *Laterally* The choice of media here may not seem obvious at first glance, but a manufacturer of cameras such as Nikon may target an outdoor pursuits or holiday magazine. After all, people use their cameras as an accessory for these activities.

Activity 9.9

Fill in the following grid for the three organizations mentioned.

	Solihull College	Seddon Atkinson	Nikon
Geographic			
Subject/trade			
Lateral			

When you have completed this, compile a list of target media for your organization (or one of your choice), including radio and TV.

Writing a press release

The initial choice here, as with many aspects of marketing, is whether an agency is used or the task is handled in-house. If it is to be handled by an agency, or a PR consultancy in this case, the criteria for initially selecting the agency, and ensuring briefing and other procedures, are much the same as with an advertising agency. However, if the writing of the press release is to be undertaken within the marketing department, then there are a few simple rules to follow:

1. Before writing, list the main points you wish to make
2. Divide the piece into short paragraphs for easy editing

3. Make your main point in the first sentence (such that if someone reads nothing more they will at least have gained something)
4. Make the main point of each paragraph in the first sentence of each paragraph
5. Include a contact point for further details and information
6. If possible, personalize or localize the contents to increase chances of publication
7. Look for an interesting photographic or visual angle, remembering that the written word is only one way of communicating
8. Remember that your release is competing for attention with many others, so make it interesting, easy to work with, relevant and, if at all possible, somehow different.

Activity 9.10

Write a press release on behalf of your company, or, if this is not possible, on behalf of another organization or your place of study. To do this properly, first compile a media hit list. Then list the points to be made, which should be about a new product or service. Finally, write the piece and consider what might be visually interesting for a photograph or TV news story.

Photo opportunities

This can be something specially organized for press photographers. It could be a new product being unveiled for the first time, or it could involve people, either employees of the company or celebrities known to the public or target audience. The local press tend to like local interest stories and pictures, and many actively seek pictures which do not feature men in suits shaking hands.

Activity 9.11

Examine the contents of your local newspaper or freesheet. On first glance, are there any pictures which particularly attract your attention and if so, why? Likewise, are there any pictures which do not appeal? One way of doing this is to quickly look at every page, then put the paper down and see what is remembered.

Press conferences

These can be divided into two categories.

- *Good news/planned* Here the general principles of conference organization and planning apply, as discussed in units 'Planning events' and 'Marketing activities and events – exploring their diversity and application'.

- *Bad news/unplanned* This can be in response to some bad news or event, and is essentially a defensive reaction. Depending upon the circumstances (e.g. an air crash), there could be a great deal of emotion involved, and this needs skilful handling to avoid making the situation worse. However, if the organization has in place an effective PR programme, the damage to the organization's reputation will be lessened.

Briefing the PR agency

Earlier in this coursebook we have seen the importance of correctly briefing an advertising agency. It is equally important to brief a PR consultancy correctly if one is used. A typical briefing document may contain the following:

- Background/problem/opportunity
- Who are our publics for this communication?
- How might we reach them?
- What might they be thinking now?
- What do we want them to think?
- What is our one single most powerful statement to communicate?
- Product/other supporting information
- Timing
- Budget.

Evaluating PR activity

It is notoriously difficult to evaluate PR activity, especially at a strategic level where the target audiences may be financial institutions and investors, or government agencies.

Even at a consumer level, it is difficult to measure such things as 'goodwill', let alone identify what aspects of the organization's activities have brought about such feelings.

However, it can be possible to measure and evaluate the effect of a discrete tactical PR event.

An example of this is an event organized by Halfords, a leading UK retailer, to promote their Christmas catalogue. Journalists from over 200 media were invited. So immediately we can measure how many arrived at the event. Following this event it was possible over time to trace how many of the media adopted the information being given on new products and offers and used it as the basis of stories in their publications or on radio/TV stations.

Using the available rate card data such as that included earlier in this unit, it was then possible to estimate how much it would have cost to buy advertising space or time equivalent to that gained by the PR press launch. This allows a monetary figure to be plotted against the cost of the event.

Sales promotion

Definition

Sales promotion (SP) – Is short-term activity undertaken with an objective of a long-term increase in sales.

Sales promotion covers an increasing number and variety of activities, some of which cross over into other elements of both the promotional sub-mix and the marketing mix itself. Before examining typical sales promotion activities, it is worth considering the above definition. Clearly, sales promotion has an objective and is subject to all the same planning rigours as any other activity or opportunity. However, in the traditional definition the emphasis is on the short-term, but more recent examples of SP appear to be long-term in their application and therefore need considering separately. Sales promotional activity falls into six basic categories, which are by no means mutually exclusive: same for less, more for same, free gifts, competitions, joint (or co-operative) promotions, and sampling.

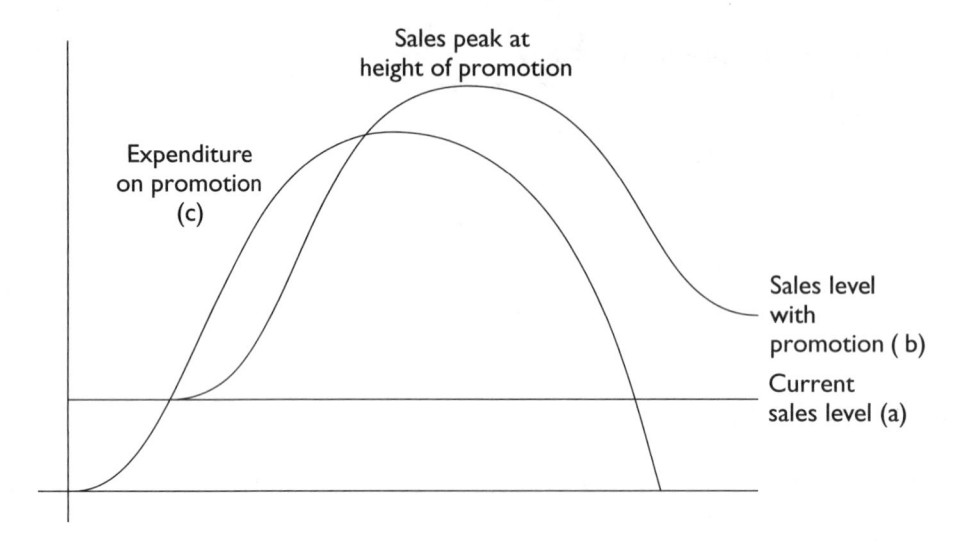

Figure 9.9 How sales promotion works

Activity 9.12

What sales promotions have you seen recently? Do they fit into the above broad categories? Did you take advantage of any of them? If so, were you previously a customer, or did this attract your custom from elsewhere? Will you continue to be a customer after the promotion has ended, or will you move on?

How sales promotion works (Figure 9.9)

Line 'a' represents sales of our product and is shown as a straight line. Now, if we undertake some activity – a price cut, limited edition or whatever – then sales will rise, now along line 'b'. However, the promotion has cost additional money and this is illustrated by area 'c'. In this illustration, it cancels out the gains made in the duration of the promotion. The payback for this promotion occurs when it is finished and sales continue at a higher level.

Sales promotion objectives

Whilst there are several types of promotion, there is only one underlying objective – an increase in sales, and hence an increase in profit. However, we need to clarify from where the additional sales will come. They could come from our existing customers, in which case we have a *loyalty* objective. Alternatively, the additional sales could come from those who are not currently our customers (and as such are someone else's), in which case we have a *conquest* objective. It is useful to clarify this beforehand, as it will have an influence on the design of the promotion.

Types of promotion

Same for less
This is perhaps the simplest form of SP, and can be little more than straight discounts (e.g. 15 per cent off or half price). As such, this is not just applicable to end-consumers, but can very much be used on intermediaries, such as wholesalers or retailers. Giving them extra discount increases their profit margin and thus gives them an incentive to sell your product, often by passing on some of the discount. On a consumer level, this is very commonly used by supermarkets, who even sell some items at below cost (loss leaders) to bring customers into their store. However, for larger purchases, products may appear tarnished or cheapened by discounting. Marketers at Chanel perfumes would be horrified at their brands being subject to such treatment, whereas other manufacturers allow permanently low prices on their fragrances. A variant of same for less for larger purchases is special finance deals, (e.g. 0 per cent finance over two years). Here the finance is subject to effective discounting, allowing the price of the car (and its image) to remain intact.

More for the same
The most obvious example of this is in special packages of products (e.g. 750 g for the price of 600 g, or six cans of drink for the normal price of four). One of the UK's longest-running promotions of this type is retailer-driven: Boots' three for two offer, to which different products have been subject over a number of years. What is particularly effective is that three for two has become synonymous with Boots the Chemists, and has thus created loyalty to the Boots retail brand rather than loyalty to the particular products or brands on offer at any given time.

A recent brand-led promotion was instigated by Punjana teas, whose premium product competes in a price driven commodity market. Their tea is nearly twice as expensive, but two packets are currently available at little more than the cost of one. People are now trying the tea, but will they continue after the promotion is ended?

A further variant of more for the same is the limited edition or special packaging. This has been popular with the car trade as a means of cost-effectively generating new interest in what may be a rather tired product offering. Here 'extras' are loaded on to give greater value to the customer.

Free gifts
Here we can see the split between loyalty and conquest campaigns. A promotion with an objective of customer loyalty may require repeated purchases over a period of time, e.g. Sri Lankan Tea. A conquest campaign may make an appeal 'from the shelf' at the moment of purchase.

In the UK the market for breakfast cereals is mature, and there is a tendency towards variety-seeking purchasing, so the inclusion of a small gift may sway the bored buyer. (The situation would be entirely different in central Europe, where the average Hungarian eats around one-twentieth of the cereals eaten by a UK resident.) The Swiss owned multinational Nestlé has been giving away gifts from the Disney film *Monsters Inc.* across its range of cereal products, and a visit to any supermarket or grocers shop will reveal other contemporary examples.

Competitions
Whilst a free gift is assured in the above promotion, the chance of winning something may appeal to certain customers. This could take various forms: a scratchcard or other instant win device, or a prize draw or something more elaborate, involving answering questions and having an element of skill or judgement in it. While all may be deemed to encourage customers, the latter two are more useful to marketers as they allow a database to be built, although it is not always clear whether the main interest is in the prize or the product.

Joint promotions

There are various ways in which companies can collaborate, competitions being one example. A recent competition involved three parties: Safeway, the supermarket chain, Volkswagen Cars, and men's toiletries. To win the VW car, a purchase of toiletries had to be made at Safeway. Each party would have their own objectives in participating, but there needs to be a match between target audiences for this to work. This way, customers can be shared to a mutual advantage.

Another form of joint promotion is to work with the media by donating a prize. The amount of advertising and editorial support generated should far outweigh the cost of the prize.

Sampling

In the food and drink industries this is very common, with promotional staff handing out samples either in a supermarket or a busy location such as a show or principal rail station. Sampling is a chance to experience the product, and this is feasible with much larger products. Test driving a car, visiting a show home, or even having a 'free' holiday to sample a timeshare complex are all examples of sampling. Incentives are often given to those sampling potentially large purchases; for example, one house builder even offers seriously interested buyers the opportunity to spend a free weekend in a show home. The greater the incentive, the more likelihood of take-up, but also the greater the number of time-wasters, so the marketer has to make judgements based on previous experience plus other factors, as in any business decision.

Evaluating the success of a joint promotion

The first point to note is that this can be judged from various viewpoints. If two companies are working together they both have objectives for the collaboration and will both therefore need to measure the outcomes.

Case Study

Joint promotions in action

Renault cars held a joint promotion with an electrical retailer. The concept was initiated by the retailer, who wanted to boost store traffic especially amongst a younger target audience than was currently visiting the stores. They set up a competition to win a Renault sports car, but competition entry forms were only available on visiting a store, thereby building store traffic from this younger group of consumers. The retailer purchased the car from Renault, whose dealers were able to set up displays and make links with their local store. The competition entry form asked for details such as age and, as a result, this information was added to the database of both companies. The retailer was able to subsequently mail the competition entrants with further offers. Renault were able to offer test drives to the people it was able to add to its database, and sales of new vehicles ensued. What is significant about such a promotion is that both parties have objectives which fit together and both are able to measure and evaluate the success of the promotion via a number of indicators.

Was the promotion a success?
From the retailer's view many new prospective customers visited their stores. Only time will tell if this translates into increased sales.

From the car manufacturer's point of view one car was bought at the outset and a small number of test drives were made. But the real feature of this promotion was that it cost them nothing!

One interesting point is that usually on joint promotions the target audiences are similar, but on this occasion the retailer was trying to raise its profile and lower its customer age profile by specifically offering a sports car.

Sales and the promotional sub-mix

Sales, or rather personal selling, is included in the promotional sub-mix. Whether this is demeaning to the sales profession, or an important reminder to the marketer not to forget the person who deals directly with the customer, is not for debate here. However, it is important to remember that sales and marketing need each other in different ways.

Definition

Selling – Is the art of influencing decisions in favour of a product or service, such that the costs involved are outweighed by the advantages.

Supporting the sales effort

This rather implies that marketing is subservient to sales, but there is a variety of tasks marketing can perform. First, product training can be provided for the sales force. This could be in the guise of a conference or in literature and manuals. Marketing could then provide background advertising activity, so that the salespeople do not have to go in completely cold. Marketing may even go as far as generating sales leads and enquiries. For existing customers, marketing can keep dialogue going from a distance with customer mailings. Sales staff, being close to the customer, can supply marketers with valuable information about the trading environment. As they know and understand customer needs, they can help in developing products and services.

Sales staff roles

Field sales staff
These are the people responsible for serving the customer in the marketplace. Job titles vary, such as sales representative, territory manager, key account manager, etc.

They know their customers well and deal with them on an individual basis. For marketers they can, if asked, provide valuable information on:

- Competitor activity
- Competitor pricing strategy
- New market entrants
- Customer reaction to our products/services
- New ideas gained from dialogue with customers.

Internal sales staff

These staff are responsible for dealing with customers, usually over the telephone. The 'CALL or CONTACT CENTRE' is a rapidly expanding area of business in the UK and it is not just high pressure sales companies such as Staybrite double glazing that employ staff in such centres. Call centres can have an outbound 'offense' function, trying to get new business, or can act as an enquiry and customer care centre such as EWS Railway's new centre in Doncaster which has as its focus the retention of rail freight customers through good customer care.

Retail staff

These staff deal with customers face to face, but in a retail setting. The marketing job is very much to supply them with a flow of customers.

Do we need sales staff?

As availability and use of the internet increases, then the customer will interface with the computer more and more, effectively cutting out the role of personal selling. This is explored in 'Co-ordinating the marketing mix'.

Relationship marketing

Here, sales and marketing converge to take a longer-term view of the relationship with the customer, with an entirely different focus as follows (Figure 9.10).

'Old' marketing (sales oriented)	'New' marketing (relationship oriented)
Focus on sale	Focus on relationship
Focus on present	Focus on future
Features sold	Benefits explained
Low customer care	High customer care
Low customer contact	High customer contact
Quality a production issue	Quality everyone's concern

Figure 9.10 Relationship marketing

Relationship marketing, when coupled with ICT, is a powerful tool, as it is now becoming possible for a supermarket with millions of customers to treat them as individuals. Tesco, via its loyalty card which rewards purchases, know what, when, how much and how often we buy any given product or category and can tailor promotions to our personal needs and lifestyles. For instance, someone who buys half a chicken each week could be offered a special price on a whole one! Someone who buys four bottles of beer a week may be offered six bottles for the price of five.

Summary

In this unit we have examined the use of the four elements of the promotional sub-mix. It is important, when answering questions and in real life, to consider fully the opportunities for different tools to be used.

Sales promotion can be used to create a short-term increase in sales activity and may be geared towards either conquest (new customer) sales or retention.

Public relations can have a wider scope than marketing, having as its audience a range of stakeholders other than end-customers.

Selling and marketing are inextricably linked, and personal selling is a highly important activity as it is talking directly to the customer.

Advertising is the most visible activity, and the world of media is changing fast, making the task of media planning increasingly complex.

Further study and examination preparation

When you have completed this unit you will be able to answer Question 3 from the June 2002 paper and Question 4 from the December 2002 paper. Go to www.cimeduhub.com to access Specimen Answers and Senior Examiner's advice for these exam questions.

Extending knowledge

Students were recommended to read the Butterworth-Heinemann coursebook on Marketing Fundamentals before embarking on Marketing in Practice, and reference to it is highly recommended.

Marketing, Campaign, Adline and *Marketing Week* are all useful sources of what is happening currently. For a more in-depth read, *Marketing – Concepts and Strategies* by Dibb, Simkin, Pride and Ferrell (1997, Houghton Mifflin) is recommended.

Websites to visit include

> www.monster.com and www.ikea.com, both companies being featured in this unit.

> Particularly recommended is www.intelligencia.com which gives much information on available media.

unit 10
co-ordinating the marketing mix

Learning objectives

In this unit you will:

- Apply the knowledge gained in previous study, especially Marketing Fundamentals

- Develop an understanding of the importance of all elements of the marketing mix – promotion, price, place and product

- Understand the growing importance of the extended marketing mix – people, process and physicals

- Examine the relationship and interdependability of all elements of the mix

- Begin to explore the financial implications of marketing mix decisions.

By the end of this unit you will be able to:

- Evaluate an organization's use of the complete marketing mix

- Understand the necessity of comparisons across activities with competitors

- Make outline recommendations on areas of marketing activity

- Begin using basic calculations to justify and reinforce your recommendations

- Appreciate the impact of a decision regarding one element on the remaining elements of the marketing mix.

This unit covers sections 4.4.4, 4.4.5, 4.4.6 and 4.4.7 of the syllabus.

The key skills covered by this unit are Problem solving and working with others. The statement of marketing practice covered is Participate in reviews of marketing activities using measurement data.

Study Guide

This is a key unit as it touches such a broad spectrum of tasks, problems, opportunities and decisions concerning the entire marketing mix (although the promotion 'P' was covered in 'Co-ordinating the promotional effort' it will also be revisited in conjunction with other Ps).

The CIM has positioned Marketing in Practice as the final module of study at Certificate-level, and, as such, it draws on the content of the other three subjects. There is a particularly strong link with Marketing Fundamentals, and this is even more relevant to this unit, where we examine what the marketer can do with the 7Ps. So, in order to gain maximum benefit, it may be necessary to re-familiarize yourself with some of the key concepts in that module?

You will need around two hours to work through this unit, plus at least a further hour on the activities.

The development of the marketing mix

Activity 10.1

List each of the 7Ps on a different sheet of paper, and then brainstorm what you know about each one in turn. This could be in the form of components (e.g. advertising is part of the promotion 'P'). Then you may list what is most important about the 'P' in question. Relevant models can be briefly sketched, and alternative approaches identified. If you are unsure, it will pay dividends to consult the relevant units in Marketing Fundamentals.

Exam hint

Marketing in Practice is exactly what it says, and is about actually doing things with marketing. The practical nature of the subject may mislead the student into believing that theory and models are less important. The reverse is true – whilst Marketing in Practice may not ask for a model to be produced or discussed, it actually calls for something beyond that. It requires the selection and application of marketing knowledge and tools to solve problems, and this cannot be contemplated without a full understanding of the theoretical background to marketing.

Originally, there were perceived to be just four elements in the marketing mix, and reference is still made to the 4Ps. We would understand this to mean promotion, place, price, product. Of these, promotion, especially in the guise of advertising, is the most visible, and this is reflected in this coursebook, where it has its own unit. A fifth 'P' is sometimes mentioned: profit – the rationale being that this would be the result if the other Ps were used correctly, and this ties in with the CIM's definition of marketing.

Unit 10 Co-ordinating the marketing mix

The next stage of evolution came as service marketing came to the fore. Here there is no tangible product, and the characteristics of a service differ in the following ways:

- *Intangible* Services cannot be touched, unlike physical products. You may have insurance, but cannot really do anything with it
- *Perishable* Service stops when the interaction ceases. However, service, good or bad, can be remembered
- *Variable* The human element is always different. And we may make a judgement on an entire multinational as a result of dealing with one employee
- *Inseparable* Again, the service is how an individual or organization deals with us, so the product is the same as the service, which is the same as the person giving it
- *Ownership* We do not own the service as it is not a physical product. We pay to hire a car, but do not own it.

The extended marketing mix

As a result of the growth of service-based marketing, three further Ps have come to the fore: namely people, processes and physical evidence. However, virtually all products have some degree of service. Consider a large physical purchase such as a house or car. How we are dealt with by sales staff has a great influence on our decision to buy, and for many the whole process is very unappealing. As important, or even more so, is the concept of after-sales service. Having already bought the product, the kind of service we receive afterwards will be a major influence on whether we buy again from that source. Also, as products become increasingly similar, many marketers now believe that service is becoming a major differentiator and a means by which an organization can compete.

Activity 10.2

How does your organization (or an organization of your choice) utilize the elements of the marketing mix? How does it promote itself and its products? What processes does it have in place for the customer, etc.? Make a brief statement against each of the Ps. How does this stack up against either known competitors or against companies in different sectors? You may find it useful to compare and contrast with other students.

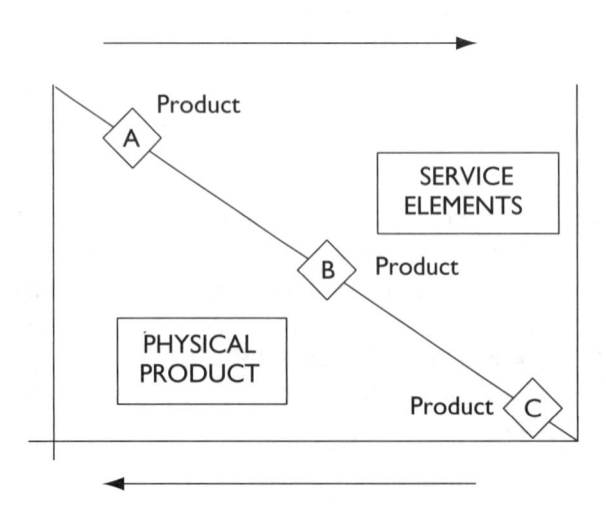

Figure 10.1

Figure 10.1 shows how products can have a varying amount of service element. Product A could be a bar of chocolate. Whether bought from a shop or a vending machine the amount of service is negligible. In the middle could be a car. Here although it is very much a major physical product, the service element, whether that be good sales advice, or aftercare, is a major part of our decision. The last example, C, is a purely service-based transaction, such as buying a pension or other financial product. Here we have nothing to show for our expenditure and the purchase is entirely based on the service Ps.

Applying the product/service mix

Knowing the figure and even being able to plot various products on it is a good start, but the marketer, realizing that there is strong competition, or even that their product is very similar to everyone else's, can use this knowledge to advantage.

By adding some extra service to the product it can be differentiated from its rivals.

For instance AOL, the ISP, offer a membership helpline; Proton cars offer a three-year warranty; IKEA offer crèche facilities.

What is also important to remember is that the service elements added must be good as consumers increasingly make judgements based not just on their own experience of service but also that received by their friends and families.

There is an activity based on this later in the unit.

Co-ordinating the mix

As we begin to look at the different elements of the mix, and make decisions, it becomes increasingly difficult to consider just one element in isolation. For instance, Nestlé may bring out a new product in South-East Asia, but they cannot do this without making decisions about the product's price and how the product will be promoted. Indeed, all elements need to be considered. This is obviously true for a new product, but to alter the price of an existing product may entail a change in distribution (place) strategy. As the price of mobile phones has fallen, distribution has widened, and the products of Nokia, Motorola and other leading brands are now on sale in supermarkets. We will now work through the remaining 6Ps and begin examining what we can do, and the implications of these mix decisions, especially financial.

Product decisions

When investigating the marketer's involvement with the product, it is useful to remember the product life cycle and its four stages of introduction, growth, maturity and decline (Figure 10.2).

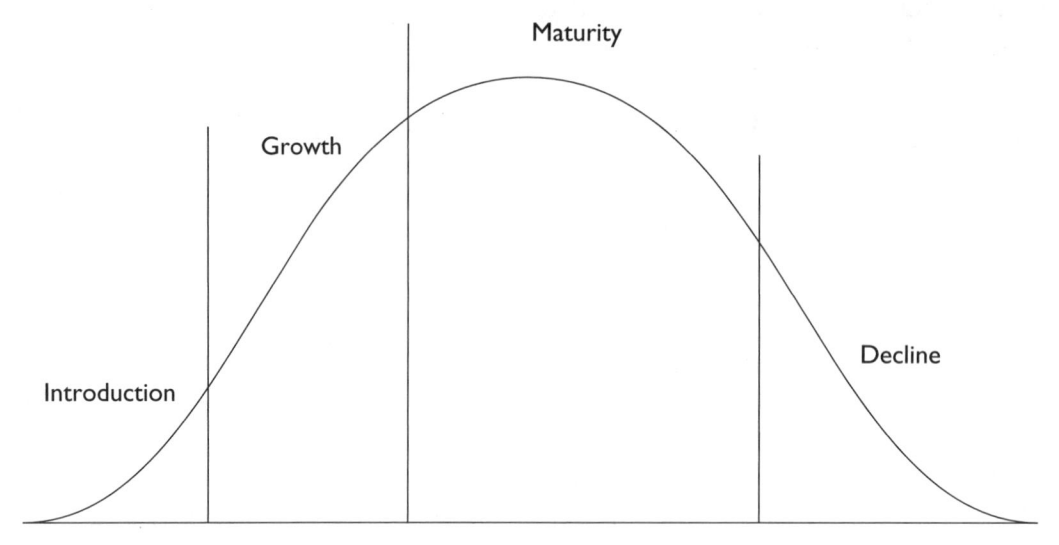

Figure 10.2 Product life cycle

Activity 10.3

The Building Brick Company

The above company manufactures a range of different bricks, and the following gives sales (in millions of units) for the past ten years of six of its designs. Where are they on the product life cycle?

	90	91	92	93	94	95	96	97	98	99	00
A	10	12	15	16	17	18	19	18	15	14	12
B									10	12	16
C	10	10	10	10	79	11	10	11	9	10	10
D											2
E				1	2	3	4	5	6	7	8
F	10	4	10	7	8	9	4	10	11	8	7

However, work on the product begins before this, as the product (or service) is developed ready for the market.

Unit 10 Co-ordinating the marketing mix

> **Definition**
>
> **The new product development process (or NPD)** – The new product development process is traditionally viewed as going through the following stages: idea generation, screening, concept testing, marketing strategy, business planning, market testing, commercialization.

Marketers can again be involved at all of these stages, although much of this initially falls within the market researcher's brief. Market testing is the final stage before full launch and needs to be carefully executed to predict the future success of the product accurately.

Activity 10.4

Market testing

Veggiepet is an American pet food manufacturer which manufactures vegetarian dog and cat food. Part of a large multinational, it has the resources to promote the brand heavily throughout Europe, but the Vice-President of Marketing wishes to test market in one country. Based on the following information, which would you choose?

Country	Population (million)	% Vegetarian (million)	Dogs (million)	Cats (million)
UK	55	8	3	3
France	55	4	2	3
Germany	65	5	3	2
Luxembourg	2	5	0.1	0.1
Czech Republic	8	3	1	1

Product launches (and relaunches)

When the product is ready to be launched, the whole of the marketing mix is available to ensure success. In most instances, the launch takes place in phases, with trade customers or distributors being the first to be informed about the new product. It is important at launch to strike the right balance between pull and push strategies (see Figure 10.3).

Push strategies
out to end-customers →

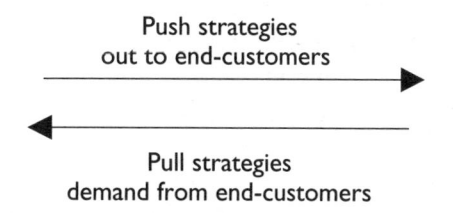

← Pull strategies
demand from end-customers

Figure 10.3

The launch to the end-customer may be very high profile and handled by a major agency, and as such create a large pull. However, the push also needs to happen, and this may involve training the sales force, devising incentives, planning a conference, and providing literature and information to intermediaries.

The product growth stage
As the product increases its sales competition may well increase. Likely tasks for the marketer at this stage could therefore include the following:

- Analysing competitors
- Widening the product range
- Improving the product
- Launching the product in new (possibly international) markets.

Analysing competitors is comprehensively covered in 'Gathering information from inside and outside the organization', but it is worth remembering that a comprehensive competitor analysis covers not just their products, but every facet of the organization's activities.

Definition

Product width and depth – Product width refers to the number of different types of product offered by a company. Depth would refer to the number of variants, and different sizes within the range. An example here would be Marks & Spencer, whose range is wide, comprising men's, women's and children's clothing (trousers, skirts, underwear, pullovers, etc.), and deep, in that these are offered in a variety of sizes, colours and patterns.

Once a volume of sales has been built up, and development and investment costs largely recovered, then variants of the product can be developed for new profitable segments of the market.

Activity 10.5

Find out how many genuinely new products have been launched by your organization over the last two years, and compare this with the number of variants developed since launch.

Fighting the competition
As we move on into the mature phase of the product, it is likely that competition will become increasingly fierce, especially from newer competitive products which may well be better than ours. We need not, and cannot, give in. Even if there is little we can now do to improve the product itself, we can make it more appealing by focusing on changes we can make to the other elements of the mix.

- *Price* This could be lowered, or at least pegged, allowing competitors to be more expensive
- *Place* Perhaps now is the time to look again at how and where our product is marketed
- *Promotion* A change in advertising or creative strategy may give fresh appeal.

Alternatively, a service element comprising the 3Ps of the extended marketing mix could draw attention away from the tired appearance of the product. Daewoo, when introducing an already obsolete car range into the UK, built their entire offering around customer service, countering the very negative perceptions held about buying a car from a traditional dealership.

Managing decline

This does not sound like the most exciting task for a marketer, but is vital for a company to maximize returns from its initial investment and also to fund new product development and launches. There is unlikely to be much budget available, and this makes it even more of a challenge. Any of the accompanying Ps may be tweaked or, like the Mini, it may have a loyal, if small, customer base.

Pricing decisions

Pricing policies fall into two broad areas: those based on cost and those based on other factors, invariably based around marketing or environmental criteria.

Activity 10.6

How does your company determine its prices? Are prices based on costs alone, or are other factors taken into account? Are some lines more profitable than others, and why might this be the case?

Cost-based pricing

This is where the price you charge is determined by the costs you incur in manufacturing, retailing or otherwise bringing the product or service to the marketplace. Issues of cost behaviour are examined briefly in 'Introduction to budgeting', but there are two variants.

- *Break-even pricing* More commonly used in a manufacturing environment, the company's costs are calculated, and the number of sales at a given price is then calculated to give a point at which a profit is made.
- *Marginal pricing* Used in many marketing environments, this is where a percentage is added to the costs of products bought in. This percentage is not all profit, as overheads such as rent, labour, head office charges and other costs have to be met. As this contributes to these costs, it is known as contribution.

Marketing-based pricing policies

To marketers, price is an element of the marketing mix and, as such, is a variable which we control. Whilst acknowledging the very real costs involved, there are many factors determining the price our product or service may command in the marketplace.

Activity 10.7

Using the model LEPEST & CO, how might these environmental factors influence price? For your organization, which is the most crucial factor and why?

Basically, in response to, or in anticipation of, outside factors there are only two things we can do: increase prices, or reduce prices. Added to this is the time dimension, as many pricing changes may be for a short time only.

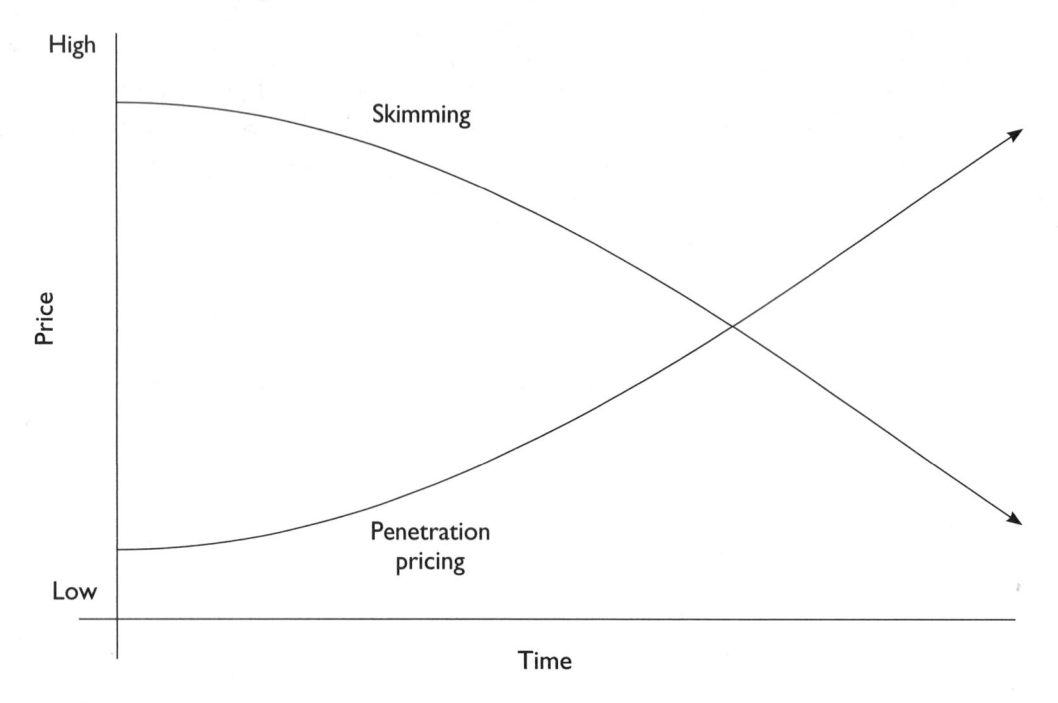

Figure 10.4 Pricing diagram

One area where there is a choice of high or low prices is when a product is launched. The two options here are known as *skimming* and *penetration*.

If price skimming is adopted, then a high, premium price is charged initially, often to recoup development costs. A reduction in price some time later can broaden the appeal of the product to new segments, as can further reductions. The classic example is currently mobile phones, but other technology-based consumer purchases, such as home PCs and internet access, are following a similar pattern.

Penetration pricing aims to build up sales rapidly and gain visibility for the product, with higher pricing to follow once established.

Price-based promotions

Sales promotion is featured in Unit 9, 'Co-ordinating the promotional effort', but interest can often be stimulated in a mature product by altering the price.

Activity 10.8

You work in the marketing department of a major importer of Swiss chocolate bars. Each month the importer buys in and sells on 100,000 bars of chocolate. Buy-in price is 15p. These are sold on to retailers at 25p, and in turn are sold to consumers at 35p. As from next month there is to be an increase in the buy-in cost to 17p. One proposal is to raise the price retailers pay by 20 per cent, giving a retail price of 40p. Alternatively, there is a suggestion that the wholesaler and retailers not only absorb the rise but cut their margins so that each only makes 8p per bar. This is a price-sensitive market, where a 1p rise causes a 2 per cent drop in sales and a 1p cut creates a 4 per cent rise. Which would you recommend for the next three months?

End of PLC pricing

Again, there are two choices: prices down or prices up. At first sight it may seem most obvious to reduce the price of a product in the latter stages of its life cycle. Development costs should be well and truly covered, and the product is unlikely to be competing fiercely for market share. So it may prove worthwhile to squeeze the last few sales out of the product by reducing the price.

However, there is an alternative viewpoint. There is nothing intrinsically wrong with a product at the end of its life cycle. Indeed, in the case of a car it may well now be in its definitive form, loaded with extras, and represent good value for money. As such, it may have tremendous appeal for the 'laggards', who would be highly unlikely to consider the new model in any case. There could even be a case put forward for raising the price of an old product, so as not to make the inevitably more costly new product appear over-expensive.

Place decisions

The next 'P' to consider is place. At first glance, this 'P' appears to concern itself with the location of an organization and its outlets. However, we need to take a broader look than that. Place can cover the whole process of getting the product or service to the customer. This may or may not involve third parties further down the distribution chain. It may well involve some logistics, from organizing a field sales force to deciding on mode of transportation. The place, in terms of where the customer sees the product, is now increasingly likely to be a TV screen or modem, the place becoming virtual rather than physical. Also to be considered alongside place is time, and this covers opening times, whether this be at a physical location or via telephone or other link. Also important is the speed at which the customer can receive his or her desired product, and this impacts on warehousing and transportation.

Activity 10.9

What is happening to 'place' in your experience as a consumer? Do you shop, eat out or buy products and services any differently than a few years ago? Is it easier or less so to buy products and services, and have you noticed any big changes in certain industries?

Channels compared

In brief, the choices for an organization can be summarized as shown in Figure 10.5.

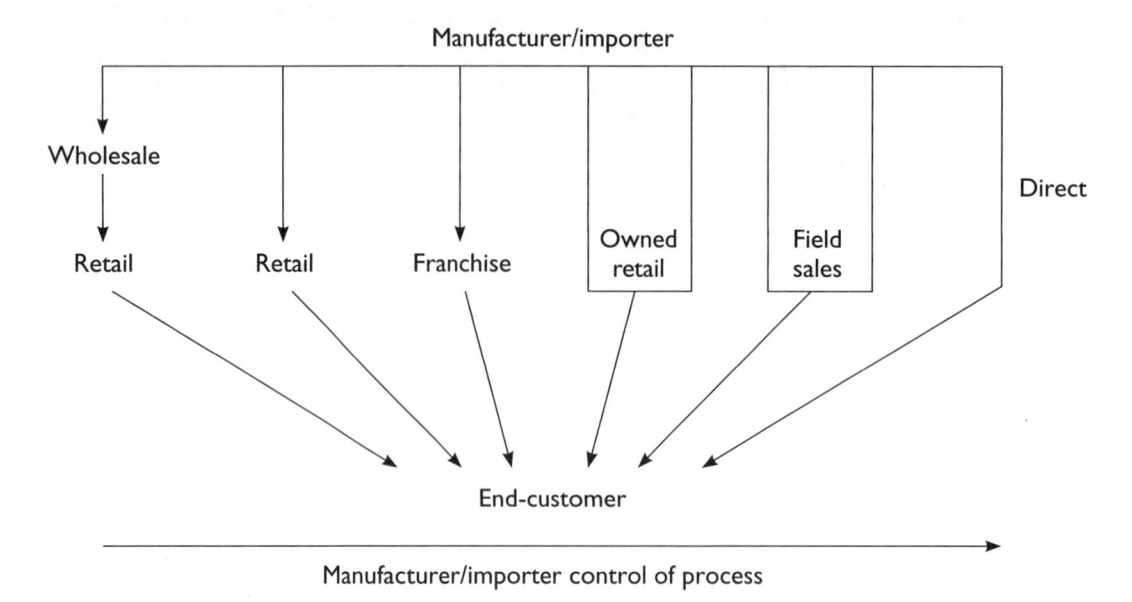

Figure 10.5 Channels compared diagram

As can be seen above, there is a variety of methods of getting our product to the end-user. The more intermediaries there are, the greater the loss of control over the final transaction with the customer. On the other hand, in wholly-owned distribution the greater the amount of capital tied up in stock.

Franchising

A rapidly growing solution is franchising, where a local entrepreneur markets the products or services, usually within a tightly specified geographical area. This is done under strict guidelines which cover everything from corporate identity, through recommended suppliers, to service standards and staff uniforms. Some of the world's best known brands, such as McDonald's, Burger King, Mercedes Benz and Toyota, are represented in this way.

Marketing support for third parties

Whilst a manufacturer or importer may spend large sums on brand-building advertising for its products, there is a need for tactical localized support for individual outlets. This can be undertaken in a number of ways.

First, the manufacturer can undertake to plan and pay for local advertising on behalf of the distributor/retailer. This is the method adopted by players in many sectors, such as Bang and Olufsen in audio, and Interflora in the floristry sector.

Alternatively, a subsidy can be given to the retailer for undertaking activity in their own area. Usually this is to a defined ratio, e.g. 50:50, and often with other conditions attached.

Either in conjunction with the above, or alone, a manufacturer can supply advertising and other materials as kits or finished artwork. This ensures a consistency of quality across the retail network.

A further means of support is to offer a consultancy service to third parties further down the supply chain. This is sometimes done on an ad hoc basis by internal staff from the marketing department. Alternatively, it can be done by appointing an external agency; this approach was pioneered by Jaguar Cars.

The final option is to give third parties the freedom to do what they wish, although this is obviously fraught with the danger of our brand being cheapened or undermined.

Activity 10.10

Comparison of outlets performance

Pizza Taberna is an expanding fast-food chain based in Central Europe, with outlets in Poland, Hungary and the Czech Republic. It is a franchised operation, and hopes to expand into Germany within the next year. Before this, it needs to know that it has got its franchising arrangements right. A section from the management accounts is included, with figures in euros to aid comparisons.

Outlet	Turnover	Staff	Profit	Ad spend	Ad subsidy
1	2000	20	130	50	25
2	1500	15	100	30	15
3	2500	25	180	80	40
4	1500	20	100	10	5
5	750	10	75	30	15

Task

Based on the above accounts, what performance can be expected from an average Pizza Taberna franchise? Comment on any significant variations from this which need investigating.

Exam hint

It is highly probable that students will need to make basic calculations in the exam, and they should be confident in their ability to perform tasks such as adding, subtracting, dividing and multiplying. Also required is a familiarity with percentages and simple ratios.

International considerations

Although international marketing is sometimes considered a separate subject, marketing is becoming increasingly international, and many students have an international dimension to their job. When considering place, we may need to make different arrangements or adopt different approaches when entering another market. The prime consideration should be one of culture, in the sense of 'how business is conducted' in another country. The main danger, therefore, is to make assumptions that somewhere else is the same as our home market, or, conversely, to have preconceived ideas that others are somehow less sophisticated than ourselves. Certainly the global village, aided by the internet and other technologies and media, is fast becoming a reality.

The internet and marketing, the ultimate 'place'

There is no doubt that the internet and e-commerce are changing the way we do business, despite the current downturn in share prices on the NASDAQ, and failures of dotcom companies such as E-TOYS.

The obvious impact for marketing is on place.

With a website, a company can:

- Have its products seen anywhere
- Trade across international boundaries with comparative ease.

However, as marketers we need to know how e-commerce impacts on and enhances what we can do across the range of marketing decisions.

Firstly we need to know that a well-designed website can:

1. Gather information about customers (e-questionnaires)
2. Be used to display/show our products
3. Fulfil a sales function (ordering online).

The rate of growth of e-trading varies across sectors and also depends on the level of access. In the UK, two of the major supermarkets, Sainsbury's and Tesco, now have an online ordering facility, with the rest about to follow. The take up remains very small, at the time of writing only five per cent of families have attempted a weekly shop on the internet, whilst over 30 per cent have bought something, usually a single purchase.

The internet's relationship with the Ps

Product
The internet allows our product greater visibility. In some cases, the 'product' is a download and only exists because of the internet.

Place
Not only does the internet allow 'place' to be expanded, it can also mean that money can be saved by not having money tied up in excessive stockholding, retailing activities and staffing, leading to...

Price
Lower prices can be the result of reduced overheads and simpler business models.

Promotion
Although the web is a means of communicating, there are so many sites and confusing clutter, that very conventional advertising methods using established media are needed to start getting hits.

People
Fewer people are needed in a pure e-business. Customers interface with a PC terminal, not a salesperson. Virtual companies can be set up with the minimum of staff and premises. But some conventional 'bricks' companies, who have invested in a chain of physical premises, such as Sainsbury's also operate in the world of 'clicks' on an internet site. Even where there is a saving in headcount over a physical business, there is still a reliance on people to deliver the product. These may not work for the company but for a strategic partner such as UPS.

Physical evidence
In a virtual world nobody knows how big you are! A well-designed website is powerful evidence of a company's credentials.

Processes
The customer's experience of using a site, ordering from a site and the fulfilment of the order are the new processes. This leads back to site and software design, and also to arrangements for delivery whether this be by the company's own staff or an outside contractor such as UPS.

People decisions

This is the most important of the three elements of the extended service mix. In recent years a whole new industry of customer service has grown, and in an era of increasingly similar products the 'P' for people is one way of differentiating yourself from your competitors. All transactions have some people element – even a vending machine needs people to ensure that it is filled, stocked with change and otherwise functioning correctly. However, the extent to which the people element matters does vary considerably.

Activity 10.11

As a consumer, consider the following purchases which you may have made or are likely to make. How important is the people element of the extended marketing mix? Have you any stories to tell, either good or bad? And is it possible to rank these purchases in order according to the relative importance of the people factor?

- Buying a cup of coffee from a café
- Buying a house or apartment
- Taking out an insurance policy
- Buying a pair of shoes
- Going on an air journey
- Organizing a loan
- Renting a car
- Attending an educational establishment.

Service and quality
As customers, we make judgements about many aspects of a company's interface. However good a company, its products and its whole offering, we are still most inclined to make lasting judgements based on our dealings with front-line staff.

In a recent survey of a private hospital, patients (or customers, as the organization regards them) spent more time with staff who delivered their meals and drinks than with the medical staff. As non-medically qualified customers, the quality of the clinical service could not really be questioned, but the food, drink and manner of those serving certainly could. The hospital had to rethink its training strategy in the light of these findings.

Relationship marketing
An important cultural shift is currently taking place in the way marketing and sales is carried out. There is a move towards valuing customers over a long period rather than just for the transaction taking place now. This requires an entirely different attitude throughout the company and will certainly necessitate training of staff at all levels. The changes can be summarized as follows: 'old marketing' focuses on the sale, product features, low customer

involvement, low regard for customer satisfaction, quality viewed as a production issue; 'relationship marketing' focuses on long-term relationship, product benefits, high customer involvement, high regard for customer satisfaction, quality is everyone's concern.

This whole customer-oriented philosophy is rooted in the financial reality that it costs far more to attract a new customer than to retain a current one. The cost of such service can be an issue, but the cost of not pursuing this direction and losing customers is a powerful counter-argument.

Marketing training

To accompany such a company-wide change towards a more customer-oriented way of thinking, many support mechanisms have to be put in place. What we are doing is devolving responsibility for marketing. Instead of marketing and meeting customer needs being the responsibility of a department, everyone now has an input. This may come as a shock to some product or procedurally oriented employees, and training programmes with considerable marketing input will need to be set up.

Activity 10.12

You work for a high street retailer whose profits have fallen in the last year. You have been asked to provide input at a staff training session for shop assistants. How would you go about this?

Internal marketing

In order to ensure that all employees understand the organization's objectives and plans, an internal marketing programme may be necessary. This can utilize any of the tools discussed elsewhere in this book, such as conferences, roadshows, media, print, etc.

Definition

Internal marketing – Is the same as 'normal' marketing, except for two important differences. First, the customer is inside the organization, not outside it, but he or she is still a customer with likes, dislikes, fears and different motivators. Secondly, what is being sold is certainly not a product in the physical sense, but more an idea, such as a customer retention scheme, a company restructuring, or some other initiative. Be careful not to confuse internal marketing with internal sales. Internal sales is a description given to office-based telephone selling.

Process decisions

Businesses are composed of many processes (production processes, accounting processes, etc.), but what we are interested in here is processes which affect the customer. It could be argued that all processes ultimately impact on the end-customer, but here we specifically look at processes that the customer actually goes through. There are four distinct phases when the customer interacts with the organization; these are as follows:

1. The enquiry/information gathering stage
2. The point of purchase, where the buying process comes to a conclusion

3. The delivery phase of the transaction
4. After-sales, when the customer has made the purchase but still may have cause to interact with the supplier.

Different modes of communication may be used at these stages: face-to-face, telephone, post or internet.

Let us now work through these stages from the customer's viewpoint, but with the objective of finding how improvements in process design can influence, win and ultimately retain the customer.

Enquiry/information search
Here the customer wishes to find out about our product or service. Choices here are to make information freely available, thereby lessening the chance of any interaction. For high-volume products, especially of low value, this makes sense. Where there is an interaction, via any of the communication modes, we need to decide to what extent we try to sell the product or service. Initially the enquiry may be logged, and the prospect's details recorded for adding to the database. Going beyond this, some attempt may be made to move the prospect further down the buying process.

Activity 10.13

Think about the last time you enquired about a product or service. This could be about buying a rail ticket, an item of furniture or a spare part for a car. How easy was it to find the information you required? Was the telephone line always engaged? How helpful was the person you dealt with – did they try to sell, or were they happy merely to supply the information you requested?

Having seen this from the angle of the customer, now put yourself in the position of the organization. What improvements would you recommend in the process?

Point of purchase
The process here varies according to the complexity of the purchase, but it is ironic that customers who have been through a decision process and are prepared and willing to buy are not always treated particularly well. Virgin is a global brand with a good reputation, but that reputation is currently being tarnished by their operation of train sevices. There are many reasons for this in a privatized railway system, but a customer wishing to buy a rail ticket on the day of travel is often annoyed at having to pay considerably more than those who have booked in advance. If this is followed by a late running, dirty, old and overcrowded train the whole experience undermines the entire brand across all sectors.

The biggest purchases a person is ever likely to make are a house/apartment, a car and financial products. These purchases are often miserable experiences, fraught with problems, and hard-sell sales techniques are frequently used.

Between these two extremes is supermarket shopping, a task most people do not enjoy.

Designing improvements
Recognizing that purchasing may be an unpleasant experience, organizations have been focusing on two areas of improvement, namely speed and simplicity.

- *Speed improvements* Sainsbury's, the UK supermarket chain, now allow customers at certain stores to scan the barcodes of products they buy, saving time and hassle at the checkout. Tesco promises to open as many tills as necessary if people are waiting. Electronic purses and smart-card technology are seen as ways of hastening smaller-scale, routine purchases.
- *Simplifying the process* One-way of achieving this is with a greater level of automation, and this is much in evidence in the banking sector with the proliferation of ATMs. Attempts have been made to simplify larger purchases. Daewoo have been mentioned elsewhere, but deserve mentioning again for their policy of fixed fair prices for their cars, rather than have customers face an intimidating and confusing system of bartering over the value of the car they wish to buy and the one they wish to dispose of. Other car manufacturers have attempted to simplify the process and create loyalty by introducing leasing packages which guarantee a car's value against a new one in the future, Ford being prominent with their Options scheme.

Activity 10.14

Following on from the previous activity, consider a recent purchase. Was this an enjoyable experience? Or could it be improved in terms of speed or simplicity of the transaction?

Delivery

The next process experienced by the customer is delivery, and one example of this is the delivery aspect of eating in a McDonald's outlet. Here a combination of speed and simplicity allows delivery to be carried out in the same manner throughout the world. Timing is important in the delivery process; other restaurant chains such as Harvester and Beefeater have controls on the amount of time customers have to wait, and this is viewed as a key performance indicator in terms of customer service levels. A recent innovation in the highly competitive UK supermarket sector is the facility to have your shopping delivered; Somerfield have taken the initiative here.

For larger products, there may well be a wait – a danger here is that the customer's enthusiasm wanes during the waiting period. Legislation in some countries allows for a period in which the customer has the right to cancel the purchase, even if agreements have been signed.

If an actual delivery does take place, what is the attitude and motivation of the deliverer? If employed by the organization providing the product or service, this person is in the front line and can easily influence customers towards or against making further purchases, especially if the delivery is late or beset with other problems.

Activity 10.15

Have you had anything delivered recently? Was this on the premises of a restaurant or service provider, or was it a physical product? Did the delivery alter your perceptions in any way, and are you more or less likely to make a repeat purchase as a result?

After-sales

A key element towards relationship marketing, and keeping customers, the view is often held that 'after'-sales actually forms the starting point of the next purchase decision. As such, a lot of marketing effort has gone into designing comprehensive after-sales programmes. These can consist of the following activities:

1. Continuing dialogue with the customer. This can comprise satisfaction surveys, information and reminders, and this is easily achieved with a well-managed database.
2. Spare parts and servicing. Larger products, such as domestic appliances, will certainly need attention after they have been in use. If this relationship is handled correctly, it can not only retain the customer but also become a source of profits in its own right.
3. Customer help lines. This has become very much a growth area in recent years. Very often this facility is outsourced, so that the person answering the telephone does not work for the company itself. This can cause problems with more complex or technical complaints.

Activity 10.16

Have you ever bought something and then felt either delighted or let down by the service you received afterwards? How has this affected your views on the product and the company selling it?

Physical evidence decisions

Definition

Physical evidence – Is that which accompanies the delivery of a product or service. This can include such things as written guarantees or policies, but could also be construed as covering the surroundings in which the service or product is delivered. The latter crosses over into 'P' for place/territory.

If you take out an insurance policy, what have you got? You certainly do not have a physical product you can take home with you, nor do you have the satisfaction of just having had a good meal. Potentially, you have nothing to show for your expenditure. This is where physical evidence in the sense of proof of purchase comes in.

Another type of evidence is that which arises when a product or service comes with a guarantee or warranty. Again, a piece of paper is the evidence that you have the right to repairs or replacement. However, if a broader view is taken as to what supports the delivery of a product or service, then other facets can be seen as providing evidence of a quality organization. We have already examined 'P' for place in this unit, but the décor and feel of a place are important for us in making judgements about the organization, and ultimately deciding whether or not to buy from there.

Activity 10.17

If you own a car, a Toyota for example, would you feel happier taking it to a franchised dealership or a non-franchised general repair garage? How much more would you be willing to pay at a Toyota dealership? What evidence do you have that the servicing or repairs will be undertaken more satisfactorily?

Corporate identity, which covers everything from paint schemes to signage and store layout, plays a major role in making the customer feel that a consistent quality service is offered.

Peripheral enhancements

Other environmental improvements also provide supporting evidence, by enhancing the point of delivery. For instance, IKEA, the Swedish furniture store, provides play areas for customers' children free of charge supervised by qualified staff. This is obviously a cost to IKEA, but is evidence of its understanding of family needs and commitment to giving customers a pleasant shopping experience.

Summary

In this unit you will have built upon the knowledge of the marketing mix you gained in Marketing Fundamentals. More specifically, you have started working with these tools of marketing and learnt the following:

- The 7Ps are very much interrelated
- There are options to select throughout the life cycle of a product
- There is a variety of different methods of pricing
- Place is becoming increasingly important
- The service Ps have a major role to play, not just in service marketing, but in the service aspect of physical product marketing.

Further study and examination preparation

When you have completed this unit you will be able to answer Question 1a of the June 2002 paper, and Question 5 of the December 2002 paper. Go to www.cimeduhub.com to access Specimen Answers and Senior Examiner's advice for these exam questions.

You may also be interested in exploring the websites of two companies featured in this unit

www.sainsburystoyou.com and

www.virgintrains.co.uk

unit 11
introduction to budgeting

Learning objectives

In this unit you will:

- See the importance of budgets and financial measurements
- Examine the scope of the marketing budget, and how it is set
- Explore the basics of cost behaviour
- Analyse different methods for allocating marketing costs
- Look at how a budget should be presented and expenditure evaluated.

By the end of this unit you will:

- Feel increasingly confident about budgetary and financial matters
- Be able to set realistic budgets by different methods
- Understand basic costing behaviour and allocation methods
- Be able to make budget and expenditure recommendations.

This unit covers sections 4.5.1 and 4.5.2 of the syllabus.

The unit covers the key skill Problem-solving. Also, as budgeting and finance is new and perhaps a little daunting for many candidates, you are likely to be Improving own learning and performance – another key skill.

The statements of marketing practice covered are Participate in reviews of marketing activity, plus Contribute to project planning and budget preparation.

Unit 11 Introduction to budgeting

Study Guide

Working with budgets – an integral part of a marketer's job role.

Unit 11, 'Introduction to budgeting' and Unit 12, which covers calculations in the examination focus on the 20 per cent of the syllabus entitled 'Administering the marketing budget'. However, dealing with figures and numbers should not just be an activity tagged on at the end, but should be an important and integrated component of marketing.

This has been reflected in the design of this coursebook and if you look back over previous units you will see how many of the activities have already involved you in some figurework. Take some time to reflect on what you have done already before consolidating your knowledge through the next two units and finally putting it to the test in the exam paper.

This unit is key to obtaining a respectable pass grade in the Marketing in Practice exam. Twenty per cent of the syllabus is on dealing with numerical and financial information. There is a thread running through the entire book whereby this is viewed as an integral part of marketing activity rather than an afterthought, or, worse still, 'somebody else's job'. This unit therefore seeks to pull all this together and focus on a subject about which many marketers have unfortunate preconceived ideas. There is a perpetuated myth that 'creative marketing types' have difficulty dealing with such mundanities as figures and finance. This may be so, but it is the marketer and the entire marketing industry that will be the losers unless we learn to speak in finance, which is the language of business. Only 25 per cent of the UK's top 500 companies have a main board director whose prime business discipline is marketing, and this is causing concern. There is a need for career-minded individuals to become, if not multi-disciplined, then at least confident and conversant with financial affairs. So this unit may prove to be a springboard not only to the next level of CIM study, but also to an enhanced and less blinkered career.

We would expect you to take around two hours reading and understanding this unit and around a further three hours to undertake the various activities.

The scope of the marketing budget

Definition

Budget – Is a plan set in financial terms. Put simply, everything we may plan to do has a cost; therefore everything can be expressed in cost terms. If we know the costs and know the resulting income, then we can evaluate the activity, and decide whether to repeat or amend our planning in the future.

This varies between organizations. If we take the CIM's definition of marketing, and consider the full mix, including product(ion), people, and the need for a marketing information system, then the scope of marketing covers the entire organization's activities. However, in reality, organizations have product development, production, logistics, human resources, operations and information technology budgets separate from the marketing budget, even though these other activities have a strong marketing crossover. The marketing budget for most organizations could more correctly be described as the marketing services budget, as it primarily covers the promotional element of the marketing mix.

The marketing budget analysed

The typical organization's marketing budget may well comprise the following budgets, which cover separate aspects of marketing activity.

Advertising budget

This covers the advertising activity undertaken, and is probably the largest part of the marketing budget. It is certainly the most visible and most subject to scrutiny. This can be further broken down and may be charged to different departments or brands. See later in this unit.

Other ways of breaking down the budget allow for different analytical requirements. Media expenditure may well be split from creative and production costs, and some organizations may have specific budgets by media (i.e. local/regional press budget), or by purpose (e.g. product launch, dealer support).

PR budget

If a PR consultancy is retained, or PR forms an important part of the organization's marketing effort, then this may well have a separate budget and again this may be split, for instance between corporate work and product support work and activities.

Sales promotion budget

Again, there may well be a separate budget for sales promotion activities. This could be split into a budget which pays for promotional materials and a discount budget. A discount budget is an internal mechanism which 'pays' for the 'cost' of special offer prices; for example, if there is 10 per cent off the purchase price, this 10 per cent is covered by the discount budget.

Conference/event budget

Depending on the focus of the activity, this could well fall into the jurisdiction of the marketing budget. However, some organizations which have conferences purely for internal staff would have the expenses met by human resources or some other corporate budget.

Print budget

Organizations with a heavy reliance on printed media, such as catalogues, may well have a distinct budget for this purpose. Retailers such as Halfords or Boots who produce a catalogue for Christmas often 'sell' the space in their publications, so this can be a revenue budget as well as a cost budget.

Staff budget

The cost of employing marketing personnel can be attributed to the marketing department's budget.

Unit 11 Introduction to budgeting

Sales and marketing budget

Although we may consider personal selling to be part of the marketing mix under 'P' for promotion, this is rarely the case in practice. Certainly it would be unusual for a marketing budget to cover the cost of salespeople's salaries, transport and other expenses. Sometimes the reverse does happen, and marketing is viewed as a sales support activity headed by a Sales and Marketing Manager, with a sales and marketing budget.

> **Activity 11.1**
>
> What activities (advertising, PR, etc.) are covered by the marketing budget in your organization? Are there other marketing-related areas, such as conferences or operations, which also have discrete budgets? Returning to the marketing budget, how is this set? How is the amount of budget agreed at the start of the year or other time period?

Methods of setting the marketing budget

This might be seen as a precise exercise executed to a laid down formula, but there are a number of different starting points for setting a budget, and many other variations in approach.

Historically based budgets

This method in its simplest form is very widely used. The previous year's budget is taken as a starting point, and then allowance made for inflation, so our budget becomes last year's budget +5 per cent. Sometimes the cost of media is not in line with inflation and rises at a faster rate or, especially in competitive situations, at a lower rate. This is known as *media inflation*.

Percentage of sales historical

Here the marketing budget is set at a certain percentage of sales revenue. This varies between industry sectors, and is usually between 1 per cent and 5 per cent. The basis for calculating the budget is historical, from the past. This could be last year's sales to give an annual figure. Alternatively, the figure could be constantly adjusted, as more recent figures become available.

Percentage of sales future

Similar in principle to the above, this works on sales projections for the future rather than the past. This therefore allows other factors to be taken into consideration, such as LEPEST factors and competitor activity, as these are taken into account when making the sales forecast upon which the budget is based.

As much as possible

This is linked to an organization's attitude towards and belief in marketing as an investment in the future just as much as other types of investment in buildings, new products and services.

As little as possible

The opposite of the above, and still a prevalent attitude, particularly in sectors which traditionally have spent very little, such as professional services.

Task/objective

The starting point here is what needs to be achieved. In a given year, there may be a need to launch a new product, open new outlets, expand into new, possibly international, markets. These needs are taken into account when planning the budget.

Peer parity

Here the budget is set according to what competitors spend. Market share is compared to share of voice.

> **Definition**
>
> **Share of voice** – You will no doubt be familiar with the term *market share*, which is a way of measuring your performance against competitors in your market. This would usually be expressed as a percentage; for example, Smith and Jones have a 10 per cent share of the UK tableware market. Share of voice would be calculated as Smith and Jones' share of the total amount spent on advertising tableware in the UK. This may well be other than 10 per cent and, if so, there is an argument that it should fall into line. However, a small player in a market, especially a newcomer, has to spend more to be noticed, while the market leader with well-known products and brands needs to spend proportionately less.

Advertising expenditure figures are published by MEAL, but with the trend towards new and diverse media, and the rise in the use of direct marketing, it is becoming increasingly difficult to estimate rivals' expenditure.

Co-operative advertising

This is a means of two parties gaining more for their advertising budget. Here the manufacturer gives a subsidy to the retailer or distributor for advertising their products, thereby gaining greater, and controlled, coverage near to the point of sale. From the retailer's point of view, they are then able to effectively spend more, as a large part of their costs are met by their supplier.

Budget negotiation

Whatever methodology is used in deciding the marketing budget, it is just part of the entire organization's expenditure. Other departments, business units or divisions all have their own claims to make. Department heads have to make their claim to senior management, or even the board; this is known as bottom-up budgeting. On the other hand, a budget may be imposed from the top; this is known as top-down budgeting. In reality, budget setting is a combination of methods, but increasingly marketing has to make a more rigorous case for itself.

Unit 11 Introduction to budgeting

Activity 11.2

Setting the budget

The Great Garden Furniture Company imports a wide range of garden furniture, including deckchairs, barbecues and parasols, and sells them through a chain of ten stores situated in major towns in the UK. In 2002 they enjoyed sales of £5 million, which has risen, backed by a £50,000 marketing spend, to £10 million for 2003. Sales for 2004 are predicted to be £12 million.

MEAL figures show the following for 2003:

Sector: garden furniture

Company	Spend	Market share
B&Q	80,000	30%
GGFC	50,000	20%
ABC	70,000	25%
Others	50,000	25%

Task

Using a method of your choice, recommend a marketing budget for GGFC for 2004.

Cost behaviour for marketing

An understanding of the basics of what happens to costs is important for marketers. It is generally true that the more we produce, import or sell (depending on the nature of our business), the more our costs will rise. Whilst it is stating the obvious to say that the more we do, the more it costs us to do it, it would also be widely expected that it becomes more economical to deal in larger quantities. If nothing else, our perceptions as consumers when buying food in larger packs would have us believe that this must be the case. However, when we start to look at a business's costs, we can see three distinctly different costs which behave in different ways. Let us now look at each of these in turn.

Definitions

Fixed costs – These are the costs which remain static, whatever the level of activity. For instance, if we have a warehouse, then it will cost the same to heat, light and pay rent on the property, whether it is empty, half-full or at maximum capacity.

Variable costs – These costs vary according to the level of activity. So if we are producing or importing, the costs of our raw materials, or the goods we import, will rise as we produce or import more.

> **Stepped costs** – This is a combination of the above two, but the result is costs which behave in a different, third way. Let us return to our factory. We have already seen how certain costs remain the same whatever the level of activity. Let us now assume that the production line has a capacity of one million units a year. The costs identified above would remain the same if we produced none, half a million, or a full million. However, if we wanted to produce more than a million, we would need a new production line or even a new factory. This would result in a sudden increase in costs, and this would be known as a stepped cost. It would therefore be better to produce 999,999 units than 1,000,001, as the revenue from the extra two units would be extremely unlikely to cover the cost of a new factory.

A key task then is to sort out the various sources of expenditure involved in our business, as a first stage towards analysing our cost base.

Activity 11.3

GGFC continued

Returning to our previous example, how would you classify the following costs incurred by GGFC?

- Salaries for head office staff
- Wages for retail staff
- Commission on sales for retail staff
- Company annual bonus
- Heat and light for warehouse
- Transportation of goods from overseas
- Transport to retail outlets
- Rent on retail premises
- Cost of imported goods
- Telephone bill.

Try sorting the above list into the three categories: fixed, variable and stepped.

Exam hint

You need only a basic knowledge of costing methodologies at this stage of your studies as a grounding for the Advanced Certificate.

You need to be familiar with the concepts of marginal (break-even) costing, flexible budgeting and ways of apportioning costs.

The flexible budget

Building on what we have learnt about fixed and variable budgets, we can now explore the concept of a flexible budget.

Unit 11 Introduction to budgeting

Definition

Flexible budget – Is derived from an original or master budget which has been prepared. The master budget is for planned achievement and performance. The flexible budget is one which shows the financial consequences of a different scenario, for instance a shortfall in sales against budgeted sales.

To explore this further, let us look at XYZ Software, a high technology information company. Their fixed costs are $1 million per year, and their sales target is $4 million. Variable costs against this budget amount to £2 million for the year, giving a healthy profit of $1 million. What would be the consequences of achieving only 75 per cent of budgeted sales?

First, we need to separate fixed costs from variable, and in this example that is straightforward. The fixed costs would remain the same at $1 million, variable costs would be $1.5 million, giving total costs of $2.5 million, against sales of $3 million, giving a revised profit of $500,000. Similarly, a flexible budget could be prepared for sales higher than originally budgeted, the key point being to separate fixed and variable costs and to make allowances for any stepped increases in costs. These could occur if a second production line was needed or a further warehouse was required to cope with a dramatic increase in activity.

Worked example: Teddy Bear Emporiums

TBE have been established for four years and are about to embark on a major expansion. Currently they have five shops trading at full capacity, giving sales of £5 million per year. Cost of goods bought in is £2 million, and the head office costs £1 million to run while each shop costs £250,000 to operate for a full year. On 1 January the company plans to open five new outlets, but these are only expected to generate half the sales of established shops in their first year of trading. What will be the impact on TBE's profits of this expansion programme?

Answer
Current trading accounts are as follows:

£ Costs fixed		
Head office	1,000,000	
£ Costs stepped		
5 shops	1,250,000	
£ Costs variable	2,000,000	Sales 5,000,000
Total	4,250,000	Profit 750,000
Next year's projected accounts		
£ Costs fixed	1,000,000	
£ Costs stepped	2,500,000	
10 shops		

Now we need to consider what will be the expected sales next year. The five existing units will continue on capacity, generating £5 million, but the new shops will generate only half their potential, £2.5 million, giving total sales of £7.5 million. We can see from the initial information that the cost of goods bought by the retailer is 40 per cent of sales (£2 million versus £5 million), so we can assume that this cost for sales of £7,500,000 is £3,000,000, so our projected trading accounts can now be completed:

£ Costs variable	3,000,000	Sales	7,500,000
Total	6,500,000	Profit	1,000,000

Marginal costing

Here we examine what the difference is between the selling price and the direct costs of marketing or buying in the product. This is called the contribution. It is not profit as overhead costs are not included... then we see how many we need to sell to cover the overhead cost. This is known as the break-even point. For example, supposing we know direct costs for labour are to be £2 per unit of product and for direct materials £3 per unit of product. The estimated selling price is given at £10 per unit of product, and total overheads (production and non-production) are budgeted for the year ahead at £100,000. How can marginal costing help us decide how many units need to be sold (a) to break even and (b) to make a profit of £50,000?

Selling price per unit	£10.00
Less Direct cost per unit	
Labour	£2.00
Material	£3.00
Contribution	£5.00

Definitions

Contribution per unit = selling price per unit − direct costs per unit.

Total contribution = sales revenue − total direct cost.

To answer part (a), how many units we need to sell to break even, we need to calculate the number of contributions it will take to cover the overhead costs as follows:

- Break-even quantity = Total overhead costs/Contribution per unit
- Break-even quantity = 20,000 units = £100,000/£5

Therefore we can see that 20,000 units is the break-even point.

To answer part (b) we can use a table like the one below which provides a fuller breakdown of volume, revenue, cost, contribution and profit. We can read off that 30,000 units need to be sold to generate the required £500,000 profit.

Sales quantity	Revenue	TV cost	T contribution	Fixed cost	Profit/(loss)
0	£0	£0	£0	£100,000	−£100,000
5,000	£50,000	£25,000	£25,000	£100,000	−£75,000
10,000	£100,000	£50,000	£50,000	£100,000	−£50,000
15,000	£150,000	£75,000	£75,000	£100,000	−£25,000
20,000	£200,000	£100,000	£100,000	£100,000	£0
25,000	£250,000	£125,000	£125,000	£100,000	£25,000
30,000	£300,000	£150,000	£150,000	£100,000	£50,000
T35,000	£350,000	£175,000	£175,000	£100,000	£75,000

TV = Total variable; T = Total.

Unit 11 Introduction to budgeting

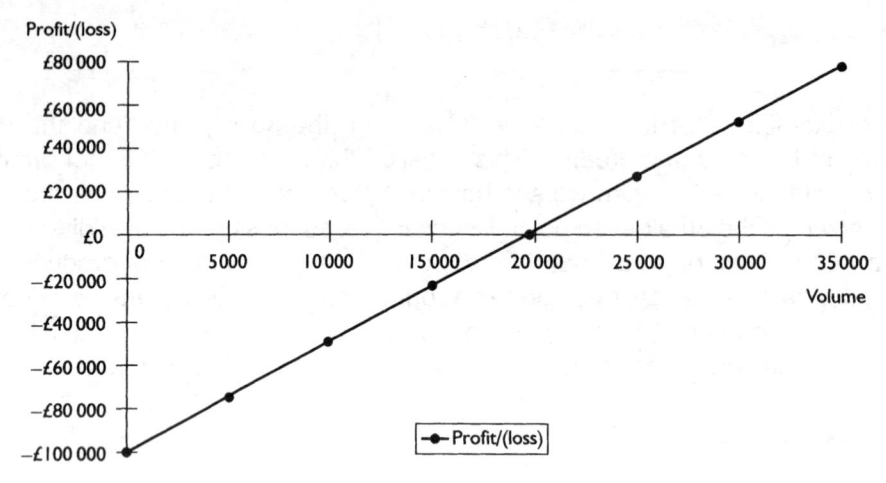

Figure 11.1 Profit/volume chart

The profit/volume chart in Figure 11.1 shows the profit or loss plotted against the sales quantities. The break-even point is where there is neither profit nor loss. In this case you can see that break-even is at 20,000 units of sale. Below the horizontal line represents loss, and above is profit.

The break-even chart shows the sales revenue, total cost and fixed cost lines across sales quantities. The break-even point indicated may be read as £200,000 sales value (being break-even this is also the total cost figure) or as 20,000 units of sale. The distance between the revenue and total cost line represents profit to the right of the break-even point, and loss to the left of the break-even point. The distance between the total cost line and the fixed cost line represents the variable cost. Break-even charts are useful to provide a visual picture of the key variables.

Apportioning the costs

Having gained a grasp of the basics of costing, we can return to more familiar territory and consider ways of evaluating the budget, whether this be an advertising budget, or a plan of action, as in the TBE example above. The prime method of evaluation is financial apportionment of costs. In today's trading environment accountability is of prime importance, and the marketer can no longer be excused for saying 'Half my advertising works, but I don't know which half'. In the quest for accountability and performance measurement, the first stage is to find a way of apportioning or sharing costs. There are several ways of doing this, as management accounting is as creative and flexible a discipline as marketing.

Apportioning advertising costs by space/time

Here let us take a press advertisement for a car manufacturer which produces three models, the 1, 2 and 3. If the advertisement just features the 2, then all costs can be apportioned to this car, which is treated as a brand, and a cost and profit centre in its own right. If the whole range is shown, then the advertising costs should be split three ways. However, the emphasis in the ad may not give equal status to the cars, so a different split may need to be made.

Apportioning marketing costs by ratio

Whilst advertising is straightforward as regards apportioning the major space or time costs, other costs incurred by the marketing department are less straightforward to split equitably. If the marketing department serves three business units in a company and one has double the sales of the other two, then the total costs of running the marketing department could be split in the same ratio.

Time-based costing

A possibility here is for the staff in a marketing department to log the time spent on projects for the different business units to be translated into an hourly service charge, so that the business units pay for what they use. Needless to say, this can cause problems and may even lead to business units deciding that they need less marketing support.

Activity-based costing

Here the basic activities involved in marketing tasks are broken down, such as writing a press release, briefing an agency, or carrying out desk research on a competitor. The total costs incurred by the marketing department on that activity in a year are calculated, then divided by the number of occasions on which the activity occurs. So, giving a cost for writing a press release as follows: time spent on press releases −200 hours; press releases produced −100; cost per hour −£35, we can then give an internal charge for writing a press release of £70.

When presenting a budget, the prime consideration will always be financial. What this will cost and what we will get in return expressed financially may well be the only information the board wishes to know. Remember that accounting is as flexible and creative a discipline as marketing, and there may well be different approaches needed to convince people. Almost certainly there will be alternative courses of action. Have these been considered and discarded with good reason, and is the chosen path the correct one? Also, have you considered what is the cost of not doing anything? There may be dire consequences of inactivity. Only when these have been considered can we move on to marketing and subjective reasons for our choice of action, such as company image and staff morale. Remember, though, that it is always the bottom line that usually counts first.

Summary

In this unit we have realized the importance of finance for the marketer. Without some working knowledge of the basics of costing and budgeting, other marketing-based arguments in favour of or against a line of action will not be heard. We have explored a variety of ways of arriving at a budget, and then examined how costs behave with different levels of activity. This then led to an exploration of flexible budgeting and cost apportionment. Finally, we looked at evaluating and presenting budget proposals and results. Throughout the unit there was a common thread of there being alternative ways of looking at the financial aspects of decisions just as much as there are different marketing approaches.

Unit 11 Introduction to budgeting

> **Further study and examination preparation**
>
> When you have completed this unit you will be able to answer Question 1a from the June 2002 examination paper, and also Question 1 from the December 2002 paper. Go to www.cimeduhub.com to access Specimen Answers and Senior Examiner's advice for these exam questions.

Extending knowledge

Publications such as *Marketing*, *Marketing Week* and *Campaign* can give you an idea of the amounts organizations are spending within their marketing budgets. These are published weekly and are available online through subscription.

unit 12
calculations in the examination

Learning objectives

In this unit you will:

- Perform calculation tasks of a similar standard to those in the examination
- Examine supplier costs
- Assess viability and effectiveness of marketing decisions
- Present your budgets.

By the end of this unit you will:

- Feel more confident about approaching numerical problems.

This unit covers sections 4.5.3, 4.5.4, 4.5.5, 4.5.6 and 4.5.7 of the syllabus.

This unit, like the previous one, covers the key skills Problem-solving and Improving own learning and performance.

Similarly, the statements of marketing practice participate in reviews of marketing activities using measurement data contribute to project planning and budget preparation.

Study Guide

It is difficult to estimate the time needed for this unit. This is a short unit, but the calculation exercises within it will greatly enhance your chances of high marks. Take your time, and if need be work in short spells. A typical student may take around three hours.

This is a short unit, but contains practical, applied exercises to help you learn from the experience of working out numerical answers.

This unit leads you into the final unit about the examination itself, and is designed to help students gain a grasp of what type of numerical skill is needed in Marketing in Practice.

Hopefully you will have followed the sequence of this book and undertaken the recommended activities. If so, you will already have gained a good grounding in the requirements and level of the section of the syllabus entitled 'Administering the marketing budget'.

As early as Unit 2 on 'Gathering information from inside and outside the organization' there were tables of figures for you to examine, and in Unit 4, 'Gathering and analysing financial and numerical information', there were show and hotel costings to work out.

In Unit 8, 'Marketing activities and events – exploring their diversity and application', you calculated the budget requirements of a stand at an exhibition.

In Unit 9, 'Co-ordinating the promotional effort', you were asked to work out detailed costs of newspaper advertising.

Unit 10 on 'Co-ordinating the marketing mix' featured pricing decisions and comparisions of performance as well as figures to translate into the PLC.

So, you have already gained considerable experience in dealing with exactly the sort of calculations you will need to do to gain a high grade in the examination. This unit consolidates on this with a series of activities for you to undertake.

Introduction

Activity 12.1

Preparing a budget for presentation to the marketing director

You work for the holding company that owns several chains of restaurants. The marketing manager has asked you to work out the annual advertising budgets for each chain according to a formula of:

- three per cent of food sales to be spent on marketing
- one per cent of drink sales to be spent on advertising.

Restaurant chain A

Good value food (approx. £5 per meal).

Sixty outlets fit this brand template, and typically serve 400 meals per week, while also taking £5000 on drinks per week.

Restaurant chain B

There are 30 outlets, mainly in city and town centres. These would average £4000 per week in drink sales, with food accounting for 20 per cent of turnover.

Restaurant chain C

Situated in more upmarket town centres, they are popular with women shoppers who call in for a sandwich, snack or a cake for £2, with some 200 such servings being made at a typical restaurant each week. At night they offer bistro-type food at around £10 per head, with some 50 meals per night being averaged by the chain of 40 outlets. Drinks account for a half of the brand's turnover.

Exam hint

Make sure you are working out exactly what is needed. These figures concern themselves with weekly takings for one restaurant in each chain. Remember that each chain comprises a different number of outlets and you have to multiply your figures for one restaurant by the relevant 'n' number.

Also remember that you need to provide an annual budget not a weekly one, so at the end you will need to multiply by 52 (the number of weeks in a year).

Activity 12.2

Examining supplier costs

Your finance director is concerned about the advertising budget, and you have been asked to investigate the possible cost savings of going 'à la carte' instead of using your current ad agency.

The agency, WBA Advertising, have given you costs of a campaign and you have asked for quotations from a creative shop and media buying company for the comparison. What is the difference in total cost?

WBA costings
Visuals	free
Artwork	£750
Photography	£575
Media	Expect to achieve 15% discount off rate card spend of £100,000

OR using a creative agency and a media buyer

Hotshop creative costings
Visuals	£200
Artwork	£650
Photography	£400

Media marvels costings
£1000 campaign handling fee
18% discount level projected

Unit 12 Calculations in the examination

Activity 12.3

Correlating promotional decisions against results

You work for a supermarket which sells packets of breakfast cereal for £2 each and this provides you with a 50 per cent profit margin. Normally you would expect to sell 1000 each month. During a recent promotion they were on offer at £3 for two packets. For the three months of the promotion, sales doubled. Did the promotion pay for itself?

Exam hint

This is a straightforward calculation, but can you spot all the numerical information? Some of the numerical information is 'disguised as words'. A tip then is to mark all the relevant numbers and 'word numbers' as follows.

You work for a supermarket which sells packets of breakfast cereal for £2 each and this provides you with a *50 per cent* profit margin. Normally you would expect to sell *1000* each *month*. During a recent promotion they were on offer and *£3* for *two* packets. For the three months of the promotion, sales *doubled*. Did the promotion pay for itself?

Activity 12.4

Your manager has asked you to evaluate four newspapers to see which offers best value in your town. These are tabulated below

Newspaper	Cost s.c.c.	Circulation	Readership	Pages
A	£2.00	20,000	40,000	32
B	£2.40	24,000	50,000	32
C	£2.50	30,000	75,000	48
D	£3.60	40,000	120,000	96

Activity 12.5

Boosting cinema audiences

The Picture House is an independant Cinema, with just one screen, and a capacity of 100 seats. It shows a film three times a day, in the afternoon, evening and night.

The cost to see a film is $3, with a third off for children (who comprise half of all audiences).

Only the Friday and Saturday night screenings are full, with other times averaging 40 people.

Currently, the cinema, with overheads of $2200 per week, is losing money.

Two alternatives are being considered to boost income.

1. Increase Friday and Saturday night charges to $5 per seat (with no special reductions for children). This will reduce attendances to ¾ capacity.
2. Kids go free with adults. Experience at other cinemas show this to increase attendances by 50%.

Summary

In this brief unit you have worked through three very realistic calculations of the kind you will face in the examination. To do this you have:

- Added
- Subtracted
- Multiplied
- Divided
- Worked out percentages
- Manipulated figures into comparable formats
- Pulled out 'hidden' numbers from text.

Now is the time to try a full examination paper – Go to www.cimeduhub.com to access Specimen Answers and Senior Examiner's advice for these exam questions.

You will notice that there is always a financial/numerical question in the compulsory part of the paper, be prepared for this. If you have worked through and can understand the four most recent papers, you should be well prepared for the examination.

appendix 1: guidance on examination preparation

Preparing for your examination

You are now nearing the final phase of your studies and it is time to start the hard work of exam preparation.

During your period of study you will have become used to absorbing large amounts of information. You will have tried to understand and apply aspects of knowledge that may have been very new to you, while some of the information provided may have been more familiar. You may even have undertaken many of the activities that are positioned frequently throughout your Coursebook, which will have enabled you to apply your learning in practical situations. But whatever the state of your knowledge and understanding, do not allow yourself to fall into the trap of thinking that you know enough, you understand enough, or even worse, that you can just take it as it comes on the day.

Never underestimate the pressure of the CIM examination.

The whole point of preparing this text for you is to ensure that you never take the examination for granted, and that you do not go into the exam unprepared for what might come your way for three hours at a time.

One thing's for sure: there is no quick fix, no easy route, no waving a magic wand and finding you know it all.

Whether you have studied alone, in a CIM study centre, or through distance learning, you now need to ensure that this final phase of your learning process is tightly managed, highly structured and objective.

As a candidate in the examination, your role will be to convince the Senior Examiner for this subject that you have credibility. You need to demonstrate to the examiner that you can be trusted to undertake a range of challenges in the context of marketing, that you are able to capitalize on opportunities and manage your way through threats.

You should prove to the Senior Examiner that you are able to apply knowledge, make decisions, respond to situations and solve problems.

Very shortly we are going to look at a range of revision and exam preparation techniques, and at time management issues, and encourage you towards developing and implementing your own revision plan, but before that, let's look at the role of the Senior Examiner.

Appendix 1 Guidance on examination preparation

A bit about the Senior Examiners!

You might be quite shocked to read this, but while it might appear that the examiners are 'relentless question masters' they actually want you to be able to answer the questions and pass the exams! In fact, they would derive no satisfaction or benefits from failing candidates; quite the contrary, they develop the syllabus and exam papers in order that you can learn and then apply that learning effectively so as to pass your examinations. Many of the examiners have said in the past that it is indeed psychologically more difficult to fail students than pass them.

Many of the hints and tips you find within this Appendix have been suggested by the Senior Examiners and authors of the Coursebook series. Therefore you should consider them carefully and resolve to undertake as many of the elements suggested as possible.

The Chartered Institute of Marketing has a range of processes and systems in place within the Examinations Division to ensure that fairness and consistency prevail across the team of examiners, and that the academic and vocational standards that are set and defined are indeed maintained. In doing this, CIM ensures that those who gain the CIM Certificate, Advanced Certificate and Postgraduate Diploma, are worthy of the qualification and perceived as such in the view of employers, actual and potential.

Part of what you will need to do within the examination is be 'examiner friendly' – that means you have to make sure they get what they ask for. This will make life easier for you and for them.

Hints and tips for 'examiner friendly' actions are as follows:

- Show them that you understand the basis of the question, by answering *precisely* the question asked, and not including just about everything you can remember about the subject area.
- Read their needs – how many points is the question asking you to address?
- Respond to the question appropriately. Is the question asking you to take on a role? If so, take on the role and answer the question in respect of the role. For example, you could be positioned as follows:

    'You are working as a Marketing Assistant at Nike UK' or 'You are a Marketing Manager for an Engineering Company' or 'As Marketing Manager write a report to the Managing Partner'.

    These examples of role-playing requirements are taken from questions in past papers.

- Deliver the answer in the format requested. If the examiner asks for a memo, then provide a memo; likewise, if the examiner asks for a report, then write a report. If you do not do this, in some instances you will fail to gain the necessary marks required to pass.
- Take a business-like approach to your answers. This enhances your credibility. Badly ordered work, untidy work, lack of structure, headings and subheadings can be off-putting. This would be unacceptable in the work situation, likewise it will be unacceptable in the eyes of the Senior Examiners and their marking teams.
- Ensure the examiner has something to mark: give them substance, relevance, definitions, illustration and demonstration of your knowledge and understanding of the subject area.
- See the examiner as your potential employer, or ultimate consumer/customer. The whole purpose and culture of marketing is about meeting customers' needs. Try this approach – it works wonders.

Appendix 1 Guidance on examination preparation

- Provide a strong sense of enthusiasm and professionalism in your answers; support it with relevant up-to-date examples and apply them where appropriate.
- Try to do something that will make your exam paper a little bit different – make it stand out in the crowd.

All of these points might seem quite logical to you, but often in the panic of the examination they 'go out of the window'. Therefore it is beneficial to remind ourselves of the importance of the examiner. He/she is the 'ultimate customer' – and we all know customers hate to be disappointed.

As we move on, some of these points will be revisited and developed further.

About the examination

In all examinations, with the exception of Marketing in Practice at Certificate level and Analysis and Decision at Diploma level, the paper is divided into two parts.

- Part A – Mini-case study = 40 per cent of the marks
- Part B – Option choice questions (choice of three questions from seven) = 60 per cent of the marks

Let's look at the basis of each element.

The mini-case study

This is based on a mini-case or scenario with one question, possibly subdivided into between two and four points, but totalling 40 per cent of marks overall.

In essence, you, the candidate, are placed in a problem-solving role through the medium of a short scenario. On occasions, the scenario may consist of an article from a journal in relation to a well-known organization: for example, in the past Interflora, EasyJet and Philips, among others, have been used as the basis of the mini-case.

Alternatively, it will be based upon a fictional company, and the examiner will have prepared it in order that the right balance of knowledge, understanding, application and skills is used.

Approaches to the mini-case study

When undertaking the mini-case study there are a number of key areas you should consider.

Structure/content
The mini-case that you will be presented with will vary slightly from paper to paper, and of course from one examination to the next. Normally the scenario presented will be 400–500 words long and will centre on a particular organization and its problems or may even relate to a specific industry.

The length of the mini-case study means that usually only a brief outline is provided of the situation, the organization and its marketing problems, and you must therefore learn to cope with analysing information and preparing your answer on the basis of a very limited amount of detail.

Time management

There are many differing views on time management and the approaches you can take to managing your time within the examination. You must find an approach to suit your way of working, but always remember, whatever you do, you must ensure that you allow enough time to complete the examination. Unfinished exams mean lost marks.

A typical example of managing time is as follows:

Your paper is designed to assess you over a three-hour period. With 40 per cent of the marks being allocated to the mini-case, it means that you should dedicate somewhere around 75 minutes of your time to both read and write up the answer on this mini-case. Some students, however, will prefer to allocate nearer half of their time (90 minutes) on the mini-case, so that they can read and fully absorb the case and answer the questions in the context of it. This is also acceptable as long as you ensure that you work extremely 'SMART' for the remaining time in order to finish the examination.

Do not forget that while there is only one question within the mini-case, it can have a number of components. You must answer all the components in that question, which is where the balance of times comes into play.

Knowledge/skills tested

Throughout all the CIM papers, your knowledge, skills and ability to apply those skills will be tested. However, the mini-cases are used particularly to test application, i.e. your ability to take your knowledge and apply it in a structured way to a given scenario. The examiners will be looking at your decision-making ability, your analytical and communication skills and, depending on the level, your ability as a manager to solve particular marketing problems.

When the examiner is marking your paper, he/she will be looking to see how you differentiate yourself, looking at your own individual 'unique selling points'. The examiner will also want to see if you can personally apply the knowledge or whether you are only able to repeat the textbook materials.

Format of answers

On many occasions, and within all examinations, you will most likely be given a particular communication method to use. If this is the case, you must ensure that you adhere to the requirements of the examiner. This is all part of meeting customer needs.

The likely communication tools you will be expected to use are as follows:

- Memorandum
- Memorandum/report
- Report
- Briefing notes
- Presentation
- Press release
- Advertisement
- Plan.

Make sure that you familiarize yourself with these particular communication tools and practise using them to ensure that, on the day, you will be able to respond confidently to the communication requests of the examiner. Look back at the Customer Communications text at Certificate level to familiarize yourself with the potential requirements of these methods.

Appendix 1 Guidance on examination preparation

By the same token, while communication methods are important, so is meeting the specific requirements of the question. This means you must understand what is meant by the precise instruction given. **Note the following terms carefully:**

- **Identify** Select key issues, point out key learning points, establish clearly what the examiner expects you to identify.
- **Illustrate** The examiner expects you to provide examples, scenarios and key concepts that illustrate your learning.
- **Compare and contrast** Look at the range of similarities between the two situations, contexts or even organizations. Then compare them, i.e. ascertain and list how activities, features, etc. agree or disagree. Contrasting means highlighting the differences between the two.
- **Discuss** Questions that have 'discuss' in them offer a tremendous opportunity for you to debate, argue, justify your approach or understanding of the subject area. *Caution*: it is not an opportunity to waffle.
- **Briefly explain** This means being succinct, structured and concise in your explanation, within the answer. Make your points clear, transparent and relevant.
- **State** Present in a clear, brief format.
- **Interpret** Expound the meaning of, make clear and explicit what it is you see and understand within the data provided.
- **Outline** Provide the examiner with the main concepts and features being asked for and avoid minor technical details. Structure will be critical here, or else you could find it difficult to contain your answer.
- **Relate** Show how different aspects of the syllabus connect together.
- **Evaluate** Review and reflect upon an area of the syllabus, a particular practice, an article, etc., and consider its overall worth in respect of its use as a tool or a model and its overall effectiveness in the role it plays.

Source: Worsam, Mike, *How to Pass Marketing*, Croner, 1989.

Your approach to mini-cases

There is no one right way to approach and tackle a mini-case study, indeed it will be down to each individual to use their own creativity in tackling the tasks presented. You will have to use your initiative and discretion about how best to approach the mini-case. Having said this, however, there are some basic steps you can take.

- Ensure that you read through the case study at least twice before making any judgements, starting to analyse the information provided, or indeed writing the answers.
- On the third occasion read through the mini-case and, using a highlighter, start marking the essential and relevant information critical to the content and context. Then turn your attention to the question again, this time reading slowly and carefully to assess what it is you are expected to do. Note any instructions that the examiner gives you, and then start to plan how you might answer the question. Whatever the question, ensure the answer has a structure: a beginning, a structured central part of the answer and, finally, always a conclusion.
- Keep the context of the question continually in mind: that is, the specifics of the case and the role which you might be performing.
- Because there is limited material available, you will sometimes need to make assumptions. Don't be afraid to do this, it will show initiative on your part. Assumptions are an important part of dealing with case studies and can help you to be quite creative with your answer. However, do explain the basis of your assumptions

Appendix 1 Guidance on examination preparation

within your answer so that the examiner understands the nature of them, and why you have arrived at your particular outcome. **Always ensure that your assumptions are realistic.**
- Only now are you approaching the stage where it is time to start writing your answer to the question, tackling the problems, making decisions and recommendations on the case scenario set before you. As mentioned previously, your points will often be best set out in a report or memo type format, particularly if the examiner does not specify a communication method.
- Ensure that your writing is succinct, avoids waffle and responds directly to the questions asked.

Part B

Again, with the exception of the Analysis and Decision case study, each Part B is comprised of six or seven more traditional questions, each worth 20 per cent. You will be expected to choose three of those questions, to make up the remaining 60 per cent of available marks.

Realistically, the same principles apply for these questions as in the case study. Communication formats, reading through the questions, structure, role-play, context, etc. – everything is the same.

Part B will cover a number of broader issues from within the syllabus and will be taken from any element of it. The examiner makes the choice, and no prior direction is given to students or tutors on what that might be.

As regards time management in this area, if you used about 75 minutes for the mini-case you should have around 105 minutes left. This provides you with around 30 minutes to plan and write a question and 5 minutes per question to review and revise your answers. Keep practising – use a cooker timer, alarm clock or mobile phone alarm as your timer and work hard at answering questions within the timeframe given.

Specimen examination papers and answers

To help you prepare and understand the nature of the paper, go to www.cimeduhub.com to access Specimen Answers and Senior Examiner's advice for these exam questions. During your study, the author of your Coursebook may have on occasions asked you to refer to these papers and answer the questions. You should undertake these exercises and utilize every opportunity to practise meeting examination requirements.

The specimen answers are vital learning tools. They are not always perfect, as they are answers written by students and annotated by the Senior Examiners, but they will give you a good indication of the approaches you could take, and the examiners' annotations suggest how these answers might be improved. Please use them.

Other sources of information to support your learning through the Virtual Institute are 'Hot Topics'. These give you scope to undertake a range of associated activities related to the syllabus and study areas, and will also be very useful to you when you are revising.

Appendix 1 Guidance on examination preparation

Key elements of preparation

One Senior Examiner suggests the three elements involved in preparing for your examination can be summarized thus:

- Learning
- Memory
- Revision.

Let's look at each point in turn.

Learning

Quite often students find it difficult to learn properly. You can passively read books, look at some of the materials, perhaps revise a little, and regurgitate it all in the examination. In the main, however, this is rather an unsatisfactory method of learning. It is meaningless, shallow and ultimately of little use in practice.

For learning to be truly effective it must be active and applied. You must involve yourself in the learning process by thinking about what you have read, testing it against your experience by reflecting on how you use particular aspects of marketing, and how you could perhaps improve your own performance by implementing particular aspects of your learning into your everyday life. You should adopt the old adage of 'learning by doing'. If you do, you will find that passive learning has no place in your study life.

Below are some suggestions that have been prepared to assist you with the learning pathway throughout your revision.

- Always make your own notes, in words you understand, and ensure that you combine all the sources of information and activities within them
- Always try to relate your learning back to your own organization
- Make sure you define key terms concisely, wherever possible
- Do not try to memorize your ideas, but work on the basis of understanding and, most important, applying them
- Think about the relevant and topical questions that might be set – use the questions and answers in your Coursebooks to identify typical questions that might be asked in the future
- Attempt all of the questions within each of your Coursebooks since these are vital tests of your active learning and understanding.

Memory

If you are prepared to undertake an active learning programme then your knowledge will be considerably enhanced, as understanding and application of knowledge does tend to stay in your 'long-term' memory. It is likely that passive learning will only stay in your 'short-term' memory.

Do not try to memorize parrot fashion; it is not helpful and, even more important, examiners are experienced in identifying various memorizing techniques and therefore will spot them as such.

Having said this, it is quite useful to memorize various acronyms such as SWOT, PEST, PESTLE, STEEPLE, or indeed various models such as Ansoff, GE Matrix, Shell Directional, etc., as in some of the questions you may be required to use illustrations of these to assist your answer.

Appendix 1 Guidance on examination preparation

Revision

The third and final stage to consider is 'revision', which is what we will concentrate on in detail below. Here just a few key tips are offered.

Revision should be an ongoing process rather than a panic measure that you decide to undertake just before the examination. You should be preparing notes *throughout* your course, with the view to using them as part of your revision process. Therefore ensure that your notes are sufficiently comprehensive that you can reuse them successfully.

For each concept you learn about, you should identify, through your reading and your own personal experience, at least two or three examples that you could use; this then gives you some scope to broaden your perspective during the examination. It will, of course, help you gain some points for initiative with the examiners.

Knowledge is not something you will gain overnight – as we saw earlier, it is not a quick fix; it involves a process of learning that enables you to lay solid foundations upon which to build your long-term understanding and application. This will benefit you significantly in the future, not just in the examination.

In essence, you should ensure that you do the following in the period before the real intensive revision process begins.

- Keep your study file well organized, updated and full of newspaper and journal cuttings that may help you formulate examples in your mind for use during the examination
- Practice defining key terms and acronyms from memory
- Prepare topic outlines and essay answer plans
- When you start your intensive revision, ensure it is planned and structured in the way described below. And then finally, read your concentrated notes the night before the examination.

Revision planning

You are now on a critical path – although hopefully not too critical at this time – with somewhere in the region of between four and six weeks to go to the examination. The following hints and tips will help you plan out your revision study.

- You will, as already explained, need to be very organized. Therefore, before doing anything else, put your files, examples, reading material, etc. in good order, so that you are able to work with them in the future and, of course, make sense of them.
- Ensure that you have a quiet area within which to work. It is very easy to get distracted when preparing for an examination.
- Take out your file along with your syllabus and make a list of key topic areas that you have studied and which you now need to revise. You could use the basis of this book to do that, by taking each unit a step at a time.
- Plan the use of your time carefully. Ideally you should start your revision at least six weeks prior to the exam, so therefore work out how many spare hours you could give to the revision process and then start to allocate time in your diary, and do not double-book with anything else.
- Give up your social life for a short period of time. As the saying goes 'no pain – no gain'.

Appendix 1 Guidance on examination preparation

- Looking at each of the subject areas in turn, identify which are your strengths and which are your weaknesses. Which areas have you grasped and understood, and which are the areas that you have really struggled with? Split your page in two and make a list on each side. For example:

Planning and control

Strengths	Weaknesses
Audit – PEST, SWOT, Models	Ratio analysis
Portfolio analysis	Market sensing
	Productivity analysis
	Trend extrapolation
	Forecasting

- Break down your list again and divide the points of weakness, giving priority in the first instance to your weakest areas and even prioritizing them by giving them a number. This will enable you to master the more difficult areas. Up to 60 per cent of your remaining revision time should be given over to that, as you may find you have to undertake a range of additional reading and also perhaps seeking tutor support, if you are studying at a CIM Accredited Study Centre.
- The rest of the time should be spent reinforcing your knowledge and understanding of the stronger areas, spending time testing yourself on how much you really know.
- Should you be taking two examinations or more at any one time, then the breakdown and managing of your time will be critical.
- Taking a subject at a time, work through your notes and start breaking them down into subsections of learning, and ultimately into key learning points, items that you can refer to time and time again, that are meaningful and that your mind will absorb. You yourself will know how you best remember key points. Some people try to develop acronyms, or flowcharts or matrices, mind maps, fishbone diagrams, etc., or various connection diagrams that help them recall certain aspects of models. You could also develop processes that enable you to remember approaches to various options. (But do remember what we said earlier about regurgitating stuff, parrot fashion.)

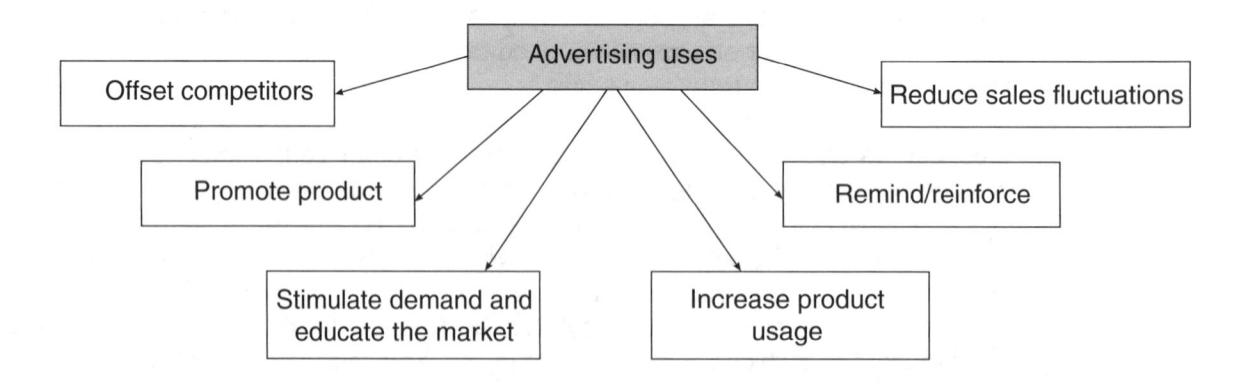

Figure A1.1 Use of a diagram to summarize key components of a concept
Source: Adapted from Dibb, Simkin, Pride & Ferrell, *Marketing Concepts and Strategies*, 4th edition, Houghton Mifflin, 2001

Figure A1.1 is just a brief example of how you could use a 'bomb-burst' diagram (which, in this case, highlights the uses of advertising) as a very helpful approach to memorizing key elements of learning.

Appendix 1 Guidance on examination preparation

- Eventually you should reduce your key learning to bullet points. For example: imagine you were looking at the concept of Time Management – you could eventually reduce your key learning to a bullet list containing the following points in relation to 'Effective Prioritization:'
    - Organize
    - Take time
    - Delegate
    - Review.

  Each of these headings would then remind you of the elements you need to discuss associated with the subject area.
- Avoid getting involved in reading too many textbooks at this stage, as you may start to find that you are getting confused overall.
- Look at examination questions on previous papers, and start to observe closely the various roles and tasks they expect you to undertake, and importantly, the context in which they are set.
- **Use the specimen exam papers and specimen answers** to support your learning and see how you could actually improve upon them.
- Without exception, find an associated examination question for the areas that you have studied and revised, and undertake it (more than once if necessary).
- Without referring to notes or books, try to draft an answer plan with the key concepts, knowledge, models and information that are needed to successfully complete the answer. Then refer to the specimen answer to see how close you are to the actual outline presented. Planning your answer, and ensuring that key components are included, and that the question has a meaningful structure, is one of the most beneficial activities that you can undertake.
- Now write the answer out in full, time-constrained and written by hand, not with the use of IT. (At this stage, you are still expected to be the scribe for the examination and present handwritten work. Many of us find this increasingly difficult as we spend more and more time using our computers to present information. Do your best to be neat. Spidery handwriting is often offputting to the examiner.)
- When writing answers as part of your revision process, also be sure to practice the following essential examination techniques:
    - **Identify and use the communication method** requested by the examiner.
    - **Always have three key parts to the answer** – an introduction, middle section that develops your answer in full, and a conclusion. Where appropriate, ensure that you have an introduction, main section, summary/conclusion and, if requested or helpful, recommendations.
    - **Always answer the question in the context or role set.**
    - **Always comply with the nature and terms of the question.**
    - **Leave white space.** Do not overcrowd your page; Leave space between paragraphs, and make sure your sentences do not merge into one blur. (Don't worry – there is always plenty of paper available to use in the examination.)
    - **Count** how many actions the question asks you to undertake and double-check at the end that you have met the full range of demands of the question.
    - **Use examples** – to demonstrate your knowledge and understanding of the particular syllabus area. These can be from journals, the Internet, the press, or your own experience.
    - **Display your vigour and enthusiasm for marketing.** Remember to think of the Senior Examiner as your Customer, or future employer, and do your best to deliver what is wanted to satisfy their needs. Impress them and show them how you are a 'cut above the rest'.

- Review all your practice answers critically, with the above points in mind.

Appendix 1 Guidance on examination preparation

Practical actions

The critical path is becoming even more critical now as the examination looms. The following are vital points.

- Have you registered with CIM?
- Do you know where you are taking your examination? CIM should let you know approximately one month in advance.
- Do you know where your examination centre is? If not find out, take a drive, time it – whatever you do don't be late!
- Make sure you have all the tools of the examination ready. A dictionary, calculator, pens, pencils, ruler, etc. Try not to use multiple shades of pens, but at the same time make your work look professional. *Avoid using red and green as these are the colours that will be used for marking.*

Summary

Above all you must remember that you personally have invested a tremendous amount of time, effort and money in studying for this programme and it is therefore imperative that you consider the suggestions given here as they will help to maximize your return on your investment.

Many of the hints and tips offered here are generic and will work across most of the CIM courses. We have tried to select those that will help you most in taking a sensible, planned approach to your study and revision.

The key to your success is being prepared to put in the time and effort required, planning your revision, and equally important, planning and answering your questions in a way that will ensure that you pass your examination on the day.

The advice offered here aims to guide you from a practical perspective. Guidance on syllabus content and developments associated with your learning will become clear to you as you work through this Coursebook. The authors of each Coursebook have given subject-specific guidance on the approach to the examination and on how to ensure that you meet the content requirements of the kind of question you will face. These considerations are in addition to the structuring issues we have been discussing throughout this Appendix.

Each of the authors and Senior Examiners will guide you on their preferred approach to questions and answers as they go. Therefore where you are presented with an opportunity to be involved in some activity or undertake an examination question either during or at the end of your study units, do take it. It not only prepares you for the examination, but helps you learn in the applied way we discussed above.

Here, then, is a last reminder:

- Ensure you make the most of your learning process throughout

- Keep structured and orderly notes from which to revise

- Plan your revision – don't let it just happen

- Provide examples to enhance your answers

Appendix 1 Guidance on examination preparation

- Practice your writing skills in order that you present your work well and your writing is readable
- Take as many opportunities to test your knowledge and measure your progress as possible
- Plan and structure your answers
- Always do as the question asks you, especially with regard to context and communication method
- **Do not leave it until the last minute!**

The writers would like to take this opportunity to wish you every success in your endeavours to study, to revise and to pass your examinations.

Karen Beamish
Academic Development Advisor

appendix 2
undertaking CIM assignments and the integrative project

Introduction – the basis to the assignments and the integrative project

Within the CIM qualifications at both Stage One and Stage Two there are several assessment options available. These are detailed in the outline of modules below. The purpose of an assignment is to provide another format to complete each module for students who want to apply the syllabus concepts from a module to their own or a selected organization. For either qualification there are three modules providing assessment via an assignment and one module assessed via an integrative work-based project. The module assessed via the integrative project is the summative module for each qualification.

	Entry modules	Research & analysis	Planning	Implementation	Management of Marketing
STAGE 3	Entry module– Stage 3	New syllabus to be launched in September 2004			
		Currently all modules assessed via examination route only			
STAGE 2	Entry module– Stage 2	Marketing Research & Information	Marketing Planning	Marketing Communications	Marketing Management in Practice
		All assessed via examination or assignment			*Exam/Integrative Project*
STAGE 1		Marketing Environment	Marketing Fundamentals	Customer Communications	Marketing in Practice
		All assessed via examination or assignment			*Exam/Integrative Project*
Introductory Certificate		Supporting marketing processes (research & analysis, planning & implementation)			

Adapted from the outline of CIM 'standard' syllabus, October 2002

The use of assignments does not mean that this route is easier than an examination. Both formats are carefully evaluated to ensure that a grade B in the assessment/integrative project route is the same as a grade B in an examination. However, the use of assignments does allow a student to complete the assessment for a module over a longer period of time than a three-hour examination. This will inevitably mean work being undertaken over the time-span of a module. For those used to cramming for exams, writing an assignment over several weeks which comprises a total of four separate questions will be a very different approach.

Each module within the qualification contains a different assignment written specifically for the module. These are designed to test understanding and provide the opportunity for you to demonstrate your abilities through the application of theory to practice. The format and structure of each module's assignment is identical, although the questions asked will differ and the exact type of assignment varies. The questions within an assignment will relate directly to the syllabus for that particular module, thereby giving the opportunity to demonstrate understanding and application.

The assignment structure

The assignment for each module is broken down into a range of questions. These consist of a core question, a selection of optional questions plus a reflective statement. The core question will always relate to the main aspects of each module's syllabus. Coupled with this are a range of four optional questions which will each draw from a different part of the syllabus. Students are requested to select two optional questions from the four available. In addition, a reflective statement requires a student to evaluate their learning from the module. When put together these form the assessment for the entire module. The overall pass mark for the module is the same as through an examination route, which is set at 50 per cent. In addition, the grade band structure is also identical to that of an examination.

Core question

This is the longest and therefore most important section of your assignment. Covering the major components of the syllabus, the core question is designed to provide a challenging assignment which both tests the theoretical element yet also permits application to a selected organization or situation. The question itself will require a written answer of approximately 2,500 words (Stage One) or 3,000 words (Stage Two) in addition to any further information you may wish to provide. This additional information should be in the form of appendices. However, the appendices should be kept to a minimum. Advice here is that they should be no longer than five pages of additional pertinent information.

Optional questions

There are a total of four questions provided for Stage One and Stage Two of the syllabus from which a student is asked to select two. Each answer is expected to provide a challenge although the actual task required varies. The word counts are also lower than the core question at 1,000 words (Stage One) and 1,500 words (Stage Two) respectively.

These are designed to test areas of the syllabus not covered by the core question. As such it is possible to base all of your questions on the same organization although there is significant benefit in using more than one organization as a basis for your assignment. Some of the

Appendix 2 Undertaking CIM assignments and the integrative project

questions specifically require a different organization to be selected from the one used for the core question. This only occurs where the questions are requiring similar areas to be investigated and will be specified clearly on the question itself.

Within the assignment there are several types of questions that may be asked, including:

- **A report** – the question requires a formal report to be completed, detailing an answer to the specific question set. This will often be reporting on a specific issue to an individual.
- **A briefing paper or notes** – preparing a briefing paper or a series of notes which may be used for a presentation.
- **A presentation** – you may be required to either prepare the presentation only or to deliver the presentation in addition to its preparation. The audience for the presentation should be considered carefully and ICT used where possible.
- **A discussion paper** – the question requires an academic discussion paper to be prepared. You should show a range of sources and concepts within the paper. You may also be required to present the discussion paper as part of a question.
- **A project plan or action plan** – some questions ask for planning techniques to be demonstrated. As such, the plan must be for the timescale given and costs shown where applicable. The use of ICT is recommended here in order to create the plan diagrammatically.
- **Planning a research project** – whilst market research may be required, questions have often asked simply for a research plan in a given situation. This would normally include timescales, the type(s) of research to be gathered, sampling, planned data collection and analysis.
- **Conducting research** – following on from a research plan, a question can require student(s) to undertake a research gathering exercise. A research question can be either an individual or a group activity depending upon the question. This will usually result in a report of the findings of the exercise plus any recommendations arising from your findings.
- **Gathering of information and reporting** – within many questions information will need gathering. The request for information can form part or all of a question. This may be a background to the organization, the activities contained in the question or external market and environmental information. It is advisable to detail the types of information utilized, their sources and report on any findings. Such a question will often ask for recommendations for the organization – these should be drawn from the data and not simply personal opinion.
- **An advisory document** – a question here will require students to evaluate a situation and present advice and recommendations drawn from findings and theory. Again, any advice should be backed up with evidence and not a personal perspective only.
- **An exercise, either planning and/or delivering the exercise** – at both Stage One and Stage Two exercises are offered as optional questions. These provide students with the opportunity to devise an exercise and may also require the delivery of this exercise. Such an activity should be evidenced where possible.
- **A role-play with associated documentation** – several questions have asked students to undertake role-plays in exercises such as team-building. These are usually videoed and documentation demonstrating the objectives of the exercise is provided.

Each of these questions related directly towards specific issues to be investigated, evaluated and answered. In addition, some of the questions asked present situations to be considered. These provide opportunities for specific answers relating directly to the question asked.

In order to aid students completing the assignment, each question is provided with an outline of marking guidance. This relates to the different categories by which each question is marked. The marker of your assignment will be provided with a detailed marking scheme constructed around the same marking guidance provided to students.

For both the core and optional questions it is important to use referencing where sources have been utilized. This has been a weakness in the past and continues to be an issue. There have been cases of plagiarism identified during marking and moderation, together with a distinct lack of references and bibliography. This becomes more important at Stage Two where the nature of the syllabus lends itself to a more academic approach. It is highly recommended that a bibliography be included with each question and sources are cited within the text itself. The type of referencing method used is not important, only that sources are referred to.

The reflective statement

This is the final aspect to each module assignment. The purpose of the reflective statement is for each student to consider how the module has influenced him or her as individuals and reflected upon their practice. A shorter piece of work than for other aspects at 500 words (Stage One) or 750 words (Stage Two), it is also more personal, in that your answer will often depend upon how you as an individual have applied the learning from the module to your work and other aspects.

A good reflective statement will comprise a number of aspects, including:

- Details of the theoretical aspects that you found beneficial within the module, and their reasons. If you have found particular resources beneficial state this and the reason why.
- How these concepts have affected you as a practitioner with examples of application of concepts from the module to your work and/or other activities.
- How you intend to progress your learning further after completing the module assessment.

When looking at the reflective statement your tutor or an assessor will try to award marks for your demonstration of understanding through the module together with how you have applied the theoretical concepts to practice. They are looking for evidence of learning and application over time, rather than a student simply completing the question because they have a deadline looming. The result of this marking tends to be that students who begin to apply the module concepts early often achieve higher marks overall.

Integrative project structure

The integrative project is designed to provide an in-company approach to assessment rather than having specified assignments. Utilized within the summative module element of each level's syllabus, this offers a student the chance to produce a piece of work which tackles a specific issue. The integrative project can only be completed after undertaking other modules as it will rely on information in each of these as guidance. The integrative project is approximately 5,000 words in length and was introduced from September 2002 at the Stage One level. It will be introduced from September 2003 at Stage Two with the commencement of the new syllabus. The integrative project is marked by CIM assessors and not your own tutors.

Stage One assignments – Marketing in Practice

Divided into five different elements, the Marketing in Practice module is the culmination of all other aspects of the Stage One syllabus. This module is assessed via a work-based integrative project. For each of the five elements, a sample question is given together with an evaluation of the type of answer that would be expected at this level. As the integrative project is based upon one organization only, the initial part of an answer will identify the organization and provide a clear background to its activities. From this further answers to questions will be developed.

Element 1 – Gathering, analysing and presenting information

Drawn from the Marketing Environment module, this element considers macro- and micro-environmental issues within the organization you have selected to base your project upon. Therefore questions will come from any part of the module. However, a typical question is shown below:

You are required to analyse the environment in which the organization operates. The purpose of the exercise is not to test your market-research skills. Rather it is to enable you to practise drawing conclusions from the application of environmental analysis techniques and models using information already available to you.

You should identify and apply appropriate environmental analysis techniques and models that enable you to analyse and draw conclusions about the environment. You should record your conclusions and the information or evidence used to reach them.

Specifically you should: Carry out MACRO and MICRO environmental analyses for the organization or a major market sector. This should include a brief commentary on each component of the environment together with the identification of major changes or developments likely to occur over the foreseeable future.

An answer to this element would be similar to any answer for the Marketing Environment module. However, here answers will relate directly to the activities of the organization within the project as a whole. A typical answer will include:

o Having given a basis to the organization, outline their business activities and areas of the macro- and micro-environment to be evaluated. This will require information on the environment detailing and gathering.

o Carry out a MICRO environmental analysis for the organization or a major market sector. This should include a brief commentary on each component of the environment together with the identification of major changes or developments likely to occur over the foreseeable future. The findings should be represented either diagrammatically or in a table. Ranking the environmental issues in terms of priority would also be advisable.

o Following on from this, a MACRO environmental analysis for the organization or a major market sector should be conducted. Cover the same aspects as above.

o The third stage of analysis is to identify the main opportunities and threats these environmental factors create for the organization. The rationale for their selection should be given. In addition, initial recommendations can be made, leading onto other aspects of the integrative project.

o The format of the whole project should be as a report and this question will only form one component of the entire project.

Element 2 – Building and developing customer relationships

This element is drawn from the Customer Communications module. As such, questions asked will again relate in part to any assessment from that particular module. However, this question will be related directly to the activities of the organization selected.

Identify the various stakeholder groups that exist for the organization and rank them in order of importance. Select one of the stakeholder groups identified above and describe its main interests, concerns and any demands, and the extent to which they can influence the organization and its activities. Suggest how the relationship with this stakeholder group may change in the future, and make recommendations as to how communication with this group could be improved.

This is a highly typical question building upon the foundations of the Customer Communications module. Requiring consideration of the organization's stakeholders, it builds upon the environmental analysis undertaken in Element 1. An answer is likely to consist of:

o Having already set the scene in Element 1, this question is a continuation of the work already written. Its purpose is to build upon the environmental analysis and evaluate the stakeholders influencing the organization.

o The first task is to identify the various stakeholder groups that exist and evaluate these. They may be shown diagrammatically or in a table. However, they do need to be evaluated in order to identify one stakeholder for further investigation.

o Following this, one of the stakeholder groups identified above should be selected. The answer should progress on to describe this stakeholders' main interest in the organization, any concerns the stakeholder is likely to have and any demands they present. In addition, the extent to which they influence the organization and its activities should be considered.

o Recommendations should suggest how the relationship with this stakeholder group may change in the future, and further recommendations as to how communication with this group could be improved should be made.

o The answer should continue with the format of the integrative project as each question comes together to form one entire answer. However, there should be an obvious gap between each answer.

Element 3 – Organizing and undertaking marketing activities

Drawing from the Marketing Fundamentals module, this element places marketing activities in the context of organizational planning and other operational activities. Questions will draw from these elements, and cover aspects such as the mission statement and objectives, as seen in the sample question below:

Give the organization's mission statement and/or aims together with a brief description of the organization itself, its constitution, size, markets etc. If you do not have a formal mission statement or aims, suggest suitable ones based on your discussions and research. Describe the sorts of operational marketing objectives set within the organization (e.g. sales, growth, market share etc). Describe how they are set and who sets them; consider the degree to which they support the overall mission and aims. Describe the marketing planning process used within the organization. Compare this with one of the various models available to marketers.

Appendix 2 Undertaking CIM assignments and the integrative project

Clearly an answer to this question will require an in-depth evaluation of the organization's activities. In addition, it is also advising that students undertake further research into the organization in order to identify planning activities and marketing objectives. A background to the organization has been given in the previous two elements and this question continues the answer from the previous two elements, whereby an answer will cover:

- The mission statement should be given, together with an explanation of the organizational objectives and/or aims. Where a mission does not exist, the analysis should lead to the construction of a mission statement.

- The marketing objectives will require evaluation. How are these objectives set? Research with marketing planners would be advisable here. In addition, relate these marketing objectives to the organizational mission and the organizational aims and objectives. Evaluating whether they support or don't support each other is advisable here.

- Following on from this, an answer would describe the marketing planning process used within the organization. Again this is likely to require research to provide an accurate answer.

- The next stage is to use a marketing planning model, with the intention of comparing the actual planning process used to the theory.

- Finally, recommendations should be made regarding planning activities within the organization. Further recommendations may centre around the setting of objectives and the mission statement.

Element 4 – Co-ordinating the marketing mix

Again drawing off the Marketing Fundamentals module, this element evaluates the use of the marketing mix within the organization already selected. Questions here will relate directly to activities from this module and are applied to the organization already selected for the integrative project. This leads to an example question of:

Carry out an assessment of the organization's recent marketing mix activities. Select a product or service (or group of products) from the organization and, using the information you have gathered in the previous tasks, comment on the performance of these product(s)/service(s) in terms of sales volume and profit.

An answer here will evaluate in detail the use of the marketing mix, concentrating on one particular product or service. Therefore a significant amount of information on at least one element of the organization's business will be required. As such, an answer will contain:

- An evaluation of the marketing mix (either 4 or preferably 7 Ps) and the marketing mix activities currently undertaken. Examples should be related to theory, preferably shown in a table to ease identification.

- Following on from this, one product/service is selected. Evaluated in more detail, this is evaluated in terms of performance.

- In addition, the previous tasks have centred upon external and internal environmental information, stakeholders and marketing planning. Therefore these need to be considered in detail for this product/service. Taking the aspect chosen, the influence of the macro- and micro-environment on this product/service needs to be considered in more detail than in the earlier question. How do stakeholders perceive this product/service. In addition, does it fit with the organization's mission statement and objectives?

o Finally, recommendations should be made following the findings.

o The question is presented as part of an entire report. However, it needs to be obvious that this is a separate question.

Element 5 – Administering the marketing budget (and evaluating results)

This is the final element of the Marketing in Practice module and the integrative project. It is designed to draw together all the other aspects into a budgeting mechanism. A question from this section will range around the use of budgeting and the process of budget-setting, as typified by the example question below:

Identify the method of budget setting used by the organization, and how this impacts on activities undertaken. Calculate the budget of the organization by another method. What would be the implications of this? Carry out an assessment of the marketing mix (4 or 7 Ps) and make recommendations for the coming year, including the implications for the marketing budget.

Clearly an answer here will require effective analysis of the earlier elements and questions. The ability to create an accurate budget will be dependent upon accurate planning, fed by clear environmental analysis. From the planning will come the process of developing the marketing mix activities. All these form an entire whole, as with the integrative project. An answer will include:

o An understanding and appreciation of the budgeting process, both in theory and within the organization selected for the integrative project.

o An evaluation of the organization's current budget-setting method. How does this operate and how effective is the process? An answer will also require the creation of a budget using an additional process.

o Building upon an answer in the marketing mix element question, significant issues resulting from the marketing mix should be highlighted. Have these been built into the budget using the original methodology? How would the organization cope with these additional budget changes?

o The final element of the answer would be to make recommendations to the organization regarding the budget setting process.

o The question is then bound with the other questions forming the entire integrative project. It should be referenced where possible and submitted as a whole document.

These provide a selection of the types of questions that are included within the integrative project at Stage One of the CIM syllabus in the Marketing in Practice module. Please note that the questions will not appear in exactly this format; these are provided as a guide only.

Appendix 2 Undertaking CIM assignments and the integrative project

Use of case studies

For anyone who is not working or has difficulty in gaining access to information on their or another organization, there are a number of case studies available which allow the completion of a module using a case-based approach rather than basing it upon an organization identified by the student. These case studies are provided on a request-only basis through your accredited CIM centre and should only be used as a last resort. Using a case study as the basis for your assignment will not mean an easier approach to the assignment. However, they do provide an opportunity to undertake assignments when no other alternative exists. Each case study comes with a certain amount of information which can be used specifically for the completion of a question. Additional information may need to be assumed or researched in order to create a comprehensive assignment.

Submission of assignments/integrative project

The following information will aid yourself, your tutor who marks your work and also the CIM assessor who will be moderating your work and moderating the integrative project. In addition the flow diagram represents the process of an assignment/integrative project from start to final mark.

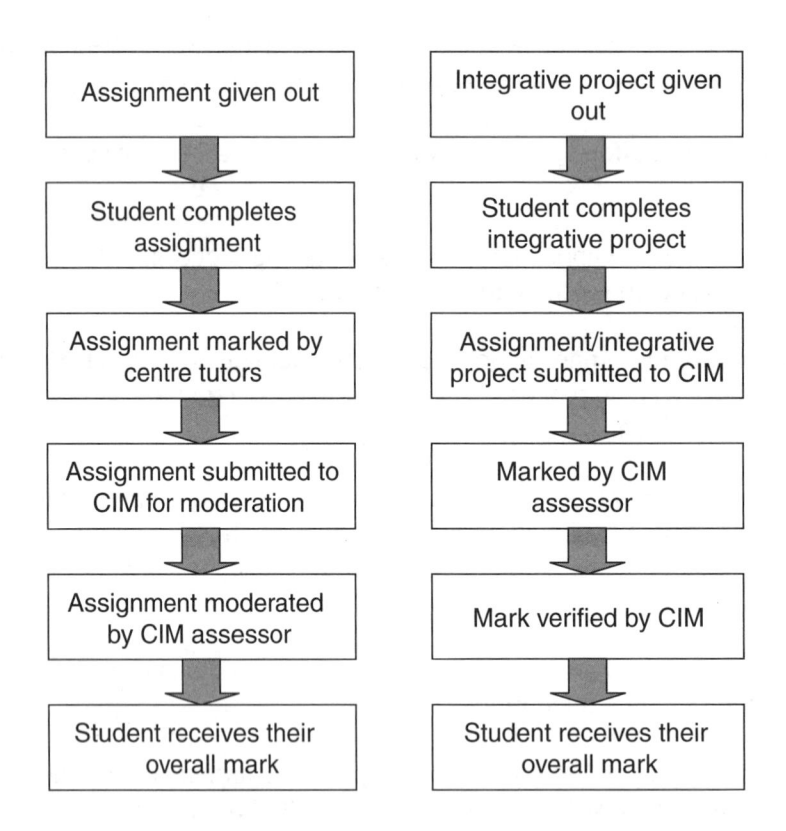

Assignment process	Integrative project process
Assignment given out	Integrative project given out
Student completes assignment	Student completes integrative project
Assignment marked by centre tutors	Assignment/integrative project submitted to CIM
Assignment submitted to CIM for moderation	Marked by CIM assessor
Assignment moderated by CIM assessor	Mark verified by CIM
Student receives their overall mark	Student receives their overall mark

Appendix 2 Undertaking CIM assignments and the integrative project

When completing and submitting assignments or the integrative project, refer to the following for guidance:

- Read through each question before starting out. Particularly with the core question there will be a considerable amount of work to undertake. Choose your optional questions wisely.

- Answer the question set and use the mark guidance given regarding the marking scheme.

- Reference each question within the assignment and use a bibliography.

- Complete all documentation thoroughly. This is designed to aid both the CIM and yourself.

- Ensure that the assignment is bound as per instructions given. Currently assignments are requested not to be submitted in plastic wallets or folders as work can become detached or lost. Following the submission instructions provided aids both CIM administrators and the CIM assessor who will be marking (integrative project) or moderating (assignments) your work.

- Complete the candidate declaration sheet showing that you have undertaken this work yourself. **Please note that if you wish the information contained in your assignment to remain confidential you must state this on the front of the assignment.** Whilst CIM assessors will not use any information pertaining to your or another organization, CIM may wish to use the answer to a question as an example.

An assignment will be marked by a tutor at your CIM centre followed by moderation by a CIM assessor. The integrative project will be marked by a CIM assessor as per an examination with moderation by the CIM. To ensure objectivity by CIM assessors there exists a mark-in meeting prior to any marking in order that standardization can occur. The senior assessor for each subject also undertakes further verification of both examinations and assessments to ensure parity between each type of assessment.

David C. Lane
Senior Moderator (Advanced Certificate)
February 2003

appendix 3
answers and debriefings

The answers that follow are indicative and are not intended to be complete. Some of the answers to the activities are embedded in the course materials, the essential text, in websites or simply in the mind of the reader.

Unit 1

Debriefing Activity 1.1

Clearly there are no right or wrong answers to this question. But you might like to reflect on the areas of difference between your job role and the areas of the syllabus. This should help you to identify your key learning needs, whilst also assisting you in drawing on your own experiences. Remember that learning does not just take place when you are reading a book or a tutor is talking, you have already learnt a great deal informally and will continue to do so.

Unit 2

Debriefing Activity 2.1

This will vary depending on the job you do. An example of what your result might look like is shown below.

Item	Why?	When?	Who?	Where?
Sales reports	Compilation of competitor intelligence and sales figures	1st week of each month	Regional sales representatives	Sent copies automatically
Database updates	Updates of contact information to ensure professional approach	Every Friday	All staff	Sent copies automatically*
Budget variance reports	Check progress to budget	End of each month	Accounts dept	Internal

Appendix 3 Answers and debriefings

Exhibition Bulletin	Details of UK and overseas exhibitions	Monthly	Self	Ordered from the London Bureau
Chemist & Druggist	To check competitor activity and trends in our industry	Weekly	Self	Ordered on subscription from publisher
Pharmaceutical Times	To check competitor activity and trends in our industry	Monthly	Self	Ordered on subscription from publisher

* I discovered that I don't know whether all notifications have been received at any one time.

The arrival of large numbers of updates at irregular intervals would suggest that some individuals are holding them until they have a number to submit. This can cause problems with data input and also could result in inaccurate information being sent out. I therefore decided to ask all individuals to send a 'Nil Return' at the end of a week when they have nothing to report. This means I can track whether everyone is sending information weekly as requested.

Other items included requests for information from customers and my manager, as well as other departments. I had also received information regarding exhibitions which we attended this year. They were trying to persuade us to have a stand during this coming year.

Debriefing Activity 2.3

The work you have done in this activity will depend on the articles you selected. However, the key points for you to remember are as follows:

- Your assistant is new, and so is unlikely to know much about marketing topics
- Key points that you have picked out for your summary should relate to your work role
- You should have remembered the KISS technique, and kept your summary short and simple
- You should have cut out all material that was irrelevant for your purpose
- You should have included all important points
- You should have omitted all diagrams, statistics and examples (unless they were important to what you are putting across, in which case you would probably include them in an appendix)
- Your document should flow logically.

Debriefing Activity 2.4

Ways to handle these types of behaviour are shown below:

Type of behaviour	Means of handling in a meeting
Aggressive	Challenge this behaviour assertively. Be prepared to manage this type of behaviour to allow less-confident participants to contribute.
Silent	Be careful not to make this participant feel as if he or she is being 'put on the spot'. If you are able to identify likely shy participants, try to encourage them before the meeting, or over coffee.

Appendix 3 Answers and debriefings

Abusive	Anger and abuse are sometimes deliberately used by participants to halt discussion. Stay calm. Be prepared to ask them to leave if the behaviour persists in disrupting proceedings.
Rambling	This can be a tactic to take the meeting away from its objective. Whether deliberate or not, be prepared to control discussion and remind participants of the objectives of the meeting.
Sniping	This can be behaviour associated with lack of confidence on the part of the participant. Sniping is a negative tactic that can be a result of misunderstanding about the objective of the meeting and its impact on the 'sniper'. Again, stay calm – remind participants of the objectives and the need to make positive progress within the time available. Recap on the facts of the situation.

It helps to research the individual members of the meeting beforehand. Sometimes you will know the participants, and you should use this information when planning the meeting.

Debriefing Activity 2.5

Prices

Daily rate for customized training	Competitor A	Competitor B	Competitor C
£750	£750	£350	£1500

There are, on further investigation, reasons for the differences in prices. Competitor B is a sole trader and does not have the same level of overheads to cover. However, equally, it does not have the strength and flexibility of our organization. Competitor C is an international business school with a well-known profile and existing client base of large blue-chip companies.

We already deal with different customer groups to Competitors B and C. Our priority is to deal with how we may best compete with Competitor A, who charges the same price as we do. How can we differentiate our service from theirs?

Debriefing Activity 2.6

This will vary depending on your industry and the size of the organization you work for. The list may include:

- Price
- Discounting policy
- Ability to supply in bulk
- Delivery in 24 hrs/7 days/28 days
- Quality of product
- Warranty
- Conform to ISO9000
- Hold IiP (Investors in People – UK award for training of workforce).

For suppliers of materials that are needed on a regular basis, criteria for continued supply may include:

- No evidence of supplier-responsible disruption to operations
- Continued evidence of commitment to cost-cutting strategies that do not impact on quality
- Continued commitment to training of their own staff
- Continued strong relationship at an individual buyer/supplier level.

Appendix 3 Answers and debriefings

Unit 3

Debriefing Activity 3.1

There are no right or wrong answers here. However, you will have immediately noticed that the Lite-stand is too tall, and the Easi-stand will take you over your budget of £1000. Your answer to this activity should either be a strong justification for exceeding budget, based on the benefits that this particular stand will offer your organization, or you will have presented the case for purchasing the Flexi-stand, on the basis that it is the only stand that meets all your criteria.

Unit 4

Debriefing Activity 4.1

There is no answer to this activity. Check the various types of chart that you have produced against the text in 'Assembling and presenting information' to see which is the most appropriate for your purpose.

Debriefing Activity 4.2

Your calculation should have been as follows:

Daily Planet (full page)	3 × $1200	$3600
Daily World (full page)	3 × $950	$2850
Daily Planet (quarter page)	12 × $400	$4800
Daily World (quarter page)	6 × $300	$1800
Weekly News (quarter page)	9 × $75	$675
Radio – 20-sec. slots	65 @ $1000 for 10 ($120 for 1)	$6000 + $600
		$20,325

Debriefing Activity 4.3

1. *Car manufacturers*
   The percentage of households owning cars is still growing, but at a much slower rate than during the 1970s. This means that car manufacturers are now marketing to an almost saturated market and it is much more important to differentiate themselves from other manufacturers.

2. *Manufacturers of 'entertainment' systems*
   Entertainment systems might be seen to include TV, video, home computers and compact disc players. There appears to be little room for growth in any market other than home computers and CD players. Manufacturers need to examine their firm's capabilities and see whether they are able to move into production of these goods. If not, they may again need to consider how they differentiate themselves from other competitors.

Appendix 3 Answers and debriefings

Unit 5

Debriefing Activity 5.1

None of the activities in this unit has definitive answers. Your answer will be specific to your own organization. Check back in the text to ensure that you have covered all aspects of the activity before proceeding with the next unit.

Unit 6

Debriefing Activity 6.1

None of the activities in this unit has right or wrong answers as they will be written specifically about you and your own work situation. Compare your answers to the text in the relevant section of this unit to ensure that you have covered all aspects.

Unit 7

Debriefing Activity 7.1

Objectives may be set around the following:

- Sponsoring a local football team – raising awareness of the company, associating the success of the team with the success of the company's products
- A stand at a trade show – generating enquiries, sales leads and eventually sales
- Presence in a shopping mall – taking the product to an audience that might not wish to visit your premises, generating enquiries
- A series of seminars – generating an understanding or conviction about a more complex product or service offer.

Doubtless you can add to this list, depending upon the specifics.

Debriefing Activity 7.2

Tata could use DAGMAR as a framework for setting their objectives and as they know the cost of attending is £10,000 they could actually work backwards through the DAGMAR model to justify the cost of attending.

If we assume that each vehicle has a profit margin of £2000, then they need to sell five vehicles for the event to pay for itself. In order to sell a vehicle, the customer needs to test drive it and Tata know that one in four test drives results in a sale, so at least 20 test drives need to be undertaken. Before a test drive can happen a customer needs to make an enquiry, only one in five of which leads to a test drive, so we need 100 enquiries.

So the objectives could be stated as:

- Generate 100 enquiries (comprehension)
- Book 20 test drives (conviction)
- Achieve five sales (action).

The above are hard accountable objectives which carry a great deal of weight. Additionally, we can have other objectives which are less measurable concerning awareness of a comparatively unknown brand.

Debriefing Activity 7.3

The situation here is one of mistrust and a need to rebuild. The objectives would centre around raising morale and communicating the benefits of the new product.

- o To raise morale of workforce
- o To unite workforce with a common purpose
- o To generate team spirit and enthusiasm for a shared goal
- o To communicate the benefits of the new product to the sales force.

The strategy would probably be a conference at a neutral location, probably with a social element. The tactics would comprise the details of this while the Ms would cover the resources needed.

The objectives set above are still a little vague, but the setting of objectives and the measurement of results are inextricably linked. So it may be that we need to do a 'health check' on employees' views to ascertain current feelings. This would give a basis, e.g. 5/10 employeees fear for their future, which could form the basis of an objective of raising this to 8/10, and subsequent future measurement.

Debriefing Activity 7.4

Your answer is personal to you, but if you were looking at an advertising campaign, you may need to consider WHY are you advertising. To maintain sales? Generate interest in a new product? To communicate new features? WHAT you are advertising may seem obvious, but WHY are you doing it? Should your efforts not go elsewhere? WHERE would refer to media selection and WHO refers to the target audience, but again continue to question WHY? WHEN makes us consider the timing, e.g. prior to Christmas for many products, and HOW MUCH refers to the budget implications.

Debriefing Activity 7.7

The following is an estimate of costs

Venue hire	$5000
Food/drink (150@$50)	$7500
Accomodation (6@$75)	$450
Printing	$10,000
Set design	$12,000
Production	$15,000
Total	$49,950

NB: staff costs are not included.

Appendix 3 Answers and debriefings

Debriefing Activity 7.8

This is about having different objectives and different target audiences. Ford are a mass market brand, who with their Ka and Fiesta appeal to young, first time car buyers, more reflected in a television audience for football. Volvo is a much smaller, more upmarket brand which appeals to a conservative, older, wealthier profile. This would be more closely reflected on a golf course than around a football pitch.

Debriefing Activity 7.9

	Entry modules	Research & analysis	Planning	Implementation	Management of Marketing
STAGE 3	Entry module– Stage 3	\multicolumn{4}{c}{New syllabus to be launched in September 2004}
		Currently all modules assessed via examination route only			
STAGE 2	Entry module– Stage 2	Marketing Research & Information	Marketing Planning	Marketing Communications	Marketing Management in Practice
		All assessed via examination or assignment			*Exam/Integrative Project*
STAGE 1		Marketing Environment	Marketing Fundamentals	Customer Communications	Marketing in Practice
		All assessed via examination or assignment			*Exam/Integrative Project*
Introductory Certificate		Supporting marketing processes (research & analysis, planning & implementation)			

Figure A3.1 Planning chart for sales conference

Unit 8

Debriefing Activity 8.1

Conference at home

Advantages	Disadvantages
Closer for most staff to attend	Overseas staff have to make complex travel arrangements
Easier logistics and planning	Not so memorable as a venue
Less time spent/lost travelling	
Nearer to home/head office support	
Usually less expensive	

210

Foreign location

Advantages	Disadvantages
Can offer good value	Will be expensive
More memorable	Logistics and planning harder
More motivating	Greater travel time lost

The above is by no means a complete list. However, it does demonstrate the exam technique of making a number of points succinctly, and this type of layout finds favour with CIM examiners.

Debriefing Activity 8.2

We may wish our employees' families to enjoy their visit with a dedicated play area, whilst we may wish to allay the local community's fears about pollution with an exhibition on the environment. This would also be suitable for any pressure groups such as Friends of the Earth who may have worries about us.

Debriefing Question 8.1

There could be several different approaches to this question. You may choose to start with a financial objective of raising funds for the hospital. Alternatively, you may go down the DAGMAR model and write down your objectives. You may prefer to assign different objectives to different target groups, such as staff, patients, their parents, the general public. What is important to remember is that this is a product nobody really wants for their children.

Debriefing Activity 8.3

It is useful to integrate knowledge gained from other sources into your studies for this subject, so talk to other people in your organization and keep an eye open for other exhibitions and store launches to attend as a visitor.

Debriefing Activity 8.4

Airbus Industries at Dubai may have the following approach:

- Objectives are likely to centre around goodwill and entertaining existing customers. It is unlikely that sales would be expected although such trade fairs are when large orders are announced.
- Activities would primarily be hospitality based and targeted at a very small number of airline buyers.
- Staffing would be undertaken by technically conversant experts who were able to handle difficult questions.
- Logistics would be a major part of planning if large aircraft are to be moved around the world.

Appendix 3 Answers and debriefings

Proton at the Malaysian Grand Prix would have a different approach:

- Objectives could focus on generating enquiries and sales but another objective would be to link perceptions of speed and modern technology with their brand.
- Activities would be aimed at the car-buying public and could include interactive displays, competitions and games. There would probably be small value gifts to give to those enquiring.

Debriefing Question 8.2

There is a variety of different staffing permutations. However, we cannot staff the entire show with salespeople as this would cost €2300 per person (€1k wages + €1050 expenses + €250 flight). Two sales staff would probably be needed to cover detailed product enquiries, whilst promising graduate recruits could also help, backed by relatively inexpensive agency staff.

Debriefing Activity 8.6

Measuring the success of a new outlet launch

The most obvious measurement is that of sales in the first few weeks of trading. Linked to this is profits made. Other measurements could include the number of people visiting the store, known as 'footfall'. The size of the average transaction could be easily obtained and compared to other stores owned by Manchester United. Other ratios could be analysed, such as the ratio of those making a purchase compared to those leaving without buying anything.

Unit 9

Debriefing Activity 9.1

The obvious message from this advertisement is that the car has good brakes and from this we infer messages of safety.

On another level of understanding it is possible to infer, by use of forest imagery, that Ford has an environmentally sound philosophy.

However, those more knowledgeable about cars would remember the stories about the Mercedes A class which during testing ran into problems, losing control when swerving to avoid reindeer in Finland.

So did you get the coded message that Ford is better than Mercedes?

But there are other ads which you understand and others don't; why not talk to some of your friends to see if they pick up hidden messages?

Debriefing Activity 9.2

Attention could be gained with a direct invocation to the target audience with a headline such as 'Do you work in IT?'. Interest could be stimulated with an indication of the salaries on offer, whilst desire could be created with the copy (detailed wording) of the ad. Action would be visiting their website, and this should be prominent.

Appendix 3 Answers and debriefings

Debriefing Activity 9.3

There is no right or wrong answer to this activity. It will vary from advertisement to advertisement. However, if you are unsure, refer back to the text on the AIDA model before proceeding with the unit.

Debriefing Activity 9.4

An ad agency is likely to make a better job of producing creative work, but is likely to cost more. In-house designers produce good work, but are prone to becoming bored with the lack of variety in their work. Media often produce free artwork, but the quality is dubious. Overall, different approaches suit different organizations, but overriding considerations are cost and control.

Debriefing Activity 9.5

While this course does not aim to turn you into a graphic designer or copy writer it is useful to have a practical understanding of putting a simple ad together.

For MONSTER.COM

Attention could be grabbed by using a **benefit headline**, such as 'Earn more money', 'Move your career forward'.

Interest could be obtained by illustrations which show people in professional jobs, or by specific copy on the kind of jobs and the success rate of users of monster.com's services.

Desire could be stimulated by quoting specific salaries and job locations.

Finally, for a dotcom operation, the only outcome for action has to be a visit to the website.

Debriefing Activity 9.6

1. £30.55
2. £1428
3. This is highly subjective. But remember to use the commercial and industrial property rate.
4. Again highly subjective and in need of further information to work out. You would really need to see the newspapers, evaluate their circulation figures and check out rivals' activities before firming your plan. Also, you would need to know when sales peaks/dips are likely to occur for that industry so that advertising expenditure can be matched.

Debriefing Activity 9.7

Your response to these activities very much depends on who you work for, what business they are in and what products or services they market. If you are studying at a college, then it would be very useful to compare and contrast your experiences with others.

Appendix 3 Answers and debriefings

Debriefing Activity 9.8

Your response to these activities very much depends on who you work for, what business they are in and what products or services they market. If you are studying at a college, it would be very useful to compare and contrast your experiences with others.

Unit 10

Debriefing Activity 10.1

If you are unsure of anything, refer to the Marketing Fundamentals coursebook.

Debriefing Activity 10.2

Your response would vary according to who you are employed by, etc. However, remember that you learn from a variety of sources and in different ways, so what you take for granted about your organization is actually valuable learning that cannot be found in a textbook.

Debriefing Activity 10.3

- A is in decline
- B is in the introduction phase
- C appears to be in maturity
- D is in the introductory phase
- E appears to be growing (although the next set of figures may show it to have peaked)
- F seems to have a cyclical pattern.

The above demonstrates that it is not always straightforward to apply this concept, and if undertaking this exercise with others you probably did not always agree.

Debriefing Activity 10.4

An initial glance at the figures in Activity 10.4 shows that three of the countries are much larger than the other two. It is logical to assume, therefore, that media costs would be much higher. Also, the UK is not typical of Europe in that it has a much higher percentage of vegetarians than the rest of the countries mentioned. The number of cats and dogs is equal in the total, but varies in France and Germany. This leaves Luxembourg and the Czech Republic, and the former is more typical of Europe as a whole in terms of numbers of vegetarians and ratios of dogs and cats to the human population.

Debriefing Activity 10.5

Your response would vary according to who you are employed by, etc. However, remember that you learn from a variety of sources and in different ways, so what you take for granted about your organization is actually valuable learning that cannot be found in a textbook.

Debriefing Activity 10.8

Before calculating the effects of any adjustment to pricing, it is worthwhile clarifying the current situation:

Buy-in	Mark-up	Sell-out	Retail	Sales p.m.	Profit p.m.
0.15	0.10	0.25	0.35	100,000	£10,000

The important point here is that we, the wholesalers, make 10p on each bar of chocolate, resulting in £10,000 profit per month (100,000 × 0.10).

Option 1: price rise

0.17 0.13 0.30 0.40 90,000 £11,700

Here, the 20 per cent rise to retailers has pushed this price up to 30p, giving us a new mark-up of 13p. However, sales have fallen by 10 per cent (1p rise = 2% drop, so 5p rise = 10% drop).

Nevertheless, this gives a monthly profit of £11,700, which equates to £35,100 over the three-month period.

Option 2: price cut

0.17 0.08 0.25 0.33 108,000 £8,640

By cutting prices, demand is considerably stimulated (4p cut = 16% rise in demand), but the reduced margins only yield 8p per bar, giving £9280 profit per month, or £27,840 over a three-month period, a difference of £9180.

Of course, reality is often not so simple, and retailers may be reluctant to accept either a 10p hike in costs or a reduction in margins. Likewise, there are all the other elements of the mix to come into play, let alone environmental factors, especially competitor reaction.

Debriefing Activity 10.9

All these activities concern your experience as a consumer. Remember that quality is judged by the receiver, not announced by the provider, so turn this around and consider the way your customers are treated.

Debriefing Activity 10.10

The totals for each column are as follows

8250 90 585 200 100

Dividing this by 5 gives us a picture of the average franchise's performance:

1650 18 117 40 20

Perhaps most important here is that this gives us an idea of ratios; for example, approximately one employee for every 100,000 euros of turnover. Also, the advertising spend averages approximately 2.5 per cent of turnover, whilst profit is around 7 per cent.

Appendix 3 Answers and debriefings

Now, analysing the individual trading figures, we can see that branches 3 and 5 spend more than average on advertising, but branch 4 underspends on advertising (only 0.6 per cent) and also appears overstaffed. This needs further investigation.

Debriefing Activity 10.11

There is no set order for the importance of people in the transactions given, as this would very much depend on your own personal experience and viewpoint. Logically, the most 'service-driven' of these are the two examples from financial services – taking out a loan and buying insurance. This is because there is no physical product at all. However, even these experiences can be very different depending on whether this is done in person, by post, over the telephone, or via the internet.

Debriefing Activity 10.12

The temptation here would be to want to talk about 'everything I have learnt on the CIM programme' immediately. Whilst this may seem like a good idea, this activity asks *how* you would go about this, not *what* you would say. So if this were an exam question you would need to look at the whole process of planning your input. This could be split into the following key stages:

- Finding out about your audience (how much do they know already, what is their attitude to customers, to the company and to marketing)
- Setting objectives for what is to be achieved (how many delegates are to be trained, what key learning points you wish them to remember)
- Method of training to be utilized (i.e. conference, small groups, written materials or other distance-based package)
- Details on the specifics and logistics of delivering the training
- Measurement (how the effects of the training are to be measured).

By now you will probably realize that this is another application of the planning framework SOST + 6Ms, which can be used in many situations.

Unit 11

Debriefing Activity 11.1

The scope of marketing varies between organizations. Remember this when answering questions, and make it clear just what you include as marketing.

Debriefing Activity 11.2

The answer to this would depend on the method chosen.

Historically 2003 saw expenditure of £50,000. Assuming inflation of five per cent, this would give a budget of £52,500.

Percentage of sales based on previous year The £50,000 spend in 2003 was presumably based on the previous year's sales of £5 million, a one per cent rate of expenditure. Therefore the spend for 2004 should be set as one per cent of 2003's sales of £10 million, which comes out as £100,000.

Percentage of sales based on projection Here we have to assume that the sales of 10 million were predicted and a budget of £50,000 set accordingly. The projection for 2000 is 12 million, a 20 per cent increase, so the marketing spend should be in alignment at £60,000.

Peer parity First, it must be made clear that this is advertising spend, not marketing spend, hence the disparity between GGFC's spend according to MEAL of £40,000 against our known spend of £50,000. If we examine the MEAL figures, the total advertising expenditure in this sector is £240,000. Dividing this by 100 gives a spend per one per cent of £2400. The implication of this is that a 20 per cent player such as GGFC should be spending £48,000 (20 × £2400) on advertising. As this is 20 per cent higher than the figure registered, we can logically assume that the £10,000 spent on other marketing activities also needs upweighting by 20 per cent to give a marketing spend of £60,000 to be in alignment with other competitors.

Other methods There is not sufficient information to consider task/objective, or other, more arbitrary methods.

Conclusion The different approaches provide different budgets, and knowing this can be a powerful tool for the marketer to negotiate from a position of strength backed by sound methodology.

Debriefing Activity 11.3

When attempting this, the important question is, as activity increases, will these costs do likewise? If the answer is 'no', then this is likely to be a fixed cost; 'yes' means a variable cost; whilst some may need further analysis and may even comprise elements of different cost behaviour. From the above list, salaries of head office staff, wages for retail staff, heat and light for the warehouse and retail rents are fixed costs, and as such would remain the same (unless of course there was a dramatic increase in activity necessitating a new warehouse or additional staff, in which case these would become stepped costs). It is also reasonable to assume that as activity increases, so commission payments and bonuses would increase. Transport costs would vary with the level of activity, becoming variable costs, although the cost of importing goods might increase in a stepped manner if importing is done by the container load. This then leaves the telephone bill. This is likely to comprise two elements and behave in just the same way as a domestic telephone bill, comprising a fixed element (line rental), plus a variable element for calls, which in a business could reasonably be expected to increase as sales increase.

Appendix 3 Answers and debriefings

Unit 12

Debriefing Activity 12.1

Chain A

Drinks	= £5000
Food	£5 meal × 400 £2000
Weekly advertising budget for one outlet	£2000 × 3% = £60 £5000 × 1% = £50 Total £110
Expenditure for chain	£110 × 60 × 52 = £343,200

Chain B

Drink	= £4000
Food	= £1000 (if food = 20% of budget then drink must = 80%, so if 80% = £4000, then 20% must = £1000)
Weekly advertising budget for one outlet	£4000 × 1% = £40 £1000 × 3% = £30 Total £70
Expenditure for chain	£70 × 30 × 52 = £109,200

Chain C

Drink	= £3900
Food	= £2 × 200 = £400 + £10 × 50 × 7 = £3500 Total £3900
Weekly advertising budget for one outlet	£3900 × 1% = £39 £3900 × 3% = £117 Total £156
Advertising budget for chain	£156 × 40 × 52 = £324,480

Debriefing Activity 12.2

	Option 1 (ABC)	Option 2 (à la carte)
Production costs	£575 + £750 = £1325	£200 + £650 + £400 = £1250
Space costs	£100,000 × 85% = £85,000	£82,000 + £1000 fee = £83,000
Total	£86,325	£84,250
Difference	£86,325 − £84,250 = £2075	

Appendix 3 Answers and debriefings

Debriefing Activity 12.3

Normal three months
£2 × 1000 × 3 = £6000 sales (£3000 profit)

Three months of promotion
£1.50 × 2000 × 3 = £9000 sales

but profit is now only 50p a packet and on sales of 6000 this is a profit of £3000, exactly the same as profit would be without a promotion. (Note for non-UK readers £1 = 100p.)

Debriefing Activity 12.4

This task is a classic example of ratio analysis. We need to find a common unit by which we can compare. In this case it is the cost to reach 1000 homes (the circulation figure gives this.) So paper A reaches 20,000 homes so we divide £2 by 20, this gives us a cost of 10p to reach 1000.

Circulation is easily measured and the results published. Less easy to measure and often the subject of wild claims is readership, i.e. how many people read the paper as it is passed around.

The results of the calculations are as follows:

Newspaper	cost per 1000 circ	cost per 1000 readers
A	10p	5p
B	10p	4.8p
C	8p	3.3p
D	9p	3p

From the above, it can be seen that if we take cost per 1000 circulation then C is best value, but for readership D wins.

However in an exam, good candidates would point out that an advertisement could easily get lost in a 96 page newspaper such as D. Also there is much we do not know, how much wastage for instance, and how credible are the newspapers, who else advertises in them etc, etc. Intelligent comments/assumptions/observations are worth marks in an exam, so share them with the examiner.

Debriefing Activity 12.5

Before looking at the two pricing alternatives we need to work out what the current income is.

Firstly, there are 21 screenings (7 × 3)

Two are full; 50 adults × $3 + 50 children × $1.50 × 2 = total $450

19 have 40 seats; 20 adults × $3 + 20 children × $1.50 total × 19 = $1710

total income $2160

219

OPTION 1

Increase Friday and Saturday night charges

2 × 75 × $5

total $750

plus other income as above $1710

total income

$2460

OPTION 2

kids go free

on Friday and Saturday nights, only 50 adults now pay $3 = $300

on 19 other screenings, 30 adults pay $3 = $1710

total income $2010

Conclusion: the first option puts the cinema into profit, despite reducing attendances. The latter has a dramatic effect on attendance but actually loses more money.

Again if this were an exam question, marks would be given for comments about the popularity of films, their suitability for children, or other factors which may affect the outcome.

appendix 4
curriculum information and reading list

Syllabus

Aim

The Marketing in Practice module is the application of marketing in context at Stage 1 and also forms the summative assessment for Stage 1. It aims to assist participants to integrate and apply knowledge from all the modules at Stage 1.

Participants will not be expected to have any prior qualifications or experience in a marketing role. They will be expected to be conversant with the content of the other three modules at Stage 1 before undertaking this module.

Related statements of practice

Hb.1   Contribute to project planning and budget preparation

Hb.2   Monitor and report on project activities

Hb.3   Complete and close down project activities on time and within budget

Jb.1   Collect, synthesize, analyse and report measurement data

Jb.2   Participate in reviews of marketing activities using measurement data

Kb.1   Exchange information to solve problems and make decisions

Kb.2   Review and develop one's skills and competencies

Kb.3   Embrace change and modify behaviours and attitudes

Learning outcomes

Participants will be able to:

- Collect relevant data from a variety of secondary information sources
- Analyse and interpret written, visual and graphical data

Appendix 4 Curriculum information and reading list

- o Devise appropriate visual and graphical means to present marketing data
- o Make recommendations based on information obtained from multiple sources
- o Evaluate and select media and promotional activities appropriate to the organization's objectives and status and to its marketing context
- o Calculate and justify budgets for marketing mix decisions
- o Develop relationships inside and outside the organization
- o Apply planning techniques to a range of marketing tasks and activities
- o Undertake basic marketing activities within an agreed plan and monitor and report on progress
- o Gather information for, and evaluate marketing results against, financial and other criteria.

Knowledge and skill requirements

Element 1: Gathering, analysing and presenting information (20%) (Marketing Environment)

1.1 Identify sources of information internally and externally to the organization, including ICT-based sources such as intranet and internet.

1.2 Maintain a marketing database, information collection and usage.

1.3 Investigate customers via the database and develop bases for segmentation.

1.4 Explain information gathering techniques available.

1.5 Source and present information on competitor activities across the marketing mix.

1.6 Investigate marketing and promotional opportunities using appropriate information gathering techniques.

1.7 Gather information across borders.

Element 2: Building and developing relationships (20%) (Customer Communications)

2.1 Describe the structure and roles of the marketing function within the organization.

2.2 Build and develop relationships within the marketing department, working effectively with others.

2.3 Explain the 'front line' role: receiving and assisting visitors, internal and external enquiries.

2.4 Represent the organization using practical PR skills, including preparing effective news releases.

2.5 Explain the supplier interface: negotiating, collaborating, operational and contractual aspects.

2.6 Explain how the organization fits into a supply chain and works with distribution channels.

2.7 Use networking skills in the business world.

2.8 Explain the concept and application of E-relationships.

2.9 Describe techniques available to assist in managing your manager.

Element 3: Organizing and undertaking marketing activities (20%) (Marketing Fundamentals)

3.1 Describe the scope of individuals' roles in marketing: meetings, conferences, exhibitions, outdoor shows, outlet launches, press conferences.

3.2 Identify alternative and innovative approaches to a variety of marketing arenas and explain criteria for meeting business objectives.

3.3 Demonstrate an awareness of successful applications of marketing across a variety of sectors and sizes of business.

3.4 Explain how marketing makes use of planning techniques: objective setting; and coordinating, measuring and evaluating results to support the organization.

3.5 Appraise and select a venue based on given criteria and make appropriate recommendations.

3.6 Explain how an organization should host visitors from other cultures and organize across national boundaries.

Element 4: Coordinating the marketing mix (20%) (Marketing Fundamentals)

4.1 Select the media to be used based on appropriate criteria for assessing media opportunities, and recommend a media schedule.

4.2 Evaluate promotional activities and opportunities including sales promotion, PR and collaborative programmes.

4.3 Explain the process for designing, developing and producing printed matter, including leaflets, brochures and catalogues.

4.4 Analyse the impact of pricing decisions and role of price within the marketing mix.

4.5 Describe the current distribution channels for an organization and evaluate new opportunities.

4.6 Describe how organizations monitor product trends.

4.7 Explain the importance of the extended marketing mix: how process, physical aspects and people affect customer choice.

4.8 Explain the importance of ICT in the new mix.

Element 5: Administering the marketing budget (and evaluating results) (20%)

5.1 Demonstrate an ability to manipulate numbers in a marketing context.

5.2 Explain the process used for setting a budget and apportioning fixed and overhead costs.

5.3 Explain how organizations assess the viability of opportunities, marketing initiatives and projects.

5.4 Prepare, present and justify a budget as the basis for a decision on a marketing promotion.

5.5 Make recommendations on alternative courses of action.

5.6 Examine the correlation between marketing mix decisions and results.

5.7 Evaluate the cost effectiveness of a marketing budget, including a review of suppliers and activities.

Related key skills for marketers

- Using ICT and the internet
- Using financial information and metrics
- Presenting information
- Improving own learning and performance
- Working with others
- Problem-solving
- Applying business law.

Assessment

CIM will normally offer two forms of assessment for this module from which centres or participants may choose: written examination and an integrative assessment. CIM may also recognize, or make joint awards for, modules at an equivalent level undertaken with other professional marketing bodies and educational institutions.

Recommended support materials (see list)

Overview and rationale
Approach
The Marketing in Practice syllabus, first launched in September 1999, requires a broad and practical demonstration of marketing, rather than any depth of understanding at a strategic level. The module will test participants' ability to draw on a wide range of subject matter and put forward practical, well-argued recommendations.

Marketing in Practice is the province of the well-rounded and versatile marketer, and aims to replicate the challenges, diversity and pace of a typical first marketing role. From an educational standpoint, it seeks to integrate the full Stage 1 syllabus, and as such is best suited towards the latter phases of Stage 1 course delivery, or, alternatively, it can be run throughout the year alongside the other three modules.

This module offers the opportunity to put into practice the entire Stage 1 syllabus, integrate key skills, and draw on participants' experience. It should be lively and fun for all involved. It rounds off Stage 1 and so provides a springboard for Stage 2, which builds on the knowledge and skills at Stage 1 and goes on to develop participants for a role in operational marketing management.

Syllabus content
As stated above, this syllabus aims to integrate fully the other three modules at this level, and assist the participant to put new learning into practice. Its integrative nature is broken down further in the next section.

Delivery approach
Element 1: Gathering, analysing and presenting information
Points to stress here are the need for business decisions to be based on information, sources of information that can be accessed, and the need to evaluate the information. There is a strong practical element, and information-gathering techniques are examined. Segmentation is also touched upon – not in any great depth but as a practical tool to use in marketing situations.

This should be used to reinforce learning from the Marketing Environment module (Stage 1) and participants should be encouraged to share practice from their own organizations.

Element 2: Building and developing relationships
This section is concerned with the people aspect of marketing. Commencing inside the marketing department, it then looks across the organization, before examining relationships outside – whether with suppliers or further down the supply chain.

This integrates well with Customer Communications (Stage 1). Tutors should combine the human aspects with the procedural and contractual to give realistic view of the real world. This section very much lends itself to a highly interactive approach. This area also supports the Marketing Management module at Stage 2.

Element 3: Organizing and undertaking marketing activities
Research has shown that many marketing assistants have responsibility for organizing a variety of events, from sales meetings to full blown conferences, and from exhibitions to corporate hospitality. Participants should be encouraged to share experiences to compare and contrast different approaches. Again, there is a strong practical element, and it is essential that participants have a grasp of costing and can evaluate the success of activities undertaken.

This builds on knowledge from both Marketing Fundamentals and Customer Communications.

Element 4: Coordinating the marketing mix
'Coordinating' is a key word – this is not strategic management of the mix. For example, participants at this level would not decide pricing strategy, but may be asked to report on the effects of a pricing decision. They may not deal with strategic advertising, but may control local advertising.

Similar demarcations apply across the mix. In line with research findings, there is a heavy emphasis on promotional activity, but all 7 Ps and their application should be explored, building on the input in Marketing Fundamentals. Budgeting and dealing with information are also important features in this section. This topic is developed further in Marketing Planning (Stage 2).

Element 5: Administering the marketing budget (and evaluating results)
This need not strike fear in tutors or participants; practical and tactical are again watchwords for this section. Company accounts, discounted cash flows etc. are not needed at this level. There is, however, a need for an appreciation of costs, how they are apportioned, and how cost effective are marketing activities. As such, basic manipulation of figures is essential. The acid test of a participant's ability is whether or not the following questions can be answered:

'How much does it cost, how do we split the costs, what will the result be, and is it worth doing?'

This section intends to provide a basic understanding of finance in business to underpin progress to Marketing Planning (Stage 2), and the critical element of 'control' at Stage 3.

Reading list

Core texts

Dibb, S., Simkin, L., Pride, W. and Ferrell, O.C. (2000) *Marketing: Concepts and strategies.* 4th European edition, Abingdon, Houghton Mifflin.

Appendix 4 Curriculum information and reading list

Syllabus guide

CIM (2003) *CIM Companion: Marketing in practice.* Cookham, Chartered Institute of Marketing.

BPP (2003) *Marketing in Practice.* London, BPP Publishing.

Hyde, M. (2003) *Marketing in Practice.* Oxford, Butterworth-Heinemann.

Supplementary readings

Butterfield, L. (1999) *Excellence in Advertising.* 2nd edition, Oxford, Butterworth-Heinemann.

Gabay, J. (2000) *Successful cyberm@rketing in a Week.* London, Hodder and Stoughton.

Gabay, J. (2000) *Teach Yourself Copywriting.* 2nd edition, London, Hodder and Stoughton.

Hart, N. (1995) *The Practice of Advertising.* 4th edition, Oxford, CIM/Butterworth-Heinemann.

Hill, Roy H. (1999) *Managing Money: Money matters for managers.* Cookham, Chartered Institute of Marketing.

Wilmshurst, J. and Mackay, A. (1999) *The Fundamentals of Advertising.* 2nd edition, Oxford, Butterworth-Heinemann.

BPP (2002) *Marketing in Practice: Practice and revision kit.* London, BPP Publishing.

Marketing in Practice: Success tape. Learning cassettes by BPP Publishing.

Syllabus guide

Index

7Ps, 121

Account handler, 55
Account planner, 55
Advertising, 125–33
   AIDA, 125–7
   evaluating media opportunities, 132–3
   media selection, 128
   objective setting, 127
   planning the campaign, 128–30
   simple communications models, 125
   use of agencies and alternative methods, 127
Advertising manager, 54
Assertiveness, three steps to, 77–9

Bar charts, 26–7
Body language, 66, 75, 76
Brand manager, 55
Briefing, definition of, 115
Budget, definition of, 166
Budget negotiation, 169–70

Competitor, 13–15
   pricing, 14–15
   promotional and other mix activity, 15
Confederation of British Industry (CBI), 19
Conference, definition of, 115
Conferences and events, 107
Contacts, list of, 75–6
Contribution per unit, definition of, 173
Convention, definition of, 115
Co-ordinating the mix, 149–64
   internet and marketing, 158
   internet's relationship with the Ps, 158–9
   people decisions, 159–60
   physical evidence decisions, 163–4
   place decisions, 155–7
   pricing decisions, 153–5
   process decisions, 160–3
   product decisions, 150–3
Cost allocation, 174–5
   activity-based costing, 174
   advertising costs by space/time, 174
   marketing costs by ratio, 175
   time-based costing, 174
Cost behaviour, 170–2
   flexible budget, 171–2
CREATE, 132
Customer, definition of, 108
Customer needs, 99–100
   basic needs, 99
   safety and security needs, 99
   self-actualization, 100
   self-esteem needs, 100
   social needs, 100
Customers, 62–4
   cultural differences when meeting people, 63–4

DAGMAR model, 103, 111, 127, 130
Database, 23–6
Database, managing the, 32–3
Database segmentation, 33–4
Decision-making unit (DMU), 62
Direct marketing manager, 55

E-relationships, 58–9
Evaluation and selection, 98
   competitors, 98
   cost, 98
   customers, 98
   synergy, 98
Events manager, 55
Exam questions, analysis of, 5–6
   job scope and career progression, 6
Exhibitions and shows, 111–15
   information and communication technology (ICT), 114–15
   outdoor events and roadshows, 114
   people staffing, 112
   promotional support and tactics, 113–14
   target audiences and objectives, 111–12
Extended marketing mix, 148–9

Financial:
   decisions, 50–2
   information, 49–50
Fixed costs, definition of, 170
Flexible budget, definition of, 172
Front-line marketer, 3

Gantt charts, 28

Halifax Building Society, 19
Hosting international visitors, 118–19

In-house facilities, definition of, 127
Internal marketing, definition of, 160

Marginal costing, 173–4
Marketing, 54–6
Marketing budget:
   analysed, 167–8
   methods of setting, 168–9
   scope of, 166

Index

Marketing director, 54
Marketing event, definition of, 87
Marketing event analysis, 104
Marketing events and activities, 108–10
   planning framework, 110
Marketing executive/assistant, 55–6
Marketing manager, 54
Marketing mix:
   definition of, 8
   development of, 147–8
Marketing-orientated organizations, 57
Marketing research manager, 55
Media production facilities, definition of, 127
Meeting, definition of, 115
Meetings and conferences, 115–18
   concept, 116
   script writing, 117
   set design, 118
   technical matters, 118
   venue and layout, 116
   working with people, 118

Network, definition of, 74
Networking, 74–5, 83–5
   bullying, 84
   ineffective communication, 85
   managing your manager, 84
   poor delegation, 85
New outlet launches, 119–21
   period of, 120–1
   planning, 121
New product development manager, 55
New product development process (NPD),
   definition of, 151

Opinion formers, definition of, 135
Organization, understanding the, 56–7
Organization information collection, 8–13
   analysing reports, 10–11
   as a participant, 12–13
   as meeting leader, 11–12
   using the intranet, 9

Personal selling, 64–6
   closing or gaining customer commitment, 66
   establishing a rapport with the
      customer, 65
   fact-finding, 65
   follow-up, 66
   making the presentation, 65–6
   overcoming objections, 65
   prospecting and planning, 65
Personal skills:
   for building relationships, 76–9
Persuasive language, 28–30
Physical evidence, definition of, 163
Pie charts, 28
Planning, anticipating and on-the-day
   management, 100–4

   construct a chart, 101
   daily management of the project, 102–3
   measurement, 103–4
Planning, approaches to, 87–94
   alternative, 92–3
   checklist for success, 93–4
   machines, 91
   materials, 91
   measurement, 91
   men, 90
   minutes, 91
   money, 91
   objectives, 89
   situation, 88
   strategy, 90
   tactics, 90
Planning, definition of, 87
Potential suppliers, 15–19
   sources of information, 18–19
   using the internet, 16–17
Press, handling the, 82–3
Press relations, definition of, 134
Print production process management, 133
Product manager, 55
Product width and depth, definition of, 152
Promotional mix, definition of, 124
Public, definition of, 109
Public relations, 133–9
   activities, 134
   briefing the PR agency, 139
   building relations with the press, 136
   constructing a media hit list, 137–8
   evaluating PR activity, 139
   identifying the publics, 134–6
   photo opportunities, 138
   press conferences, 138
   press releases, 136
Public relations manager, 54

Sales and promotional sub-mix, 143
   relationship marketing, 144
   sales staff roles, 143–4
   supporting sales effort, 143
Sales manager, 54
Sales promotion, 139–43
   definition of, 139
   evaluation of joint promotion success, 142–3
   objectives, 140
   types of promotion, 141–2
   works, 140
Selling, definition of, 143
Seminar, definition of, 115
Spreadsheets, 37–45
   calculation with, 38–41
   customer satisfaction survey, 42–5
Statistical techniques, 45–8
   averages, 45–6
   probability, 46
   time series, 46–8

Status report, definition of, 102
Stepped costs, definition of, 171
Suppliers and distribution channels, 67–71
Syllabus, 4–5
   administering the marketing budget, 5
   building and developing relationships, 4
   co-ordinating the marketing mix, 4
   gathering, analysing and presenting information, 4
   organizing and undertaking marketing activities, 4

Target audience, definition of, 109
Time series, definition of, 46
Total contribution, definition of, 173

Variable costs, definition of, 170
Venue selection, 94–5
   criteria for, 95